DOGPOO &

67 Proven & Implementable Truths, Tactics & Hacks To Create Better Content, Promote Your Products, Grow Your Audience and Make More Sales

Ravi Jayagopal

DogpooBook.com

Coolest Geek On The Planet

My name is Ravi Jayagopal.

I'm an Entrepreneur, Business Coach, Marketing Consultant, 8-time Author, WordPress Developer, Digital Marketer, Speaker, and Podcaster.

I've been selling online since 1997. And I've created and sold a wide range of products and services: Information products, Desktop Software, WordPress Plugins, Membership Sites, Online Courses, E-books, Real Books, Kindle Books, Audiobooks, Premium Podcasts, T-Shirts, Agency Services (Marketing, SEO, Website & Membership Site setup), Webinars, Local Meetups, Consulting and Coaching.

I'm the Co-Founder of DigitalAccessPass.com (DAP), a leading membership plugin and marketing automation platform for WordPress.

I have a podcast at SubscribeMe.fm where I talk about creating Membership Sites & Online Courses, how to Create, Sell and Deliver digital content, WordPress, Podcasting, Creating Audio, Video, & Reports, and tools and tips that you can use to create a long term, profitable online business.

I am also the creator of S3MediaVault.com, a secure file protector and media player for Amazon S3, CoolCastPlayer.com, the "Prettiest Podcast Player on the Planet", and PodcastReviews.me (check your Apple Podcasts reviews from all 155 countries, for free), and more.

I live in sunny San Diego with my stunningly beautiful, super-smart wife Veena Prashanth (Co-founder of DAP, Creator of

SmartPayCart.com, SmartQuizBuilder.com, and more), 2 amazing kids, and a male dog inexplicably named Vanilla!

Learn more about me at SubscribeMe.fm/ravi-jayagopal

I am the Coolest Geek on the Planet (Google can confirm) and I love to play with dol… er, I'm an amateur Ventriloquist ☺

Table of Contents

DOGPOO & DOSAA

In 2014, I coined two new words to describe a Subscription-based business model:

DOGPOO and **DOSAA**.

No, not referring to the mouth-watering Indian dish, *Dosa*. Nor am I referring to actual dog doo-doo ☺.

DOGPOO stands for "**Do Once, Get Paid Only Once**".

DOSAA stands for "**Do Once, Sell Again and Again**".

Creating something once, and then selling it over and over again - like an Online Video Course, Software, or a Book – is usually way more profitable, scalable, and fun than simply putting a lot of your time and effort into something that is done just once where you get to benefit from it just once.

DOGPOO: Performing live on stage: You get to charge for tickets only once. The show happens one time. You can't charge for that same concert again.
DOSAA: Recording your live event and repeatedly selling it to many, for a long time. Or recording an album.

DOGPOO: Speaking live on stage or doing a show live on the radio/TV/etc.
DOSAA: Selling the Video/Audio recordings, doing a Podcast, and getting people from all over the world to listen to it, and even paying for it.

DOGPOO: Working with a client 1-on-1 & getting paid for your time and skills. You cannot re-use or re-sell time already spent.
DOSAA: Creating a productized version of your knowledge that

can be sold as a Book or a Course, over and over again, to many clients.

DOGPOO: Writing custom software for a client: You only get paid once for that project. Once it's done, your work cannot be leveraged further.

DOSAA: Creating a customizable, off-the-shelf Software product – like a WordPress Plugin or SaaS – that can be sold over and over again to a large number of people.

One thing stands out in the above examples: **Scalability**.

In the DOGPOO examples, you will see that all of the products – like a live concert, writing custom software for one client, or speaking in front of a live audience - are all one-time events. You do them once, you get paid once, and you can't really leverage your past work and get paid for it again.

Now, there are opportunities in the DOGPOO model too. You could record your live concert, or your presentation at a seminar - and then sell the recordings as a product, over and over again. But a recording of a live concert is not the same as a digitally mastered studio recording, and probably only your 1000 true fans (more on this later) will both watch it live and pay for the recordings - unless of course, you're a big-time artist.

Similarly, if you are a developer or designer and do custom work for a client, the copyright of the work you have created almost always belongs to the client. Sure, you could leverage some of the code, the framework, or design patterns for later use in a different project, but most of your work is still largely unusable in another project, mainly because a new client usually brings different requirements. Plus you might get sued if you copied your old client's work for your new client.

And that's where creating a product - that can be repeatedly sold to a large audience without too many changes or customizations - can be a game-changer for you, as both an entrepreneur and digital creator.

A software product like DigitalAccessPass.com (a membership plugin for WordPress that I co-founded) can be sold over and over again to thousands of different customers without any tweaks. If you design the software to be customizable, then each client can modify it to suit their needs without you having to write custom code for each one of them individually.

But it's not just software that can be scaled. Much of the intellectual property you create can be repeatedly sold as well – like, a Video, Audio, How-to Article, Document, "Secret Sauce" information, and even Services.

"So what's the big deal? I already know about digital products!", you say?

Enter: **DOSAAS**.

DOSAA(S): With an Extra "S"

The extra "S" might as well stand for putting your DOSAA efforts on "Steroids".

It's not just about selling digital products that you can sell one-time.

It's not just about digital products that you can sell again and again to different people.

It's not even about selling the same product to different customers.

It *is* all about selling it again and again - to the **SAME** customers.

So let's revisit the crazy acronyms one last time.

DOGPOO: Do Once, Get Paid Only Once.

DOSAA: Do Once, Sell Again and Again.

DOSAAS: Do Once, Sell Again and Again - to the *SAME* Customers

And those are the ideal properties of a *Perfect Product*.

Having a Day-Job Sucks - especially for the enterprising ones like you and me.

And so does Selling One-Time Products – which is like depending on a paycheck from your day job.

Day Job (DJ): You have to go to work every day.
One-time Products (OTP): You have to make sales every day.

DJ: You stop working, you no longer get paid.
OTP: You stop selling, you get no new customers, you no longer get paid.

DJ: You start every month at $0.00 from your employer. You work first, then you earn (you have to work for a certain period even to get paid vacation and other benefits).
OTP: Your business starts with $0.00 in sales each month.

DJ: All of that work you did last month isn't going to mean anything when it comes to getting paid next month.
OTP: All of the selling you did last month isn't going to mean anything when it comes to making sales next month.

DJ: You have one source of income: Your employer. And there is no guarantee that you'll be employed next month.
OTP: You have one source of income: Your *future* customers who haven't purchased yet – and you don't even know if anyone will. There is no guarantee that you will get new customers next month.

DJ: You have no job security.
OTP: You have no revenue security.

You can see how dangerously similar they both are. If you have a business selling one-time products, you could boast all you want that you own your time and that you are your own boss. And if you have a job, sure, you get to boast about being able to leave your work behind at the office (for most people) and take vacations without worrying about what your employer is dealing with back at the office (in most cases). But the bottom line is that there is no stability or security in either case.

When you are selling one-time products, a big problem is that no matter how well you do this month, you have absolutely nothing to show for the next month.

Let's say you made $3,000 this month. What about next month? On the first day of the next month, and the very first day of every single month going forward, you start back at "Square 1" – with an income of $0.00. And that really sucks.

But this doesn't mean that you start by selling a subscription-based product. When you're getting started, you may not have the product library or the marketing chops to charge a recurring subscription for what you're selling.

So it's best to get started with a one-time product, which helps you build a list of buyers, to whom you can continue selling other products in the future as both a product owner and as an affiliate.

Launch Fatigue

If your business model is to keep creating products that will help you keep selling to those who have already purchased from you, then over the next 2, 5, or 10 years, think about how many darn products you will need to create and launch, just to get those past customers to come back and buy from you again?

No one can realistically create 5, 10, or 20 new products every single year, year after year, just to stay in business. My wife Veena Prashanth and I are both software architects, prolific product creators, and we're also very good at software development. We know multiple programming languages, database design, system architecture - you name it. We can pretty much develop and launch any kind of plugin or software we want to, at any time.

We are capable of coding night and day, doing tech support ourselves if required (which we did in the beginning before we could afford to hire a team), writing the documentation, and we also know how to market it and sell it. *And* we have a full-blown software development business. We also have an in-house team for support, design, and other tasks.

But even we cannot sustain launching new plugins all the time, even if we can "do it in our sleep". That is just a very exhausting and draining business model if the only way to continue making money as a business is to...

A) Keep creating more products to sell to your existing customers,

-or-

B) Keep hunting for new customers every single day, 365 days a year, year after year.

That is *not* a sustainable business model. It doesn't work for the long term and involves a lot of risks.

It's exhausting not just for you and your team, but it is also **very exhausting for your customers** if you keep promoting offers about your "next big thing". And they have to read a sales page, watch your videos, understand your offer, get through your pitch, decide if your offer is right for them, and then buy again. And again. And again.

When you constantly keep pitching new products to your customers, after a point, it won't matter how great your products are, how useful they might be to them, or how much it extends the power and functionality of what you've previously sold them. They're going to tire of your constant pitching and will unsubscribe from your list, stop buying from you, and tune you out entirely.

80% Failure Rate

You've probably heard of the statistic that 8 out of 10 small businesses eventually fail. Just ponder that for a second: 8 out of 10 small businesses go belly up. A whopping 80% failure rate. Only 20% survive.

That doesn't necessarily mean that the remaining 20% are *super* successful - or even *really* successful.

It just means 2 out of 10 somehow manage to survive. Out of that 20%, only a very few go on to actually *thrive*.

If we apply the 80/20 rule, only 20% of that remaining 20% will be successful. So only 4 out of 100 businesses will be successful. And 16 out of 100 will just survive.

That's a *huge* difference between surviving and thriving. This is why you can't sustain in survival mode for very long.

Back to the 80% of businesses that fail.

Why did they fail?

One immediate answer is that they failed to make more money than they were spending. So they went out of business.

But why did they not make enough money?

Because they couldn't make enough sales to pay their bills and earn a profit.

Let's go one more level deeper. Inception movie-style, "dream-within-a-dream-within-a-dream" deeper.

Why couldn't they make enough sales? Did they not think it through? Did they overestimate their product? Did they not do enough market research?

The person who started a bakery figured since they're good at baking and making cupcakes and cookies, and they have seen many successful bakeries, so they believe that they can make better cookies, and they believe that can lead to a successful bakery. They figure that there will always be people who love cupcakes and cookies and bakery products.

But what they don't realize is that there are a lot of things other than their baking skills that go into creating a successful bakery that pays its bills and also makes a profit.

That person who started a web development shop and went and hired a designer, a developer, a database person, and a marketing person, because they had a few clients on hand and figured those clients would keep them afloat while they looked for new clients? Those clients will get their work completed at some point, and leave, and may not have more work for you any time soon. What then?

The reality is that constantly finding new customers is tough. The problem with one-time products and services is that you could have a huge surplus of business for a month, and then almost nothing for the next three. So if you hired extra help when your business was doing well, you may have to let people go when things get real slow (like during a pandemic or some extraordinary global/local event).

And if the fluctuation of business is happening every month, there's no way you can hire people one month and fire them the next month. You're just not going to be able to attract and keep great talent if you do that. You cannot plan for anything. And it's really hard to build a long-term business using just freelancers and part-timers, who may not always be available to you if they find a higher-paying, more consistently paying, longer-term contract with a different client.

Back to the "Day Job" example from earlier – imagine that at the beginning of the month, you had a decent job. You work hard for a month and earn, say $5,000. Now on the last day of the month, you're given your paycheck - your manager walks in and says "Thank you, Ravi. Here's your paycheck for last month. Your services are no longer required."

You are now basically fired from your job at the end of the month. And on the first day of the next month, you now have to start applying for a job, go attend multiple job interviews, go through written tests and multiple rounds of interviews, and by the end of the first week of the month, let's say you land another job.

This next job pays you just $3,000 ($2k less than the previous job). You work hard for another month, only to be let go again at the end of that month - not because you did anything wrong, but in this scenario, imagine that's the norm — you get to stay at your job for no more than a month. You now have to start looking for another job and let's say this time, you don't get a job for 3 months.

How long can anyone live like this? How can anyone make an honest living with a spouse, kids, and a home when you have such an insanely fluctuating income? Think you can even dream of buying a house or a car or going on vacations or saving for college or retirement when you know you're *probably* going to be working only 7 to 8 months a year, and even that you're not exactly sure about? And you still don't know if those jobs will be any good, whether you'll make enough money at each job, how far you have to commute or travel for the job, what benefits you get, etc.

Imagine what a crazy life that would be. *No one* in their right mind would willingly agree to live like this for the long term.

What everyone wants is a reasonably steady income - one where they know how much money they'll take home each month. And then, they can budget for rent/mortgage, car payments, vacations, etc.

That's what selling one-time products is like. This is why so many people shut down their businesses, forget their dreams, and go back to the "stability" and "security" of a "job".

How unfortunate is it that working for someone else is considered a better option?

Back to the 80% small business failure rate: The reason why such a large number of businesses eventually shut down, is not because they're not good at what they do - but it's because they cannot consistently bring in revenue – i.e., make sales - month after month. The monthly revenue fluctuates so badly because they can't get new customers consistently, so they can't plan for hiring people or buying computers or office space or taking out a loan, etc. *Nothing* can be planned because *nothing* is predictable, and everything changes month to month.

And that happens because most of these failed businesses were trying to sell one-time products or services. They needed to get new customers every day to walk in and buy their cakes and cookies, needed to get new clients month after month for their web design service, new customers for their plumbing business, new customers for their restaurant, for their car wash, for their dental practice, for their plugins, for their video course – you name it.

Their lives get consumed by having to get new customers every day, for the rest of the life of their business, and eventually, many run out of steam – and money.

So here's the bottom line: With a one-time product or service, there is no way to predict how much money you'll make each month. The **lifetime customer value** – probably *the* most important metric in a business - is impossible to predict.

And might only be a matter of time before you run out of customers, or run out of money to run the business. And eventually, there is the ever-growing pressure from the family to "go get a job like everyone else and give this family some peace of mind with a consistent income".

This chapter was about showing you the value of getting your existing customers to buy more stuff and pay you more often – preferably in an automated way. And nothing brings in consistent revenue like **recurring revenue**. And that comes with creating subscription-based products and services.

Finally, here's one last (and critical) reason why you ought to think about a recurring subscription model: At some point in your life, you're going to want to sell your business. It could be because you just want to cash out and retire and enjoy your retirement traveling the world, or because you have a bigger calling in life that you have always put off, or maybe you just want to chill and watch sports and go to your grandkids' basketball and soccer games and hang out with your family.

Whatever the reason, most people will want to sell their business at some point. After all, you've built a valuable asset over the years. If you can't run it any longer, you're not simply going to just let it die and let such a precious asset go to waste.

And when it comes to selling your business, one of the first things that a prospective buyer will look at is not just how much you have earned the last year, or last quarter or last month. What they really want to know is if there is a way to predict how much money your business is going to bring in next month.

How much you sell your business for depends on one key factor:

- Your **Monthly Recurring Revenue (MRR)**

How many customers do you have who are paying monthly? If you answer that is "none", that means all of your current customers are already paid up (past purchases) – which means the prospective buyer of your business has to start looking for new customers from the 1st day they buy your business and then do that, again and again, every month thereafter. Not having recurring revenue is how the value of a business just plummets to the ground.

There are other important metrics like **Customer Acquisition Cost (CAC)** and **Customer Lifetime Value (CLV)** which will show how profitable each new customer is. If the ratio of CLV to CAC is just 1:1, then that business is not worth too much, because what the customers are paying you is what you're spending to acquire them, to begin with. So it's a net loss.

But the key metric is still recurring revenue (which includes Annual Recurring Revenue (ARR)), and if your MRR is zero or very low, then either you may not be able to sell your business at all and might have to simply shut it down or hand it off to a family member - or you'll have to sell it for pennies on the dollar at a great loss.

Either way, there goes your retirement dream and dreams of funding your kids' and grandkids' future.

So the key to a long-term, profitable business is **Subscriptions**. And I go into great detail about this in my book "Subscribe Me: Making, Marketing & Monetizing Online Digital Content with Membership Sites, Online Courses and Recurring Subscriptions"

The "Perfect" Product

The *Perfect* product, if ever there can be one, is…

(1) **Created once** and the same product/service can be sold to **different customers** (digital info products, downloadable software, intelligence & intellectual property, mobile apps, online tools, packaged services)

(2) **Customers pay repeatedly** for your product/service that is **delivered repeatedly** over time (SEO/Consulting/Coaching services, a Membership site with new content being added every month, subscription program for Car Wash/Flowers/Razor Blades/Baby Needs, etc.)

If you can create something that can do *both* (1) and(2) – a product that can get each customer to pay for it every month, *and* can also be sold to thousands of different customers, both at the same time - you have potentially a *huge* winner on your hands.

But it's OK if you can't create a product that can do both - for most businesses, getting your product to do even just *one* of those two (#1 is easier than #2) can bring in big profits.

The biggest common factor among the world's most successful companies is that they have been able to create something that does both #1 and #2.

Microsoft: Created Windows and Office, sold the same products to millions of customers, then they get them to repeatedly pay when they buy newer versions of those products and have now switched to subscription services for the same products as well, where you pay for them monthly.

Apple: They design world-class products once (even if they have to be manufactured repeatedly – which is why they outsource that), and get repeat customers from newer versions of their hardware (most people upgrade their iPhone every 2-3 years). And they created the "App Store" where the same apps can be sold to millions of users, and Apple also gets a cut (of about 30%) from all app-generated income. And they have several recurring revenue streams like Apple Music, Apple TV+, iCloud, and Apple Arcade.

Adobe: They created a library of products for creators – like Photoshop, Dreamweaver, Acrobat, and Lightroom. And they've not only sold millions of copies of those products separately, but they've also packaged that into a subscription called "Creative Cloud", where you must sign up for a monthly subscription to get the same software that used to be previously available for a one-time purchase.

Google: Their search engine and other online properties bring people back to the site repeatedly, which allows them to sell billions of dollars worth of ads on their various online properties. And they have their fingers in a hundred different pies, including their Cloud Services and Google Play, which brings in recurring revenue.

While you and I may not be able to create the next Google or Apple, the cool thing is that you don't *have* to model these companies just to have a successful business.

Whatever products and services you currently offer can be creatively modified and enhanced to create subscription-based versions of those exact same products and services.

I Came Home and the Dog Was Bald

My precious Vanilla, swaddled like a baby by my daughter

I've always been intrigued by the psychology of persuasion (and am a big fan of the book by Cialdini too). And one of my favorite past-times is reading random stuff about "Ninja" copy-writing and persuasion and marketing techniques, as I've always been, and will always be, a student of marketing.

One of the techniques I love is a Neuro-linguistic programming (NLP) Technique called **Pattern Interrupt**.

This is where you do something so different from the rest of your competition, that it completely throws your audience off-balance, and lowers their guard just enough for you to make your presence felt - and grab their attention for a few fleeting seconds. (What you do with that next is a completely different story for another day, another book.)

This technique can be used in many aspects of work and life.

Stand out from other typical websites...

... by offering a free report, without asking for their email address first.

Stand out from the thousands of marketers crashing your prospect's inbox with "offers"...

... by offering just honest-to-goodness, *awesome*, instantly usable, valuable content.

Stand out from your competitors...

... by putting your personal phone number on your website.

Stand out from most other bloggers...

... by generously publishing outgoing links to all kinds of posts and pages and sites (like this blog post) without worrying about "losing your readers" (an awesome technique I learned from Seth Godin).

You may have heard of Roy H. Williams, the "Wizard Of Ads" and one of my idols.

Here's an excerpt from one of his newsletters that I even today eagerly await every Sunday at midnight. In this, he tells the story of one of his seminars, where he asks his audience to volunteer ridiculous, over-the-top subject lines, so he can demonstrate how to tie it to their marketing, all of it in front of a live audience.

"The stagecraft begins when I ask everyone in the room to write a statement that would catch the ear of any person who overheard it. "The statement doesn't have to make sense," I say, "It just needs to be larger than life, evocative, difficult to ignore. The kind of statement that would make a passing stranger turn and say, 'Huh?'

I then ask 6 volunteers to bring their statements onto the stage. I'm now going to craft real ads for real businesses using the statements written on those papers as the opening lines for the ads. 'Do I have any business owners in the room?' Six business owners take the stage. I randomly pair them up with the colorful statement-holders. I have no idea what businesses are on stage or what statements are written on those papers.

I owe Tom Robbins (not to be confused with Tony) for this little bit of stagecraft. In a magazine interview that accompanied the release of his novel, *Fierce Invalids Home From Hot Climates,* Tom said, "Everything in the universe is connected, of course. It's a matter of using imagination to discover the links, and language to expand and enliven them."

Business owner number one. Tell me about your business.
'I have a plumbing company.'

Name a profit center you'd like to improve.
'I'd like to get more calls for our 24-hour emergency service.'

Crazy person number one. What did you write on your paper?
'I came home and the dog was bald.'

The room roars with laughter as I walk to the front of the stage and balance there - my toes hanging over the edge - as 2,000 people hold their breath.

'I came home and the dog was bald. I haven't been that surprised since I woke up at 2 AM to pee and stepped out of bed into an inch of water.

Thank god Martindale Plumbing never goes to sleep. At 2 AM they were just sittin' there, hoping someone would call.

They fixed the problem while I made coffee. Great guys. Thank god for Martindale Plumbing, 24 hours a day. But I still got no idea what to do with a bald dog."

<end>

(Back to me)

I started laughing so hard at 3:45 AM while reading this newsletter on my phone, in my bed, getting ready to fall asleep, that I became wide awake, and couldn't fall asleep for a while after. That's how much it tickled me, inspired me, and got my juices going (this was many years ago - I no longer use electronic devices right before going to bed - other than listening to a podcast while I brush my teeth).

Remember, it's not just about writing something ridiculous, larger than life, and simply shocking for the sake of shocking. That usually ends up like a bad joke.

The key is to start your copy (email subject, blog post, book title) with something exciting, curiosity-inducing, ridiculous, outrageous, and maybe even shocking – but somehow tie it all together with your main story.

That's when you make people laugh in a dark room in the wee hours of the morning, and inspire them so much that they lose their sleep.

Sign up for the free Monday Morning Memo newsletter written by one of my favorite people in the world.

A Mini Headline/Subject-Line Challenge

Imagine you're sending out an email to your list - something to do with your product (any product or service, or even yourself).

I challenge you to come up with a "pattern interrupting" headline - and also tell me how you would tie it back into your story.

You can email it to Ravi@SubscribeMe.fm and I will share it in a future content piece, giving you full credit, of course.

The Most Powerful Word

"What is the Most Powerful Word in the English language for Entrepreneurs and Digital Creators?"

If you asked me that question, I could make a case for any one of the following:

- You (referring to customers)
- Empathy (being able to put yourself in the shoes of your audience)
- Free (Billions of dollars have been made off of free products)
- Customers (the lifeblood of any business)
- Subscriptions (recurring!)
- Influence (ability to affect someone or something)
- Audience (everything starts here)
- No (saying no to distractions, no to mediocrity, etc)
- Selling (we're always selling to someone or the other)

But I'm here to make a case for an entirely different word, which I believe is the *perfect* answer to that question.

The Most Powerful Word in the World is... **"PROOF"**.

And let me, er, p*rove* it to you ☺.

"Proof" is such a powerful, influencing factor in everyday life. In the forthcoming examples, I will be loosely combining "Hints", "Signs", "Feelings", and "Hunch" as part of the Proof umbrella. E.g., if your personality gives someone a hint that you might have a massive anger management problem or that you're flaky or creepy, they are not exactly going to wait for absolute "this will hold up in court" kind of proof before they stop dealing with you. Rightly or wrongly, a bad feeling or hunch based on your words and actions will be good enough for them to judge you.

So even when it comes to things like establishing Trust and Credibility, you still have to earn it, by proving to them that you're worthy of that – nothing will be given to you without you proving it to them first.

Here are some examples.

- Wish to date a boy/girl (or keep dating them)? You've got to show proof consistently that you are worthy of being with them. That you're not a sleazebag. That you won't try to sneak into their phone at midnight and send compromising pictures to their friends. Or that you're not the snooping type, that you're not a creep or stalker, that you don't have a bad reputation from previous relationships. You have to prove that you're reliable, that you will keep your word, and your promises (like you won't cheat on them), that you are actually who you say you are (unlike Dexter Morgan), etc.

- You have to prove with friends that you will be loyal, never sell them out, won't share private conversations, that you'll always have their back, you won't talk about them behind their back, you will be there for them when they desperately need you, and you will be there not just during the fun times but also during the rough times.

- Parents have to prove to their children all the time, that the parent is fair, that they'll keep their word, they'll follow through, there are consequences to actions, that good behavior begets praise and rewards, and bad behavior will be punished. The parents have to consistently prove by their actions, words & decisions that they're trustworthy, honorable, that they won't say one thing and do another, that there isn't a different rule for the parent when it comes to most things, that they treat all of their kids equally, that character matters, that sportsmanship matters more than winning, etc. "Do as I say (not as I do)" won't fly with children.

- An interviewee has to show proof, in their resume, with their words, actions and demeanor during the interview, as well as with many other things both tangible and intangible, that they're the right person for the job.

- The hiring manager has to show proof that they're not a sleazeball, that they're going to be fair and open, that they know what they're talking about, why the company is a great place, why you should work there, and what kind of great opportunities are in store for you there.

- A politician has to show proof that they are a decent person, have a good character, are not corrupt, have a track record of making the right decisions that their voters consider important, etc. Of course, they could still get elected without all of that, but it's going to be much harder, more expensive, and bigger compromises.

- Proof of concept, also known as proof of principle, is a way to quickly figure out whether a certain idea or project is feasible, to verify if a concept or theory has practical potential, before investing a large amount of time, money, and effort.

- A product creator has to show proof that their product works - with demo videos, testimonials from others who have used it and recommend it, positive reviews from the community and third-party sites, and a good word from leaders and influencers in your niche (or at least, a lack of negative PR).

- Fitness- and Weight loss products that have a lot of "Before" and "After" pics and videos and testimonials from their users, tend to do well.

- Direct Response TV Marketing showing you how to remove a car scratch with their spray, or how their vacuum cleaner works so well in removing dirt and grime, or how guys have gone from half-bald to a full head of thick hair, are so successful and sell so many products with their demonstrations and testimonials, that they buy up entire hourly slots on TV just to sell their products (infomercials).

- You need Identity Proof for a lot of things, from buying alcohol to getting onto an airplane.

- Proving that you know what you're talking about, with consistent messaging on all platforms. That you're willing to give before you ask. That you're willing to provide value for free, upfront, before asking for money.

- That you're patient, and willing to "court" and "woo" your customers, and are not doing the equivalent of asking someone you met 5 minutes ago to go home with you for the night.

- Boasting about offering great support and customer service on your website? You have to back that up by actually responding to questions and issues promptly.

- Even if it's not easily demonstrable, how far are you willing to go and how creative can you get to show that your product works, and works well?

- Are you trying to fake credibility by publishing brand logos of unrelated news and media organizations (there are actually people online selling courses on how to fake this!)? Or are you only linking to legitimate, unpaid, earned media?

- Is your website indirectly showing signs of a fly-by-night operation, with popups and flashing banners and showing a downsell offer the moment you try to leave the page, and a fake scarcity timer that always says "Hurry! Offer expires in 2 hours!!" and only resets and never really expires?

- Are your offers treating your visitors like they're gullible and naïve? Are your scarcity tactics off-putting and appear scammy?

Not all "proof" is tangible – sometimes there's nothing specific to show, no documents, papers, screenshots, or badges.

But there are intangible ways to provide proof, and intangible ways in which others look for proof about you, your business, products, and services.

Past actions, words, and choices.

And what you did when no one was watching (or when you thought no one was watching).

Social Profile: Tweets, Instagram, Facebook, and other social posts. Social Media Influencers show proof of their influence with the number of followers, the amount of engagement they get on their posts, and the willingness of their followers to buy what they recommend. The bigger the following, the more they get paid to post sponsored content.

Social Proof: What others are saying and writing about you. On social media, in forums, on review websites, and blogs. Testimonials from other industry peers and mini- and micro-celebrities in your niche.

Have you refused a refund to someone even though they were eligible? Have you insulted a customer? Or treated them unfairly?

In the case of crowd-funded products, showing proof about how it *would* work, with a believable, working prototype.

When it comes to becoming a highly-paid sports star, it's not enough if you have one great game. Can you do it again next game? How about doing it all month? How about for an entire year? Can you come back and do it again next year? So to become a superstar and legend like Serena Williams or Steffi Graf, you've got to constantly prove over and over again that you can win at the highest levels.

Want your book to be turned into a movie? You've got to prove that your book has a large fan following. That it's a hit in its own right, that you have built a legion of fans who will come to your book signing tour and Q&A's, that they follow you on social and engage with your content. It doesn't matter if you are a musician or podcaster or YouTuber or social media influencer – to get sponsorships or book/movie/show deals, you have to prove that your work is amazing, and also that you have a big audience and a passionate following.

Sometimes it's hard to exactly prove something in the positive – that's when the lack of negative information could be a good thing. And vice versa.

E.g., it may be hard to prove you're cheating on your significant other without having photos of you with someone else. But if your comings and goings are starting to get questionable, your timings have suddenly changed and don't seem reasonable, you're suddenly spending entire nights away from home even though you're not traveling, you're heard whispering on the phone in the middle of the night in the bathroom, etc – sometimes you don't need hard evidence to prove something. Those kinds of signs and hints are enough to create doubt.

And in the legal court, one must be proven guilty beyond a reasonable doubt. But there's no such thing in other parts of life.

Partial proof, hints, signs, and feelings are enough to sow doubt. And that can lose you whatever it is that you're after – whether that's a sale, a partnership, a job offer, a date, or even a spouse.

The belief that there is a God (or Gods) is just about the only thing for which most people don't require proof – that's why it's called faith. But for everything else, you need proof.

No one is going to have a relationship with you or do business with you because of blind faith. You can't tell a stranger "just trust me". You have to prove your mettle, character, intent and value, and everything else, every step of the way.

And providing proof just once is not good enough today. Like we expect of legendary figures, everyone is asking: Can you do it once? How about again? And again?

If you can, then you can build a great business and lifestyle with your 1000 True Fans and beyond, to whom you've repeatedly proved yourself, and about your products and services, and they'll buy pretty much anything you publish (or point them towards).

Seth Godin Ruined the Internet

(And How to Be an Expert in 1 Simple Step)

I say that with the utmost sarcasm because I'm one of Seth's biggest fans. I've read every single one of his books - and most of the ones I bought were real paperback books that I still proudly display on my bookshelf in my home office.

One of his books/reports is titled "Everyone is an Expert", which he released as a PDF. Now, what he means is that everybody's an expert at *something*. But there are a whole bunch of people who completely ignore the *something* part, and try to pretend like they're an expert at *a different thing*, because they believe that whatever they're an expert at is not good enough, cool enough, monetizable enough, etc. And they feel compelled to act like they're an expert at something that they *think* others care about.

And that's how you end up with someone who earns a few hundred dollars selling something online and immediately considers themselves a "Marketing Expert". Or someone who has launched a membership site for a few clients, and calls themselves an "Online Course Expert". Or someone who has run a few ads on Facebook and suddenly they're now a "Facebook Ads Expert". Or they've read a few books and attended a few self-development seminars and webinars, and now they're a "Life Coach" at age 21. Or someone who has always had a day job, has never run their own business, happens to consult with one business client and suddenly they're a "Business Coach".

No, you cannot fake it until you make it. People can sniff fake "experts" from a mile away.

Here's how to be perceived as an expert, the right way, in 1 simple step:

Don't give me information. Give me your perspective.

Do you want me to think of you as an expert? Then don't just regurgitate information that I can find online for free. Instead, give me your experiences and your perspective about that information, and what I can and cannot (and should and should not) do with it.

That's it! That's the main thing you need to know to position yourself as an expert in just about anything. Simple, but not easy.

This goes back to one of my favorite quotes that I said on someone's podcast where I was being interviewed. When asked about what kind of content someone should be creating, I said...

People don't pay for Content. They pay for Perspective.

Let me show you how to use this to become an expert and authority in your niche with some examples.

One day, I was listening to a podcast about WordPress. And the host started talking about the latest version of WordPress that had just come out. And he just started reading the entire feature list, line by line, probably the same stuff that was published on the WordPress website, point by point.

And I was thinking to myself, Dude! If I wanted to know the exhaustive feature list, I can go to their website for that. Or, when I upgrade, WordPress is going to give me a complete list of what has changed. Why the heck are you wasting 10 precious minutes of my time simply reading it verbatim from the WordPress site?

Now, if that were my podcast and I was the host, here's how I would've made it a lot more interesting and valuable for my listeners:

1) I wouldn't read the entire list. I would first give out a link to the WordPress website where they've listed it, for anyone who wants to go over it word-by-word. And then I would've cherry-picked a few really important ones and talked about them specifically.

2) I would read the actual feature, and then add my commentary on it with *my perspective*.

3) I would talk about which features I thought were missing in this release, and which features are overdue.

4) I would talk about why a certain feature doesn't do justice to what it can do - or something deeper about that feature.

5) Why someone should or shouldn't upgrade to that version.

6) What happens if you upgrade and you have other plugins that haven't upgraded yet.

7) What else you should consider before you upgrade.

And those were just a few things I randomly came up with for this example, but you get the idea. If I had a podcast about it, I can guarantee you that I would do a lot more than just read out a feature list - I would be giving out a lot more specific tips, strategies, and recommendations.

So instead of reading aloud a boring press release word-for-word, I would tell you about stuff that you cannot just read on some website. I would tell you things that only someone who has actually "been there, done that" can tell you; someone who has installed the latest version of WordPress, and also used other plugins, and knows enough to tell you that there will be a problem with X, Y, or Z plugins if you upgraded. Or, that some security issue will be fixed if you did an upgrade.

We're taught right from an early age, the difference between Facts vs. Opinions. That's exactly what expertise really comes down to:

The ability to absorb information, and tell me why I should care about it.

Fact vs. Opinion. And why someone should care about *your* opinion.

Information vs. Perspective.

News vs. Education.

If you simply report the news, you're a reporter (or aggregator). There's nothing wrong with that. There are a lot of people who have made a career out of aggregating information. But that's not very valuable to the average person, which is why, if you have a news website, you are probably going to have to monetize it with ads, as you may find it hard to charge for a news article. Because you're just one of several websites (or people) reporting the news, that I can find elsewhere just as easily, for free.

However, if you tell me your informed, educated, researched opinion about something, and it is smart and intelligent and comes from personal experience, and helps me learn something new, maybe breaks something complex down for me, gives me an "aha moment", or helps me make decisions, or improves my life somehow (make money, save time/energy/effort, lose weight, etc), *now* you're well on your way to being considered an expert in my eyes. And that's when you can charge for your content, and many will pay for it.

Brilliant 5, Blah 95

When I published my first, real, paperback book back in 2007, called "No Business Like E-Business", I wanted to quickly figure out how to promote my book. Back then, if I wanted to learn about something fast, I just went to Amazon and bought the best couple of books on the subject.

So for promoting my book, I bought a book called "1001 Ways to Market Your Books". Back then, it had a massive number of reviews, highly rated, lots of folks all over the web singing its praise. So naturally, I bought the book.

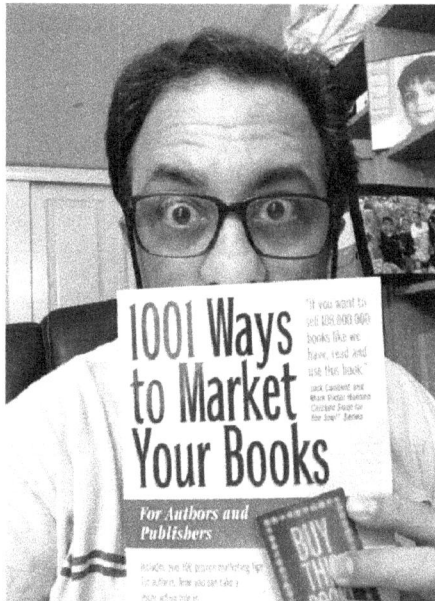

Long story short, there's a reason why it has a whopping 1001 ways to promote a book because it lists every dang method there is, however silly or basic.

Imagine if you bought a book today that claimed to give you 1001 ways to promote your website. And it had "ideas" like printing a business card, attending local meetups and handing out your cards, telling your friends and family by email, posting the link on Facebook, Twitter, and Instagram, etc.

So if a list is showing you 1001 ways of doing something, that list probably has a bunch of obvious things and is so watered down that only 5% of it is actually going to be useful and impactful.

I call it the **Brilliant 5, Blah 95** rule.

5% is brilliant, 95% is blah.

So to promote a blog, some of the "Blah 95" of promotional tactics would be contacting other bloggers in your niche to ask them if you can write guest articles for them, submitting articles to article sharing sites, and linking back to your main site via the signature, posting in old-school online forums and using links in the signature, participating in Facebook groups and sneak-promoting your articles (only in context).

Similarly, to promote a podcast, the Blah 95 tips would be: Post the link to your episode post on your website, on Facebook and Twitter, post your MP3 link on Twitter a couple of times, create a post on Instagram, create an Audiogram and post it on Facebook, Twitter, and YouTube, etc.

[Sidebar] An audiogram is a video version of your audio. It's a static image superimposed with a moving audio waveform, which you might have seen on a TV or sports show, where someone calls in, and they have their picture on the screen, and there's a visual, animated waveform of the audio on the screen as if to show that they're talking and that waveform is the sound waves that they're creating.

So you can take a small clip of your audio, add an image to it, and a waveform, and turn it into a video - basically an mp4 file. You can then publish that video on Facebook, Twitter, Instagram, YouTube, and any platform that accepts video content. So it's another way for you to promote your show. [/Sidebar]

Will it get you a ton of engagement and new listeners? Possibly, depending on your niche, your audience, their demographics, which platforms they use the most, etc. But it's still better than missing out entirely on YouTube viewers. Audiograms are a huge part of what I call **Native Marketing**, where your content is native to the platform where you are promoting it. And the audience doesn't have to leave the current platform to check out your content - they can consume it right there.

All of the Blah 95 tactics are fine. While they may not make a *massive* difference, you still need to do them, because they're a part of the basic foundation to move your project further. They're a part of getting one reader at a time, one listener at a time, and one customer at a time. But focusing on getting one audience member at a time, requires a lot of time, effort, and patience, and the results can be excruciatingly slow.

One of the biggest differences between successful *entrepreneurs* and the not-so-successful *wantrepreneurs* is that the successful ones focus primarily on the Brilliant 5, while the rest of us spend more time worrying about the Blah 95. The Blah 95 is usually low-hanging fruit, it's cheaper, you spend more time than money on these, it's labor-intensive, and it can be done by putting in a lot of time and hustle. And most people getting started have more time than money, so they tend to choose the Blah 95 strategies.

But the big guns go right after the Brilliant 5. And one of the Brilliant 5 is Paid Advertising. That's right - spending money to promote your product or service. Imagine not goofing off on Facebook for 3 hours a day and calling it Networking, or Content Marketing, or Relationship building. Imagine putting your money where your mouth is, and stop talking big-game, and mustering the guts to invest some money, even if it's just $10 a week, to promote whatever it is that you're promoting.

Using High-ROI tactics – like advertising on social media (wherever your target audience hangs out the most), forming partnerships with other product owners in your niche who are not direct competitors and don't have a conflict of interest, paying influencers - in cash or in-kind - to promote your product, hiring a PR person or agency to get you interviewed on big media as well as on podcasts, etc – are all part of the Brilliant 5.

Forget advertising - even if you're just in content-creation mode, let's say you are writing an article or creating a list post or a list episode, where you're listing, say, the Top X Ways to do something. Don't list the Blah 95 - go after the Brilliant 5.

I can't tell you how many reports or list posts I've read, where they listed way too many things.

I once read a report that was titled "The Top 100 WordPress Plugins You Need On Your Web Site".

Really? 100 plugins?? Did the author even realize that your site's performance will go down the drain if you installed and activated 100 WordPress plugins? Did this person even try installing all of those plugins at the same time?

How about something better, like 27 "Must Have" WordPress Plugins For Your Business Website where you also tell me that you should *not* install all of them unless you absolutely need those features?

The article above was written by me, and I made sure I don't waste your time and give you only the essential plugins. Not 100, not even 50, but just 27, all based on personal experience. Every single one of them is what I use and recommend. And that's how you differentiate yourself from all the other list-post creators.

The biggest difference between a Performer and a Pretender is that the Pretender will go on Google, and do a search "top ways to promote a book". They'll see about 173,000,000 results. And the first few results are 50 Surprisingly Simple Ways To Promote Your Book, 15 DIY Book Promotion Tools You Need to Know, What's The Best Way To Promote My Self-Published Book?, 71 Ways to Promote and Market Your Book, 101 Book Marketing Ideas to Promote Your Book.

And just from the articles found on the first page of Google, you can get at least 200 ways to promote a book. Don't you think anyone can take 200 of those tips, and whittle it down to a list of 30? Of course, they can. Some do. And that's why they're a Pretender. A fake expert.

Back to the 1001 ways to promote a book – imagine if you took that entire list, collated and curated them, applied them to your own Kindle or Paperback book, and then came up with the blog post or podcast episode title, like this:

"8 Incredible Ways to Promote A Book That Helped Me Sell 75 copies of my own book in just 3 days – Plus 45 more ways that you should ignore because they won't work in 2021".

I just quickly made that one up for illustration, but you get the point.

So at first glance, your title tells me, alright, you are not giving me 1001 ways, not 101 ways, not 50 ways - just 8 ways to promote my book. And this is one of those times where less is more.

I would be skeptical if it feels to me like you've inflated the numbers just to look more valuable, or to make it look like you have more content. In today's world of content tsunamis on all platforms, more content is not the answer. 8 ways sound more believable, realistic to implement, and seemingly of higher quality than 1001 ways.

If you have something to teach me, teach me in the shortest time possible. Fastest way possible. Most efficient way possible.

The improved title above shows me that you cared enough to whittle down the list. And then you're saying it helped *you* sell 75 copies of your book - that means, you have probably experienced the book promotion process yourself. Then it says you sold 75 copies, and that too in 3 days. Is it groundbreaking? No, but it sounds more believable and authentic than if you had said that these 1001 tips will help the reader sell 1 million copies.

You'll see a lot of fake marketers do just that - they'll take their own results, or the results of one of the outliers in their niche, and say "How You Can Make $17,546.21 From a Single 45-minute Webinar".

Ok, just because ONE person did it that ONE darn time doesn't mean I can duplicate those results. So a more believable version title would be "How I Made $17,546.21 From a Single 45-minute Webinar". This tells me that you're going to show me how you did it, but you're not promising that I can do it too. Way less hypey, way more authentic.

Also, becoming an expert is not the same as others knowing that you are an expert. You may be very good at something. But if I don't *know* that you are an expert, if you say or do things that don't demonstrate that you're good at that thing, or if you say things that make you look or sound like a newbie, like someone without much experience, or like you don't know what you're talking about, then there's not much of a chance that I'm going to think of you as an expert.

Let's reverse engineer this quickly.

To become an expert, you've got to teach me something, give me your opinion about something. You've got to have not just an opinion, but a strong one to the point of appearing a bit opinionated, and you believe those things so strongly *because* you're an *expert*, and you've got to convince me with facts, reasoning and logic and proof, that you know what you're talking about.

But how do you form an opinion about something in the first place?

By knowing about it, reading about it, researching it, using it, working *on* it, working *with* it, executing on it, testing it, tweaking it... basically by doing a lot of *stuff* with *it*. Whatever "it" is.

You can go one step further: You need to participate in discussions on it, debate it, answer others' questions about it, tweet about it, write a blog post about it, a Kindle book about it, podcast about it, make videos about it... you get the idea.

And somewhere along the way, you will form opinions – about "it", about the journey, the process, the mistakes, the wins, the failures... because you've immersed yourself in it. You now know so much about it - and THAT is when you are on the path to being an "expert" (level of expertise notwithstanding).

So don't just tell me that WordPress released a new version. Tell me your opinion about it. Your perspective about it. The good, the bad, and the ugly.

Don't just tell me that Facebook has just released a feature called live video. Don't just give me information that Google is moving its live video platform from Hangouts to YouTube. Tell me how it affects me, tell me what I should do about it, what changes should I make, show me how I can take advantage of it, should I still keep using it, or should I use something else? If it's something else, then how does it stack up against YouTube live? What are the differences between YouTube Live, Facebook Live, Instagram Live, etc? When to use what?

Simply by using the different platforms, you'll quickly know the quirks, the differences, and if you use them all for a webinar as well as for a live video, if you use them all to do a vlog, etc you'll quickly know which platform works best for which task.

When Twitter first released Periscope years ago (no longer exists), there were a huge number of early adopters. I was one of them too. I signed up real fast and watched a couple of "scopes" from Guy Kawasaki and Gary Vee.

But even though a lot of us signed up for the service, there were only a few who tried out all of the features, played with the tech, made how-to videos about it, started a channel on YouTube, etc. And just by doing that, they went from being *just another user* of the platform to being a *teacher*, because they could now teach this stuff. And if you can teach it – however little you can – that means you tried it and learned it. Because you executed on it. And *teaching* is considered a higher level of expertise than just *doing*.

There were a few who used that to build an audience, documented what they did and how they did it, and they earned another level of credibility because they didn't just show you how to use a tool, they also showed you how to use it accomplish something – like building an audience and using it to promote a book or online course or webinar.

And then the next higher level of expertise is to live it, breathe it, do it all the time, go deep into live videos, do a live video every day – on Facebook, Instagram, Periscope, etc. build a big audience, show others how they too can do the same, put all of the tips, tricks and techniques into an online course, sell a whole bunch of copies, and now you see this person as the ultimate "Periscope Guru".

And those folks are interviewed on podcasts, become guests on video shows, get PR on local news, and get invited to present at live seminars. And they become even more famous. They do a live video from the stage, which is then watched and shared by thousands. That gets them even more followers. They add what they're learning into their course, and re-release it as version 2.0. They sell even more copies of their course. They get even more famous. They keynote a major social media conference in Las Vegas.

And that's what I call ascending the ladder of authority, or authority ascension, that leads to becoming the ultimate expert in just about anything.

A Programmer and a Marketer Walk Into a Bar

This is one of the most fascinating true stories of my life.

Back in 2000, I, along with my wife, 1-year-old daughter, and my father-in-law, had just moved from India to the US. At the time, I already had a website called BabyNamesIndia.com, which I had started in 1997. It is no longer active and hasn't been for about 15 years, but if you want to see a blast from the past, then check it out.

And I had just started dabbling with PHP, JavaScript, and MySQL. I had created a Contact-us Form for BabyNamesIndia.

One day in 2001, out of the blue, I got an email from that same Contact-Us form on my baby names site. And this person – let's call him "R" for now – wrote to me and said that he would like to use my Contact-Us Form PHP script on his website. And he asked if I could sell it to him.

This was way before WordPress and content management systems. That means, even if you needed something as simple as a contact-us form, where you had the First Name field, email, subject, and the body of the email, and you wanted it to be emailed to the site owner, and maybe even send an auto-response email, you needed to either program it yourself or hire a programmer. And that programmer just happened to be me.

I find out that R was a college kid and he had a website and wanted a similar contact-us form on his website.

I had no idea what to charge for something like this. Up to that point, I had never thought about what my time would be worth, how to charge for it, or for writing a piece of code, etc. So I just pulled a random number out of my behind and told him the script would cost $30, and I could install it for him for another $10.

He immediately agreed without any hesitation or negotiation. He even gave me a $10 tip once I had completed the job. And that was the easiest $50 I had made in my life up to that point.

Now, when I was still in India (before 2000), I had already made a couple of thousand dollars online selling a popular baby names book on my website. I would basically get an order online, then I would physically go to the local post office, and then pack and ship a copy of the book that I had previously bought in bulk from a local book distributor. But I was only making a few dollars per book in profits, and there was a bunch of physical work involved. But selling an existing PHP script that I had already created, and delivering it online, without ever leaving home, while still wearing shorts and a t-shirt, just blew my mind. Needless to say, I was ecstatic!

A few months later, he comes back again and says, hey Ravi, there's this awesome script on this other website, can you create something like that? So I checked it out. It was a JavaScript pop-up. This is not a regular HTML pop-up that you see today. This is like the alert prompt that you would get when you try to delete something, and it gives you two options, OK or Cancel. And you can't do anything else on that browser tab until you choose one.

So if you went to a web page that had this script installed, you would get an alert that says, "Hey, do you want to sign up to a newsletter? OK | Cancel". So if you clicked OK, it will try to open the default email client on there.

Back then, there was no Gmail. Hotmail existed but was also web-based. But the good thing was back then, a lot of people had an email client installed on their computer, like MS Outlook or Eudora (which became Mozilla Thunderbird, which is what I use to this day, and have been using it from back when it was still called Eudora).

So once you clicked OK on the alert which asked "Would you like to join my email list?", the script would open the local email client with the to-email and the subject line already pre-populated, and the viewer just had to hit send, and it would send an email to that to-email address and then they could be added to your email list – basically, an ugly replacement for an email signup form.

It was a super-basic **mailto:** command, and I could code that in 5 minutes. So I created the script for him and sold it to him for $50. I somehow had the sense to retain the copyright for the code, because I had written it from scratch. A few months later, we were emailing back and forth about some other project, and he mentioned that he had a girlfriend and he was planning on proposing to her shortly.

So he needed to quickly come up with a couple of thousand dollars for the engagement ring. So he needed cash fast. So I thought I was being super smart when I offered him the resell rights to that same script that I had previously developed for him. I told him that he could sell it online to whoever he wanted and keep all of the profits.

Back then, "Resell Rights" and "Private Label Rights" (PLR) and "Master Resell Right" etc were all pretty popular in the make-money-online niche. So once again, I pulled out a random number from my behind and told him that he can have full resell rights for $500.

I was fully expecting him to pass on the offer, and I was ok with that happening, which is one of the reasons why I priced it rather high (at least for me, at the time).

He thought about it for a few days, and came back and agreed to pay! I was on top of the world because I had just figured out the "power of the internet", by selling pre-developed PHP and Javascript scripts online. That aha moment is what led to me creating my scripts website, MyWebmasterInABox.com, which probably earned me well over $200,000 while it lasted. And the core foundation of ideas from this website is what turned into DigitalAccessPass.com (DAP) a few years later.

Of course, I can't take any credit for what DAP is today. I haven't written a line of code in many years now, and my wife Veena Prashanth is the brain and the brawn behind our plugin business, managing the tech team, the development, marketing, and everything in between for DAP and her other plugins. So while she works hard, I hardly work lol.

Anyway, back to the story: I sold R the resell rights for $500.

A week later, I received an email from one of the newsletters that I had subscribed to at the time. I had subscribed to way too many lists because I was constantly trying to learn marketing and selling and launching and list building and so on. I have always been, and will always be a student of marketing, and I like learning from what others are doing. There's a saying in marketing and life in general: do as they do, not as they say - because people tend to say one thing and do another thing. They don't always practice what they preach.

So don't just go by what they're saying. Look at what they're doing, whether it is parenting, sports, marketing, list building, launching, etc. Kids always look at parents to see what they do, and not necessarily what they say. So I was always trying to follow people, subscribed to a whole bunch of newsletters and websites and blogs, and downloaded every lead magnet I could get my hands on.

So back to the email – it was from one of the biggest newsletters I had subscribed from a renowned marketer. In the email, the marketer was promoting a new "software program" that can automatically get people to subscribe to your email newsletter the moment they visit your website. Wait, that sounds an awful lot like the script I developed and later sold resell rights to.

Turns out, he was promoting R's script. R had cut some kind of a deal with the publisher of the email, and she was promoting the script that he had renamed and made it his own.

He even had a domain name and an awesome sales page for it. I didn't have a sales page, I didn't have a domain, heck, I hadn't even thought about selling it to others. I wasn't selling anything online other than baby names books. I was just so focused on BabyNamesIndia.com, trying to sell more books, more eBooks (I had created one myself by hiring someone to make the world's biggest list of Indian baby names), and trying to apply all of my online marketing knowledge to make it better.

I was also doing ads via AdSense and Chitika (defunct) and earning about $1500 a month just from AdSense alone. Plus another $1000-$1500 a month in eBook and physical book sales. And all of that was on my nights and weekends. Plus I had a full-time job. So I was thrilled with making close to $3K per month on the side, with just my side-business.

So I was not yet in that mindset of trying to sell software online. So, it turns out this R went to a whole bunch of newsletter publishers and made a deal with them. And they were all promoting his script – *my* script that I had sold him! He absolutely crushed it! He paid me $500, but he must have made at least 10x his investment, if not 100x or 500x.

Now for the big reveal: Do you know who R is? It's Ryan. As in… (drum rolls)…

Ryan Deiss, Founder of DigitalMarketer.com and Scalable.co, and one of the biggest names and celebrities in the world of digital marketing.

And as Paul Harvey would say, "and now you know... the *rest* of the story".

This was a pivotal part of my career, so thank you, Ryan!

I've since attended Ryan Deiss' Traffic & Conversion conference several years and paid him back 10x in conference tickets, and I've walked into the hotel bar where he was mingling with the premium ticket holders, met with him and his wife, and even had a drink with him (though I may have had that drink by myself while had water or something).

So the biggest problem with a lot of us creators is that while we may be great at our craft, we're not naturally great at marketing our products and services or even ourselves. That's why someone who's a great cook will probably fail at running a restaurant because the restaurant business is not just about good food. This is best explained in the book "The E-Myth Revisited: Why Most Small Businesses Don't Work and What to Do About It", one of my favorite business books.

And that's how I learned the biggest business lesson of my life: it is not enough to simply create, you need to also promote. And I carry it with me till this day.

Which to Launch First: One-Time Product or Subscription?

Short answer: It depends.

If you have never launched a website before, or sold anything online, especially digital products, then I would not recommend launching a subscription-based product right out of the gate. And you should also not start with a high-ticket product either.

The reason is that when you're just getting started, you will not have the copywriting skills, the marketing skills, the positioning skills, product development skills, the ability to recruit JV's and affiliates, the savvy to put it all together, or even a product or library of content that is worth charging a recurring subscription.

No matter what kind of a superstar you've been in your day job, you simply won't have those skills when you are first starting your membership site and online course. Even if you set up membership sites for clients for your living, it's still not the same as doing it all yourself, *for* yourself. And you may not know to hire the right people for the job, because you may not know how to gauge other people's skills, may not know what that involves, you may not ask the right questions, and you certainly won't know what you don't know.

You will hear people say that it takes the same amount of work to sell a $10 product as it takes to sell a $100 or $1000 product. That's a bit misleading. Sure, the basic elements of selling a product online – like the landing page, title, subtitle, body copy, pricing table, buy buttons, etc - may all be the same. You may even use the same kind of platforms – free and paid – to promote them. But the level of proof (of the product's benefits, your expertise, etc), authority, and positioning you need to sell a $10 course, is nothing compared to what it takes to sell a $1,000 coaching program or online course.

I recently encountered a 17-year-old teenager on Twitter who grew his audience quickly starting from scratch. Soon I started seeing his tweets more often, via other people's likes, comments, re-tweets, etc. Soon thereafter, he started selling an eBook on growing your audience with Twitter using DM's. He had about 3,000 followers at the time and was selling his eBook for $15. A couple of others I was following were also tweeting about him, so I figured that for that low price, it was a no-brainer for me to check it out. I was expecting $15 worth of value, and I can say I go that for the most part.

However, if that same teenager was selling a course for > $100, I would've wanted to research it some more. And if it was sold for $500-$1000 or more, I would have wanted a ton of more proof before I bought it – social proof, testimonials, specific results from reputable names, case studies, and definitely a few free training videos that showed me something that would show me why I should buy it and what is the payoff for me. I would've wanted $1000 worth of value this time, and that's a lot harder to do as a marketer.

DIY, DWY & DFY

There are 3 basic digital product monetization models: DIY, DWY, and DFY.

DIY stands for Do It Yourself, DWY stands for Done With You, and DFY stands for Done For You.

Imagine a pyramid with three tiers.

DIY (Do It Yourself) is usually the lowest tier of the pyramid – it's the basic, fully automated online course where everything is delivered digitally. This is similar to the 1-site license we offer at DigitalAccessPass.com (DAP). The buyer who downloads the software can watch documentation videos and read how-to setup documentation and set up their website themselves. Of course, we offer ticket-based support, but they don't get any 1-on-1 calls with us. Software as a Service (SaaS) like a hosted platform (podcast hosting, social media marketing tools, online tools that store/modify your content, etc) are in this tier.

DWY (Done With You) is the middle tier - slightly more advanced than DIY, where you do things along WITH them. In my business, we set up our users' membership sites by working alongside our Platinum and Elite members. They pay a subscription fee for DAP and also get a number of our plugins with their subscription. We do it on a live, 1-on-1 call. We get on a call with them, go over their goals, the kind of content they wish to create-, sell- and deliver, and we tailor the setup of DAP to fit their specific needs.

That's your classic DWY: Done With You. You can charge more for DWY compared to DIY.

Then there's the top-most tier - at least it is, in most niches - which is DFY: Done For You. We don't offer a DFY option in our business at this time. In this model, the client does not wish to do it themselves; they also don't want you to do it *with* them. They just want you to do it FOR them and tell them it's done, and send them a bill.

Examples of DFY are SEO services, marketing funnel set up, set up of CRM's like Infusionsoft, traffic generation, lead generation, online ad campaign set up, etc.

If you add 1-on-1 coaching and consulting, where you work with your clients first, find out their needs, customize the solution specifically for their needs, and then also offer the backend services to get it done FOR them, that's where you can charge the most.

And my recommendation would be to slowly start value-stacking.

Presuming you already know your niche, and have figured out who is your target audience, start by creating a low-cost, one-time product first. It could be a Kindle book, a Report, a short video course, an audiobook, etc.

Start building an audience from day 1. Build an email list of free subscribers as well as buyers.

As a separate exercise, create a sales page for your future subscription product, even if you're not going to promote it right now. Put together the entire offer ahead of time. It doesn't matter if you haven't created any products yet. Just creating the offer, the pricing table, and the landing page will give you a lot of ideas about what it's going to take to create a subscription-based membership.

You could create 3-tiers - (say) Silver, Gold, and Platinum - with each tier offering more benefits than the other, and that could include not just your team's time, but also your own ongoing consulting and review of the business roadmap.

You can take a look at my offer for my Digital Creators Academy to get an idea of the 3 tiers I'm referring to.

Pricing also plays a role in the kind of marketing that will be needed to make some sales. A $1,000 product buyer's mindset is going to be much different, in a good way of course, compared to a $100 buyer, which will be different when compared to a $5 buyer. No offense to anyone or any product - that's just human psychology in action.

The kind of marketing aimed at a person buying at the $1 Store will have to be different from the person shopping at an expensive jewelry store. Now, I'm sure there will be a small group of people who may buy both expensive jewelry *and* also shop at a dollar store. But that is a minority.

In general, the more expensive your product or service is, the less hand-holding your product probably needs, which means less support, and they tend to be more generous with their praise and recommendations and may refer more clients to you.

So if someone buys something from you for $1,000, the chances are pretty high that they can afford to continue paying you a $100/month continuity afterward. Because if they could afford to pay you that much upfront, then they probably have at least somewhat of an established business, they probably have more money than time, and if you can demonstrate the value of what you're offering, they will not have a problem paying you a small fraction of the value that they're going to be getting from you and your product.

An ideal revenue model would be to get paid a decent amount up front, followed by a continuity program (recurring retainer). Especially because the standard stick rate for the average membership is between 3-6 months. It will differ from niche to niche. But if you're getting lock-in from them to the equivalent of 10 months upfront, and then add to that the mindset advantage you have with such customers paying for high-ticket items, now you have one of the best membership models there can be.

Big Chunk Upfront Plus Backend Continuity Shall Maketh Thy Successful, Such a Membership Model - Yoda, probably ☺.

No Such Thing as Too Long, Only Too Boring

How long should your sales page be?
How long should your podcast be?
How long should your blog post be?
How long should your webinar be?

I have one simple answer to this...

There is no such thing as too long, only too boring.

And as much as I would love to take credit for that quote, it's not mine, and I don't know who originally said it.

That is such a fantastic premise, that it applies to pretty much every aspect of life.

The movie "The Godfather" is arguably one of the greatest movies ever made. A few years ago, my wife Veena (co-founder and co-developer of DAP) and I watched the first two Godfather movies on Amazon, a few days apart. I had watched it when I was much younger but wanted to watch it with her again. The Godfather 1 was 2h 58m. It was absolutely mesmerizing. And the crazy thing is, we only noticed that after The Godfather 2 had ended, and we paused the video player, and we sat there in silence, hungover (in a good, non-alcoholic way) from the impact of the movie. And when the splash screen came up, we realized that The Godfather 2 was a whopping 3h 22min.

Lord of the Rings (LOTR) Part 1: 2h 58m. The combined running time of all LOTR movies: a whopping 9.2 hours! And that was not even including the Hobbit series. I remember watching the Fellowship of the Ring (Part 1) in the early 2000s. I had just arrived from India a few months earlier. I had never heard of the book - I doubt many people in India had. And I remember, at the end of the movie, the credits started rolling and the lights came on, and I was sitting there in shock that the movie had ended. I had not realized that I had sat there for almost 3 hours, and I thought that the best part was just getting started, as the fellowship formed and they started their journey. I have never been more mesmerized by a movie, that I not only had not sat there for 3 hours, but I was kind of upset that they ended it so "abruptly", just when I thought they were getting into the thick of things.

On the other hand, I have seen some terrible movies, many of which I have stopped watching after about 15-20 minutes hour, and then some I have endured for a full hour and a half only because I was in a theatre with my family eating popcorn, and didn't have the heart to ruin everyone's evening. I have walked out after watching a movie thinking, oh boy, there goes 2 hours of my life that I will never get back. I would have probably paid five times as much just to erase that movie from my memory and get back that time.

I have been to live seminars where the speaker was on stage for 3 hours, and I have had to hold my pee so badly because I didn't want to miss a second of the presentation. And then there are presentations where 10 minutes in, I get up and leave the room because this speaker is there only to pitch their products, or is as interesting as watching paint dry.

One of the most popular and most downloaded podcasts is Dan Carlin's Hardcore History, where the average episode is about 4-5 hours long - each episode! And he gets millions of downloads a month. Yet, many under-20 minute podcasts promise to pack a lot of content quickly and cut to the chase, but I have unsubscribed from those shows after listening to just a few episodes because their intro was way too long, too much unrelated small talk and banter, appearing disorganized and fumbling and bumbling for ideas to talk about, the appearance of making it all up on the fly. After all, the hosts couldn't be bothered to prepare for 10 minutes in advance, too many ads right up-front (sometimes up to 5 minutes), poor audio, or worse, terrible audio. One of the podcasts by the famous internet marketer Neil Patel and his partner, was so bad in the beginning, that it sounded like one of them is recording it from the toilet. And I remember unsubscribing because the podcast was releasing episodes 7 days a week, and I just couldn't keep up. And I started deleting them, and then I couldn't delete them fast enough because they just kept coming and coming.

Let's say you love Pizza. So you order it Monday evening watching the game. Then in the evening, there are leftovers, so you have more pizza. Then when you wake up, your significant other says, there's so much pizza, you have to have it for breakfast. For lunch, the same thing. More pizza. And then for dinner, he or she orders a fresh pie from the same pizza place. Just about that point, you're probably ready to throw up if someone offered you one more slice of Pizza, or even mentioned the word pizza. That's what happens when there's too much of a good thing, thrown fast and furiously at you.

Same thing when it comes to blogging: Seth Godin writes the smartest, shortest blog posts that'll leave you doing a double-take on the depth of what he wrote, and then on the flip side, I also love the extremely long and detailed posts by, yup, that same guy whose podcast I mentioned earlier: Neil Patel. I love Neil's blog posts and most people, including me, would think, why doesn't he just take this massively humongous insanely awesome blog post and create a book out of it. But no, he publishes all that amazing content as one massive blog post (it's been nicknamed as a "Skyscraper Post") that gets him millions of visitors a year and was the launching pad that turned him into an internet marketing celebrity many years ago.

Let's take YouTube videos - most amateur how-to videos are incredibly boring because there's usually not enough lighting, bad sound, loud thumping noises as the person is typing or showing something, extremely long gaps between transitions or thoughts, way too much setup time, spending way too much time moving the mouse around the screen and clicking and typing up long descriptions and titles and so on, especially with screencast videos, and almost zero editing to remove all of the fluff. The creator is just rambling along randomly, making up thoughts and words on the fly, without an agenda or point, and then not removing any of it, which would make the video way more interesting. And the video doesn't even have to necessarily be long for me to exit after 20 seconds. I don't care how long the video is if it's interesting and giving me "value" (something that everyone has to define for themselves, as to what that is for them).

It's the same thing when it comes to online webinars as well. Most webinars suck because first, a lot of them pretend like it's a live webinar when there are a hundred different tells that it's just a stupid pre-recorded video trick, there are all the fake "alright guys, let's get some feedback here. Type into the comments box if you are foolish enough to not know that all these names on the side are fake made-up names with your name at the top, to make you think that you are on a live call with 50 other people, most of them with their first and last names neatly spelled, with the first letters capitalized, because they're all such awesome folks".

Then there's the obligatory "Let me show you a few amazing pictures of me with my kids and spouse and dog, and then the income report screenshots, and me telling you how much money I made last month without ever telling you how much I spent to make that money." And the numbers are always perfectly random, like "How I made $17, 536.55", you know because if you didn't say a perfectly nice and round number, no one would know that you're BS'ing, right? Yeah, you get my point.

So, let me repeat that awesome quote: "There's no such thing as too long, only too boring".

Ultimately, it all comes down to how awesome your content is.

The length of the videos in your video course, or the audio in your audio course, or the length of your podcast episodes, or the length of your sales copy, or your email, none of it matters, if your stuff is boring as hell, or irrelevant, or doesn't deliver on the promise of your title or description.

There's this famous quote, that has been strangely attributed to several different people, like Mark Twain, George Bernard Shaw, Voltaire, Johann Wolfgang von Goethe, Winston Churchill, Pliny the Younger, Cato, Cicero, Bill Clinton, and Benjamin Franklin. But a lot of online research seems to agree, that it was indeed the French mathematician and philosopher, Blaise Pascal, who once ended a letter that he wrote, with this sentence:

"I have made this longer than usual because I have not had time to make it shorter."

You almost always have to put in more time to make something shorter – whether it's a podcast, live video, or a movie. It's a lot easier to just wing the whole thing and keep recording and hit publish as soon as you stop the recording. I know a lot of podcasters and marketers who do exactly that with their podcasts or video shows. No editing, no optimizing, "good enough" lighting, "OK" audio, barely any preparation.

They just think they're doing their listeners or viewers a favor simply by hitting publish, because their excuse is, hey, at least I'm able to get this out the door as is because if I were to edit it, I would never be able to publish it.

Well, that's just lazy, and disrespectful of my time, in my humble opinion. There are certain things for which it's better to just ship it as Seth Godin says than sit on it and dilly dally and never put it out there. But most audio and video are not among them. It's just plain disrespectful of your audience's time if you take content worth 10 minutes and stretch it out for 30 minutes, just because you could not be bothered to plan and take a few minutes to get your audio and lighting correct.

Just because something is long doesn't mean it's better and doesn't mean it's boring.

And at the same time, just because it's short doesn't mean it's worse, or that it's to-the-point, either.

Length doesn't matter - what truly matters is the substance in your content, and how quickly and in the shortest time possible you're delivering education, empathy, emotions, and/or entertainment.

Product First or Audience First?

This is a burning question for anyone starting an online business. As much as it seems similar to the "Chicken or the Egg" argument, it's not that complicated when it comes down to the core nature of these two strategies.

Unfortunately, there is no simple one-size-fits-all answer, so I'll break it down as best as I can, given my own experience selling several products online since 1997, and then add to that my experience coaching and consulting with clients since 2003.

1) Create a product first, and THEN find an audience for that product.

2) Build an audience first, and THEN create a product(s) for that audience.

In Strategy #1, you start with the skills and resources you currently have and create your product or service first, based on your knowledge and experience. Then you try to find an audience for what you've already created or are in the process of creating. For many product creators, they create it to scratch their own itch, so it comes down to finding people like them.

Then you keep improving the product, extending it, and creating other products and services around your core product or core niche, as you get more feedback from current, past, and future customers.

In Strategy #2, you build an audience first, that is hopefully big enough, hungry for a solution for a problem they have, can afford to pay for it, are easily reachable, and easy to work with. And then you create something for that audience.

There are a lot of tangents I can go in when talking about some of these things – like, how big of an audience do you really need to make it work?

The answer to that depends on what kind of a product or service you're selling, how much it costs, and what is your revenue target?

For eg., if you're selling something for $100, and your goal is a one-time revenue of $100,000, then you need 1,000 buyers/members/clients.

But if you're selling something for $20, and your goal is still the same $100,000, then you need 5,000 buyers – 5x more than in the first example, to achieve the same revenue target.

When I say "Product", I'm referring to anything that you create and sell - whether it is a digital product, physical product, actual service, online course, membership site, SaaS product, WordPress plugin, etc.

Both strategies have their pros and cons. And both have been proven to work over the years by probably millions of entrepreneurs. The main question is, which of these is better suited for *you*?

Let's start with Strategy #1: Creating a product first and then finding an audience for it.

If you look at any successful company, movement, or even a cult, in the history of the world - it always started with the vision first, and then came the audience, who resonated with that vision.

Henry Ford famously said, "If I had asked people what they wanted, they would have said faster horses."

Steve Jobs once said, "It's really hard to design products by focus groups. A lot of times, people don't know what they want until you show it to them."

Larry Page and Sergey Brin were two Ph.D. students at Stanford University, California. They saw that online search was deeply flawed and needed a better product. Search engines that existed at the time ranked results by counting how many times the search terms appeared on the page, and these two figured that a better way to determine a website's relevance was by the number of pages that linked back to a website and the relevance of those other pages themselves.

So back in 1996, if Google had surveyed the entire planet of a few billion people, and asked them what their top 10 issues were in their life that they would like to get solved, I can guarantee you that having a better search engine would not have been one of those top 10. Heck, it may not even have been one of the top 1,000 things that 99% of people in the world wanted.

Nobody knew that we needed a better search engine until Google created it.

I'm going to quickly toot my own horn here for a bit: Many of the products I've created have been things that most people didn't know that they needed until I created them, and then an entire industry was born out of them.

When I created the first-ever PayPal Download Protector PHP script in 2001, most people didn't know that their download files needed to be protected after someone had paid, because those using PayPal to sell eBooks didn't know that one could simply do a view-source of your sales page where you had the PayPal buy button, and the button code would actually have the thank you page URL embedded in it, and they could go to the thank-you page directly without having to pay for it and download the ebook or video or audio.

It was one of my most successful products back in the day, and all I had to do was explain to people how their digital products were getting stolen from right under their noses, and I sold tens of thousands of copies of this script. And then I went on to create a similar script for ClickBank and called it the ClickBank Download Protector. Once again, thousands of copies were sold.

Back in 2007, I created DigitalAccessPass, and that's one of the very few things I can take credit for at this point, because my lovely wife Veena Prashanth who is also the co-founder & co-developer of DAP, has taken it to dizzying new heights that I never could have done myself, not in a million years. So kudos and a big shout out to my lovely lady.

So when I started working on DAP back in 2007, the world didn't know what content dripping was and didn't know why they needed it.

Online Marketers were creating entire new websites for each time they re-launched their product once or twice a year, and they manually published the content little by little on this new site, because if they did a new launch using their website from last year, all new members coming in could access all of the content from day 1, they could download all member-content in a few days, and then ask for a refund.

And this was very much true in the make-money-online and biz-op niches. So the marketers would create a fresh new website every year, with a fresh new domain, and would upload all of the content manually, little by little, throughout the course, and create a new forum with a new content management system and a new group of buyers with new comments and so on. What a terrible waste of time, money, and resources. But the world didn't know of a better way until I invented Content Dripping in late 2006. And that's how DigitalAccessPass.com - fondly known as DAP - was born.

I didn't go around surveying thousands of people for what kind of software I should create. Maybe I should have, and maybe I would've done a lot better, but that's just splitting hairs at this point. Based on my knowledge and experience in the industry, and simply having coded some of these solutions for my personal use, not just hearing someone tell me about a cool new niche, but simply by being in the trenches, participating in different online forums, and answering questions from people, and having walked the walk and talked the talk, I had a pretty good idea of what I thought was missing in the industry.

I remember going to a conference in San Diego in 2008. At the conference, everyone was allowed to take the mic at the end of the last session, and ask questions or offer their feedback. So I went to the mic and said that I had a new piece of software coming out, where, just like you can queue up emails ahead of time in an Email Autoresponder, you could queue up content ahead of time, to drip over time. I called it a ContentResponder. And the moment I said that, every single famous marketer on stage all but jumped up, and everyone was like, dude, sell it to me right now. I got a big round of applause from the 2000+ people present there, and when I went on and said that I would be happy to give everyone a copy of it for free, I got the biggest applause I've ever received, from the biggest audience ever at the time for a marketers' seminar. I'll tell you more about that story in an upcoming chapter.

Stephen King is the king of the Horror/Fiction genre. It doesn't matter how many millions of dollars romance novels make, Stephen King is never going to write a Fifty Shades of Grey type of novel. And J.K. Rowling is never going to write a non-fiction book about Space, Time, and Matter. They're not writing books based on which genre of books sell the most - they're writing books based on what they're the best at.

When I started selling digital information products, I realized the need to protect content. I created a plugin for that.

When I started doing launches and saw others doing launches, I saw what was missing, and invented Content Dripping.

In 2009, when I realized I need to host large videos and audio PDFs outside of my website (for performance and security reasons), I developed S3MediaVault.com, an Amazon S3 Video Player, Audio Player and File Protector for files stored on S3. It supports Amazon S3 & CloudFront, Impossible-to-download True Video & Audio Streaming using HLS, Video & Audio Playlists, and more!

When I started a podcast called SubscribeMe.fm in 2015, I saw that there was just one other podcast player plugin, and even that didn't have all the features I wanted and thought it should have. So I developed CoolCastPlayer.com.

When I saw that one of my websites had a bunch of errors on the home page, and realized that it might've been that way for who-knows-how-long, I created WhatChangedWhen.com (now defunct).

And to promote CoolCastPlayer.com, I needed to build a list of podcasters. I knew that podcasters wanted an easy way to download and view their Apple Podcasts Ratings and Reviews from 155 countries. So I created a free website PodcastReviews.me that did just that.

So the point of all these examples is that I had an itch, and I wanted to scratch it, so I created something that would scratch it. And then I go to where everyone like me with a similar itch hangs out, and try to let them know.

When I first tried to let people know about WhatChangedWhen, from the few people I polled in my network on social media, one person said they didn't understand what the site does.

Another said they don't see the value in this.

One person said they don't have a website or a podcast.

Another said they have only one website and they're working on it every day so they don't need content monitoring even if it's free.

But on the flip side...

I got feedback like "I think a service such as yours can be incredibly helpful. Being able to quickly discover and identify potential problems allows podcasters to respond very quickly."

Another said "Hey Ravi! Thank you make this amazing resource."

Another said "Stud! You're crushing... Just shared with my mastermind group."

Another said "Yes!!!"

And finally, the best one yet is when a friend said "Dude, this is a crazy good idea, wish I had thought of this first."

See how different the feedback can be for the same idea? So instead of worrying about those who don't need what you've created, or those who don't get it, or don't get the value, you just keep moving on and keep trying to reach new people who understand the pain, maybe because they've experienced it themselves, or maybe because they just get it right away.

Anyway, I can give you probably a million examples of someone who first created a product or service based on their passion, dreams, vision, skills, experience, domain knowledge, being in the trenches, from first having an itch, then wanting to scratch it, and then wanting to find other people just like them who had the same itch.

Now, this simple yet risky strategy is why a lot of businesses fail. I could totally argue against this strategy, and tell you that most businesses and online courses and membership sites and software products fail, because you created something that not enough other people need, or want, or they don't care enough to pay for it, etc. There are so many factors that can cause a product or service to fail.

But still, this is BY FAR the most popular strategy for creating products and services, because starting with what you already know, with that itch, is the most natural thing for entrepreneurs. It's second nature to pretty much everyone. This is exactly how the greatest products and services in the world were created. This is how most of the inventions and discoveries in the world were made.

Most people don't need any advanced marketing skills or entrepreneurial skills to be able to identify their pains, figure out how to solve them, and how to then see if others have the same issue.

If you have watched Shark Tank, maybe like 95% of the products that are pitched there, come out of the creator's pains, in their inability to not be able to do something, or wanting to do something better, easier, faster, less pain, more gain, etc.

And if you've noticed the questions asked by the Shark Tank investors, they're always interested in knowing the entrepreneur's background. Do they have any experience in the industry? How long have they been doing this? How deep is their knowledge? Have they paid their dues, so to speak?

Guess why they're asking all of that? Because as an investor, if you have to bet your money on something, you should bet on the entrepreneur, not on the product. The product itself might flop, it may never sell. But if the entrepreneur behind it is really good, they can improve the product, they can reinvent it, or create something altogether new based on what they've already learned, they can hustle and work hard and be in the trenches. That's what the Sharks are looking for because they cannot - and will not - do any of that. All the sharks can do is to lend money, lend contacts, lend the network, lend their name and credibility, and offer some guidance and mentoring. Everything else has to be done by the entrepreneur.

So while the product has got to be great, what gets the Sharks into a bidding war, is the entrepreneur behind it.

To be honest, there are no perfectly original products anymore. Whatever you can think of, whatever you can imagine, has probably been thought of by hundreds if not thousands of people worldwide, and someone has already created some version of it. Even the idea of living in space is no longer just an idea - people are working on it! So just having an idea is not good enough. It's all in the execution, and the product development and how quickly you can test it, get it to market, get market feedback, iterate it, evolve it, and then the hustle and heart and expertise of the person behind it.

And don't forget - the first version of the product is just that - the first version. It's not set in stone. Like Dave Jackson from the School of Podcasting says: Your podcast is not a statue, it's a recipe.

In the same way, your product is also not a statue, but a recipe. It can change, it can evolve - it HAS to evolve. YOU have to evolve. Even a statue that's set in stone needs repairs and maintenance - there is no such thing as set-it-and-forget-it.

And that's why, it's totally fine to create the product first and THEN find an audience, and this strategy is what is going to work for 99% of entrepreneurs, especially first-time entrepreneurs. Of course, you shouldn't wait until the entire product is ready for release, and then 2 days before launch, you tell everyone that this is what you've been working on.

No need to keep your product creation journey shrouded in secrecy. Nobody is going to steal your idea. Ideas are abundant. It's the fulfilling of the idea from scratch to launch, is where most people fail. So start building your audience even as you start working on your product. The process of pre-selling something that hasn't been created yet is such an extensive skill in itself and probably requires a separate book. Which I may write myself, or maybe I'll add it to this book as a new chapter.

But the fact remains that you can do very well with Strategy #1: Product First, Audience Next.

Now on to Strategy #2: Audience First, Product Next.

So Building an Audience First and THEN creating product(s) for that audience.

Which is WAY easier said than done.

And I'm also going to let you in on a crazy little secret... that Strategy #1, which is Product First, Audience Next, and Strategy #2, which is Audience First, Product Next, are not mutually exclusive at all.

You don't HAVE to choose just one or the other. You can do both.

You MUST do both - but in a specific order.

I do have to say this about Strategy #1. The cool thing is that once you've accomplished that ("Product First, Audience Next", then Strategy #2 ("Audience First, Product Next" becomes moot, because now you already have an existing audience who have already bought your first product. So creating additional products for an existing audience is going to be a lot easier than finding or building a new audience.

I have a phrase for this. I call this: **Go Deep, Then Wide**. I have a separate chapter about this.

When you find a niche where you have already created a product and you're starting to build up an audience in that niche, it is a lot easier to go deep into that niche, than to go wide and start with new niches that are unrelated to that product.

Almost every single successful entrepreneur or company almost always tends to go deep, before they go wide. There are very, VERY few companies - only the ones with billions of dollars in revenue – that can afford to get into completely new territory, throw stuff up on the wall, and see what sticks.

For eg., Tesla, which is into electric cars, Solar Panels, HyperLoop (an underground bullet train), and SpaceX which builds rockets and spacecraft and wants to send people to Mars.

Electric cars and solar panels are related (batteries, renewable energy), but Hyperloop and SpaceX? Completely unrelated industries.

Similarly, there's Google, which started with search, then built Adwords, which offered the ability for advertisers to advertise in the right-side column of Google search. Then they extended it to AdSense, which allowed people like you and me to put ads on our blogs and websites and earn a tiny piece of the ad revenue.

I used AdSense way back in 2003-04 when it first came out. At the time, I had a website about baby names, called BabyNamesIndia.com. It's still there, but I haven't updated it in over 10 years. You can check it out if you want to see a blast from the past. An all-HTML, hand-coded website, and I monetized it by selling a physical book on Indian baby names. Later I created my own eBook on Indian Baby Names. I also had AdSense ads on it. I also tried ads from multiple companies like Chitika, Bidvertiser, another service that offered websites where you could buy links (I think it was linkexchange.com), and promoted my website WebmasterInABox.net (also defunct).

At one point, I was averaging about $1,500 per month just from that website, like clockwork, primarily from Google AdSense. And I probably would've made at least 10x more - at least 10,000 dollars a month – if the traffic were from the US. But unfortunately, it wasn't. Most of my traffic was from India, and like 5% of it was from the US. So because the traffic wasn't from the US, there weren't too many advertisers showing ads to visitors from India, because, most of the traffic around the world is much harder to monetize compared to traffic from the US, and maybe even Canada and the UK. So that's why I made only $1500 instead of $15,000 a month.

And that sucked!

So Google created most of their products around Online Advertising: Ads on Google.com search, ads within Gmail, ads on their other properties like Google Maps, YouTube, Google+ (RIP), etc.

They dug pretty deep into the ad-revenue space, before going into other niches. But even with their deepest of pockets and massively brilliant human resources, they are not guaranteed any success – they failed with many products like Google Plus, Orkut, Boston Dynamics (BD - remember those scary robots), Google Nexus, Google Talk, Inbox... you get the idea.

They did eventually sell off BD as manufacturing robots were not suited for Google's strengths in the digital world. And that's why Google manufactures so few physical products today. Almost 87% of Google's revenue comes from advertising. And only about 13% from all of their other products, of which, a HUGE chunk is actually from their cloud services - like Google cloud hosting and Google Play store.

Even a 1+ TRILLION dollar company like Google goes deep way more than it goes wide. And even they fail – a lot - when they stray too far from their core niche.

And that's why, when you're building a new product in a specific niche, it makes NO sense to go and start from scratch in a completely brand new niche, try to establish credibility and authority and trust of an entirely new audience that you would have to build from scratch. It makes no sense to go off on a complete tangent. You would be better served to create more products for your existing audience, and just keep building on top of it, keep stacking the value.

Strategy #2 becomes way easier if you started with Strategy #1.

But what if you're directly starting with Strategy 2?

After all, it is one of the most overhyped, overwhelming strategies that you'll hear from a lot of marketing gurus, and it's easily the most difficult one to start with, especially if you're just getting started with your first-ever business venture.

So when you hear someone tell you "Oh, that's easy - just pick a hungry market, create products for them, and boom, you now have a flourishing business.", know that it's never that simple.

When it comes to building an audience first, you still can't just wake up one day and say "Alright, I'm going to build an audience today".

You can't just manifest an audience out of thin air. You have to think through a whole bunch of things before you even take the first step to building an audience.

You *have* to start with the niche first because you cannot build a "one size fits all" audience. It has to be specific to a niche. That's why Billboard advertising is so un-targeted because you can't choose who should see it. You just "Spray and Pray" and hope that out of all the people who hopefully do see your billboard, some of them will be your target audience.

Let's say you try to pick a trend. Go to Google Trends at trends.google.com and you can, according to Google, "Explore what the world is searching".

So right now, at the time of writing this, Google is showing that people are searching for Taylor Swift, Kim Kardashian, FIFA World Cup, and American Football.

I don't know how easy it would be to create products or services based on Taylor Swift or Kim Kardashian, and Soccer (football). You might think, hey, I can write juicy gossip columns about those topics.

Sure, you may write one blog post... or 10, or 50. What then? How are you going to be found? You would have to rank very high in search, do a bunch of SEO, depend on a long-tail search where you're trying to rank for specific keyword combinations, and not just for the search "Taylor Swift".

Let's say you somehow got 10,000 visitors. What next? How're you going to monetize it? AdSense ads? Handpicked sponsors? It's not like you can create an online course about the "royal wedding". You can't create t-shirts and caps and pens with the picture of the royal couple without getting sued into oblivion.

You've probably seen specialty pop-up stores come up during certain times of the year. In the US, if you go to the mall before Halloween, chances are you'll see a massive new store that wasn't there even a month ago – entirely dedicated to just Halloween costumes, toys, and decorations. Thousands and thousands of products, massive collections, for everyone from babies to teens to adults.

It's a well-known fact that Halloween means big business for stores. According to the National Retail Federation's website at nrf.com, people spend about $9 Billion during Halloween!

So there it is - a huge and hungry $9 Billion market. People looking to buy stuff in the stores and online and in their local grocery stores and department stores. Hungry buyers who'll pay a lot of money to deck out their front yards with spooky and scary creatures and lighting and buy tons and tons of candy for kids to ruin their teeth and run up their parents' dentist bills.

Think you can compete in that market and get a slice of that?

Not as easy as you might think. There's no way the average person like you and me, without any prior experience in selling physical products, with no experience in sourcing products or running a physical store, or in all of the setup that goes into launching a physical store - with ZERO experience in the industry or anything even remotely related to the niche - there's no way you or I can launch a store in the middle of the mall, with thousands of SKU's (products). Try sourcing and selling just one physical product - like maybe a scary mask - on Amazon.com. It's super-tough competition, and super-hard to break into if you're a first-time seller on Amazon with no selling experience, no merchant reviews, no product reviews, no nothing.

Now imagine selling tens of products on Amazon. A *lot* harder. And to think that you can rent a store paying thousands of dollars in rent, and manage the kind of inventory control and product sourcing and billing and returns and refunds and part-time employees who can work the store and the billing system and monitor fraud and theft? You'll burn through your funds and lose your life's savings if you went after this business for the only reason that it's a huge and hungry market.

So just because Halloween is a huge industry doesn't mean you or I am qualified to build a big business out of it.

Now, on the other hand, let's say you already had a small local store. You already know about inventory control, billing, hiring people, sourcing products, and managing a physical store. So you already have the tools, the knowledge, experience, contacts, vendors, experience in dealing with vendors, delayed payments, refunds, restocking, damage, fraud, theft, and everything else that goes on in a store. And that is when if you wanted to expand beyond your little local shop, and add a new source of income, even if it is seasonal, you could easily do that by expanding into the Halloween Store business.

And you don't even have to have owned a local store - you could have worked in a store for a few years and you could easily gain the knowledge and experience through that as well.

(NRF Halloween Trends)

Here's another example: A couple of years ago, Crypto Currencies were a massively trending topic. You couldn't go a day without reading or hearing about something related to Crypto, like BitCoin, or Ethereum, or BlockChain. But just because it was hot and heavy, does it mean you could latch on to it and start pumping out online courses, books, a YouTube channel, and a podcast about Crypto Currencies? Sure, you could try - nothing preventing us from trying.

But if I did it, I would probably fail, because I have zero interest in that topic. Even if I have some interest, doesn't mean I would know what I'm talking about. I would either have to team up with another crypto expert, or I would have to first learn a lot about it myself. It's not practical for me to become an expert in that subject, as it would take too long, and it's not in my zone of genius.

That means I have to depend on someone else to create the content, whether that is for the paid content or the free content - like YouTube videos and podcasts and social media content for

Facebook and Instagram. Basically, someone else becomes the face of the business. If you're OK with that, that's great, because that's what it will require. And if this Cryptocurrency expert I would be partnering with is going to create all the content and be the face of the business, they're going to want to know what exactly I'm bringing to the table.

Now, if I'm already a big name in a related industry, and I have an established audience, it wouldn't be too hard to convince the expert that I'll do all the heavy-lifting on the back-end - the marketing, the technology, the funnels, the website, etc.

Let's say they agree to this deal. 6 months down the line, they get bored (happens to almost everyone), and they're no longer all that excited about the niche. Maybe because the hype and the fad died, or they came across a shinier object. What now?

It's like any other partnership: What do you do if one of the partners stops performing? Loses interest? What happens if they don't show up and deliver on their promises? So because I wasn't the front-facing guy, and also not the Subject Matter Expert (SME), I really can't do much about it other than hunting for a replacement, or shutting down the business.

So, the bottom line is, you can't pick a niche in a vacuum just because it is a trending topic in a hot niche. But because we're now covering Strategy 2, which is building an audience first, and then creating the products for it, the problem remains:

What kind of audience are you going to build?

Let's say you start with their likes and dislikes, wants and needs, demographics and psychographics, sex, gender identification, age group, cities or countries they live in, the language they speak, are they on social media (and which one) - are they on Facebook, or Twitter, or Instagram, or Snapchat - where do they hang out, can they be reached online, or do you have to go to in-person events, do you have to sponsor live events, do you have to advertise on the radio, is that local radio, or national radio, do they listen to podcasts, and on and on and on.

If you've ever run Facebook ads, you know what I mean. When you want to run an ad on Facebook, the most important part of a Facebook ad - even more than the actual ad copy and headline and image and branding and colors, etc, is *who* should be seeing that ad.

The audience selection is probably *the* most important piece of the puzzle because it doesn't matter how awesome your promo video is, or your image, or your call-to-action. If you show that ad to the wrong person, to an audience to whom your product or service is irrelevant, your ad is not going to convert, and you'll waste a lot of money.

That's why you'll see a lot of first-time or new Facebook advertisers saying Facebook ads don't work. They'll blame the strategy itself. But the reality is that their ads probably didn't work because of several things they didn't get right, the most important one being selecting the right audience for the ad.

So to build an audience, you have to create a detailed avatar of that audience first, because building an email list is different from building a Facebook group which is different from growing Instagram followers which is different from growing your podcast audience.

Building an audience of millennials is different from an audience of gen-Xers which is different from an audience of baby boomers. You get the idea.

This is why there are some HUGE caveats to this audience-first strategy. And one of them is, like I just talked about, knowing what kind of an audience to build.

But before you even *think* about building an audience, you need to select your niche first, because you can't create an audience in a vacuum, without knowing what niche or industry you're building this audience for.

If you build an audience of women aged between 20-40 who are interested in health and fitness, you will not do well selling them men's shaving and grooming products. Sure, some of them may buy it for their boyfriends or husbands, but they would be a minority.

But if you build an audience of men between 20 and 50, who need to shave frequently, and who can use quality razors at a cheap price, that's a great start.

But how are you going to build this audience of men?

How are you going to do that without creating anything for that audience first? Or without even knowing if you can create grooming products, to begin with?

Let me give you an example: Two guys - let's call them Mark and Michael. They meet at a party, and over drinks, they start talking about how razor blades are so darn expensive. And there are such a large number of men who need to shave often, but it's insane that there are no quality products at an affordable price. So they start poking around that idea, one thing leads to another, and they start a company with their own money and from some additional investors. They create a great product: Cheap razors at a great price. Then they realize that there's no way they can sell these razors one box at a time. There's no way they can compete with the marketing power of popular shaving companies like Gillette. So they wonder, what if we sold these as a subscription? No one had ever done this before. Would it work? They wouldn't have to wait too long to find out.

They create a brilliant marketing campaign with funny, homemade-style videos. The company grows insanely fast. Fast-forward to a few years later, they're acquired by a large company for 1 Billion Dollars. Yes, Billion with a B.

And that is the *true story* behind DollarShaveClub.com. And the founders were Mark Levine and Michael Dubin. And the company that bought them for $1 Billion in cash was Unilever.

So let's revisit the highlights of that story:

It started with Mark and Michael talking about their own frustrations.

Scratching your own itch: Check.
Big and proven market: Check.

But they didn't build the audience first. They built the product first. Cheap but quality shaving razors. That's all they started with.

Product First: Check.

And then once they started selling those well, *now* they had an audience. They had a built-in list of buyers. That was paying them every month.

Recurring Revenue: Check.

So far, everything they did was Strategy #1: Product First.

And now that they already had an audience and they knew who they were, it was such a simple strategy to create more products for this EXISTING audience.

Strategy #2. Create Products for an Existing Audience.

They didn't sell just razors for too long. They started selling shaving cream, after-shave products, shower gels, soap, cleansers, oral care like toothbrushes and toothpaste, hair gel and hair care products, skincare, travel products, and even butt wipes! Yes, soft, moist butt wipes to clean yourself after you do doo-doo.

None of these would've happened if they'd just sat around thinking they'll simply build an audience of men between 20 and 50, and *then* figure out what they want, and *then* build products for them later.

Unfortunately, for 99% of people, trying to build an audience first, will probably not work.

And if someone manages to pull that off, it means they've probably already had a lot of experience in creating a business, maybe created one or more businesses, made mistakes, learned from them, know how to hire content creators, how to hire influencers, how to market a product, already have a team that can launch a new product in any niche, because most of the tools and tactics you need are pretty much the same.

The skills that are needed regardless of which niche you are getting into, are things like a techie to help you with the website tech, a social media person, an ad person, a writer, a graphics and branding person, someone to take care of creating the funnel, like your sales pages and landing pages and email marketing, a CRM person to set up all of that, someone to write all the copy, someone to manage all of these skills, etc.

Now, you, the marketer, can go into any market, partner up with a content creator or expert in that niche, who can create the content for you, give you the know-how, someone to be the face of the franchise, so to speak, and you can have the full support of your team to figure out the rest.

Obviously, I'm over-simplifying things. But that's the kind of team and skills you already need to have to go into a brand new market, brand new niche, where you have no expertise, or ability to create content, and build something that works.

It's like the Sharks on Shark Tank – they don't care about building the products, running the business, sourcing the raw materials, etc. They won't be involved in any of the day-to-day runnings of the business. They just want to partner with the product creators and entrepreneurs, and then help them with funding, contacts, marketing, etc.

Regardless of the niche, you need to be able to create a lot of content today. A lot of it will be free. You need to be able to write articles, create content for Facebook, Instagram, YouTube, create a podcast, content for your lead-magnets to build a list, and on and on. And *after* you've created a ton of content, now you still need to be able to create content that someone will pay for.

I have created a bunch of episodes in my podcast SubscribeMe.fm where I talk about how to do content marketing, content repurposing, cross-posting content between social media platforms, how much content is too much content, etc.

But still, at the end of the day, you have to be able to create a lot of great content, and you need to be able to talk about your topics from a position of authority if you want to build a following and create influence and credibility and on and on and on.

Here's my bottom line advice for most people: Start with a Product first.

Once you have a small following, email list, or customer list, you can then not only improve your existing product and keep adding layer upon layer on top of that, but you can also start expanding into selling them other things that they need, that you *know* they need, that you *know* they'll want, because you've asked them, and they've told you.

That is why, **Strategy #1: Product First, Audience Next** and **Strategy #2: Audience First, Product Next**, are not mutually exclusive.

But for many of us, we will be well-served if we started with a Product First.

Sell First, Create Later

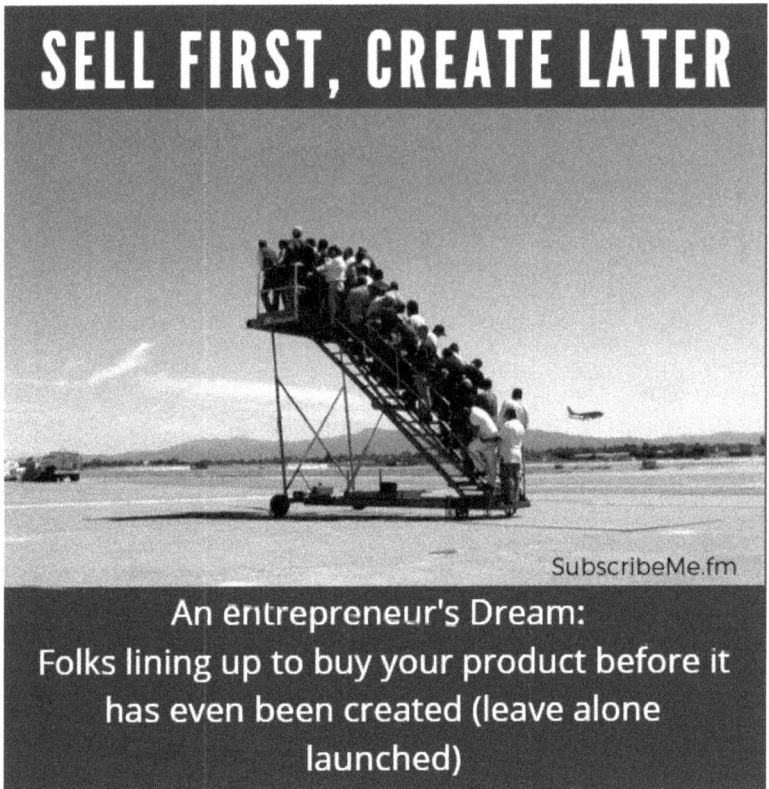

SELL FIRST, CREATE LATER

SubscribeMe.fm

An entrepreneur's Dream:
Folks lining up to buy your product before it has even been created (leave alone launched)

I frequently encounter entrepreneurs and digital creators online who spend a lot of time creating an elaborate online course, spend months, or even a year, creating a single course or sometimes an entire digital library, working on the content, setting up the membership site, hiring a copywriter to write the copy for the sales page, lining up affiliate partners to help them with the promotion, setting up a bunch of Facebook ads, priming their list. And then they launch it to their list and then... <crickets>.

On the flip side, I also see people posting something like this: "I'm creating a fantastic new course about Cat Juggling. Comment

'YUP' if you want a copy." Or "Would you buy it for a 90% discount?".

They may end up with a bunch of people commenting and engaging with their posts. But it's so easy for people to engage with your content because commenting is free - they don't have to buy anything, and talk is cheap. And free opinions and free advice should always be taken with a boatload of salt.

You: "Hey, would you like to know how to become an expert at Cat Juggling?"
Them: "Of course! I love this!| I want it now!!!"

You: "Would you pay $50 for it?"
Them: "Abso-frickin-lutely! It's a steal"

You: "Cool cool! Ok, here's a link to buy it for just $10 - go ahead and sign up now".
Them: "Um, I am currently working on an overdue project for a client. Once I finish it, I'll get back to you".
Or: <no response>
Or: "I am launching my membership site next week. After that, I'll check this out".

You get the idea. People will say anything in the spur of the moment, especially when they see a whole bunch of engagement on your post. It looks exciting and new and shiny. But the moment you ask them to take the next step, a lot of them will suddenly become very busy.

I've encountered this over and over again with not just paid stuff, but even with free stuff.

In the past, every time I've launched a new Kindle eBook, I like to seed it with reviews as soon as I publish it, even before I officially launch it to my list. So I'll go on Facebook, both in my personal feed as well as highly relevant Facebook groups (after getting permission from the group admin, of course) and post something like this:

"Hey, I've just launched a new Kindle book titled <insert title>. Would love to give you a free copy if you would be willing to check it out and leave me an honest review on Amazon. Feel free to add that you received a free copy in your review. Thanks!"

I'll get tons of "Yes, I would love to". And then I PM them, ask them for their email, and give them a free copy, by giving them access to my membership site powered by DigitalAccessPass. If they haven't left me a review, I'll even remind them with automated follow-up emails and even personally message them. Over half of them won't respond at all. That's ok – I was still able to add them to my email list, and I hope that by delivering great value over time, I'll be able to convert them.

Then I modified my offer by adding a deadline to it, to see if that changes anything: "Hey, I've just launched a new Kindle book titled <insert title>. Would love to give you a free copy if you would be willing to check it out within a week and leave me an honest review on Amazon. Please let me know only if you have the time to read it within a week. Cheers!".

But many of them will come up with every imaginable excuse, practically everything except "my dog ate my review". Life gets in the way for all of us, work and business pressures, deadlines, family and personal health, etc can all derail what we had hoped to get done. But saying you'll read it and review it within a week, and then multiple follow-ups and weeks later, saying you've been busy with your launch, are just a sign of indifference, procrastination, or just not caring to follow through on your "promise".

Now, you could say that they were so indifferent because my book was free, so they didn't value it much and didn't care about taking action, and they might have taken action if they'd actually paid for it. Trust me, I've seen people pay for courses and never get past the initial login – they don't download the content or watch the videos. I can tell because I use S3MediaVault to deliver all of the digital content, and it shows me reports about every user – how many times they've logged in (via DigitalAccessPass.com), how many times they've viewed the videos and how many times they've downloaded the PDF's (both features of S3MediaVault).

But on the flip side, you could also say, if they won't follow through on their promise for something free, why would they follow through on their commitment to buying your product when it launches?

That's why the phrase "Put your money where your mouth is" is so powerful, because it's one thing for someone to say "Sure, I'll buy it", and another thing to pull out their credit card and make an actual purchase.

So until you make people put their money where their mouth is, and make an actual offer and give them an incentive to pay you now, nothing else they say about how they will buy it or want to buy it or need it, will matter.

Also, if you post something like "Comment below if you want a copy", there's a good chance that a lot of your followers will assume it's free, even if you haven't explicitly said "free copy". So if you private message (PM) them later with a link to your offer page where they have to pay for it, you will get a lot of disappointed and angry folks upset that you did a bait-and-switch and intentionally misled them into thinking it was free.

So sure, go ahead and ask the "Would you be interested in buying it?" question, get some engagement going, let people know what you're working on, maybe even ask them for advice about the title of your course (oh, how we all love giving their opinions!) or about the modules or chapters.

But don't get too excited about the engagement for that post, because that doesn't mean anything for your bottom line when it comes to making sales.

The only way you can know for sure is to create an actual offer, which should include a huge discount and a bunch of great bonuses, make it an irresistible offer, and then see how many will vote with their dollars, and not just with a like or comment.

What you're doing here is Product Validation, or PreSelling: "to precondition (someone, such as a customer) for subsequent purchase or create advance demand for (something, such as a product) especially through marketing strategies", or "to sell in advance" (*merriam-webster.com/dictionary/presell*).

One day, I was chatting with a good friend who is also my coaching client. He wanted me to coach him for free and help him launch the membership program that he was going to be working on. He was confident that he would be able to charge $100 per student, and after the launch, he would then pay me my coaching fee using the payments from the first 30 students (my yearly unlimited coaching fee is $3,000). And then he would also pay me a few hundred dollars extra as a bonus, and he would keep all profits from that point.

So he wanted me to help him launch upfront, and then get paid later. And my time would become my investment into his business.

Instead, I asked him, why spend weeks or months working on something that you don't even know if it will sell? You don't have an email list, not much of a social following, and those you're connected to are probably not your potential buyers (lots of friends and family).

And even if someone comments on social media that they will buy it when it's ready, there's no guarantee that they will actually follow through on that commitment. The only way to truly know for sure is to make them put their money where their mouth is.

Sell First, Create Later.

If you're going to charge, say, $99 for your online course when it's completed, offer it to your audience for maybe a 50% discount. See if they're willing to pay for it today before you've even created it. Or maybe even a 90% discount for the first group of "Founding Members".

Let's say you give the early birds 50% off and charge them only $49 in total. You don't even have to make them pay it all upfront. You could simply charge them $1 today, with another single automated payment of $48 in 7 days.

This gives them the incentive of not having to pay in full for something that's not yet created, it delays the majority of their payment to a week from now, and they still get the early-bird discount and bonuses.

And this strategy gives you a major incentive to finish it within 7 days. If you make it 30 days, then you'll probably end up procrastinating for 23 days and probably still end up doing it in a week. Instead, put all of the pressure on yourself to work fast and ship fast.

Also, you don't have to have the entire course ready in 7 days. You can create just 1 or 2 main modules and release those to whet their appetite. As long as you keep them informed of the content schedule, they'll be happy to wait, because you're (hopefully) over-delivering with your price, bonuses, and your content.

And even though you're offering it for a massive discount, you've still got to create some *really* cool bonuses for these early birds (see chapter "Badass Bonuses").

Preselling works very well if they already know-, like-, and trust you a little, especially because you want them to actually pay for something that you've not even begun to create yet.

But if you do already have an audience (however small) that knows-, likes-, and trusts you, then buying your upcoming course or other digital product at a 50%-90% discount with a payment of just $1 today, with all of the bonuses, should be a no-brainer, provided your content is a good match for what they're looking for.

I prefer to charge them the full payment (after the discount) upfront so that they don't back out later out of sheer buyer's remorse. But just because they paid upfront doesn't change anything about refunds – if they want a refund, just give it to them, no questions asked.

If it's a low-ticket item and the price is already pretty low to offer a big discount, then I prefer to offer some extra expiring bonuses, instead of a discount.

So it all depends on the niche, your relationship with your audience, and your level of confidence in the course topic and content.

Selling it first will allow you to validate the interest of your audience. If they won't buy it for a whopping discount and an irresistible offer, there's no way to know if they will buy it at the full price down the road.

And if people who already know-, like-, and trust you won't buy it now, it's going to be even harder to get strangers to buy it.

Doing this will also give you a lot of insight into your audience, niche, your offer-creation, and marketing skills.

[Cat Juggling is a funny term Frank Kern (one of my favorite marketers) uses when he wants to give an example of a niche]

Create First, Sell Later

Or you could also call it "Keep Creating, Keep Promoting".

With this, you simply continue to create the content that you're really good at creating and teaching, that which you excel at yourself, content that you think will be useful to your audience because you've been there and done that yourself, something you mastered while scratching your own itch.

This is similar to the YouTube Creator model, or the Podcaster or the Blogger models, where you strive to keep creating great content, keep hitting publish, promote it to your existing audience, and let the chips fall where they may. You could easily fall into the rut of too much creation and too little promotion, so you'll have to learn how to continue promoting your content while also adding value to your audience, without it becoming too much of a "buy my stuff, buy my stuff" all the time.

You should also continue to test, tweak, ask your audience for feedback, learn from that feedback, do more research, experiment with your content, and use that in your future content.

Every time you launch a new product, similar to the **Sell First, Create Later** strategy, launch it at a massive discount to your entire list, offer a great affiliate program so that they can promote it to their network while the discount is still active, add a few early-bird bonuses, and you continue adding to your customer base with each new mini-launch.

For this model to work, you have to be able to release content quickly. You cannot take months to create a new product, and it cannot be a massive course with 20 modules and 50 lessons. You should niche-down really hard, and create short-and-standalone pieces of content – like a mini-course – that you can create within a week or two. And all of your content should build up towards a larger goal in the long term. It's like selling them individual pieces of the puzzle which will eventually help them complete the whole puzzle and reach their end goal, which is whatever they set out to achieve.

Even if a particular course doesn't sell by itself, you would've still created valuable new content for your library, which will be very useful to enhance the overall value of your membership, especially if you wish to charge a recurring subscription fee for your "online school" or "academy" - something you should consider doing at some point anyway.

Or if you don't have enough products for a subscription, you could treat this mini-course as a great free bonus when you promote other courses in the future. Or imagine offering an entire digital library of DIY content when they sign up for your more expensive coaching program.

Also, every time you launch a new mini-course or promote any kind of content that is valuable to your niche, even if you don't get a lot of sales right away, your audience will notice that you're frequently creating and publishing great content. They may not buy your product or even engage with you, but there are always lurkers who are quietly paying attention to the fact that you're a prolific creator. That will establish your brand and authority in your niche over time, as they start associating you with your niche and start thinking of you as someone who is an expert in your niche. And they will slowly get to know/like/trust you – which will make it a lot more likely that they'll eventually become a paying customer.

Start With the Last Thing First

The strategy of selling first and creating later is great, but that doesn't mean you can simply start promoting your product without creating an offer first.

I've seen people create a short landing page with some super-basic details about the product, slap a single buy button on it, and right away start promoting it. It's not necessarily a bad idea, because simplicity can help you ship faster, and *done* is better than *doing*. But that is taking my "Sell First, Create Later" strategy a little too far. Because there is a better way to do it. And that is to create the offer first.

The offer is not just the product and not just a short landing page with a few bullet points about the product and a buy button.

As legendary Harvard Business School Professor, Theodore Levitt once said, "People don't want to buy a quarter-inch drill – they want a quarter-inch hole."

Your sales page could be as simple as "here's what I've got, here's what it does, here's what it will do for you, here's what it costs, and here's why you should get it, and why you should get it now". But you'll get better conversions if you have a more complete offer.

An "Offer" is a complete package that leads to a total value that is far greater than just the price of the product they're buying. And it includes many components: the headline, subheadline, what problem or pain it solves for the buyer, its unique selling proposition (USP: why you, why your product, and why now), its benefits, features, pricing, bonuses, scarcity, urgency, call to action (CTA), social proof, delivery, shipping, refunds & cancellation, support, etc.

So before you start promoting your product that's not even been created yet, start with the last thing first: The Sales Page.

Most landing page design tools today come with ready-to-use templates, which already have many of the components built right in – like hero image, a place for a video at the top of the page, headlines, subheadlines, features & benefits section, testimonials, pricing table, etc.

Import one of those templates, and remove things that may not be immediately relevant – like testimonials or a sales video. Or if you can create a quick sales video, and get a few testimonials from past clients who've used your product in some format, definitely include those. It's critical to have a bunch of really good bonuses, which I talk about in the chapter "Badass Bonuses".

You should be able to create a decent sales page with a great offer in a day or two (at worst). Don't focus too much on the copy for the first draft. Just get all the components of the offer onto the page first.

But even before you get into creating the entire offer, you've got to do one thing first. And that is...

Start With the Pricing Table

Whether you are selling access to a membership academy, online school, SaaS product, WordPress plugin, or agency, before you create the offer and sales page, start by creating the pricing table first. Even if you're selling a single eBook, you should create the pricing table first, and you should always offer more than one option, like **eBook Only | Audiobook Only | eBook + Audiobook**.

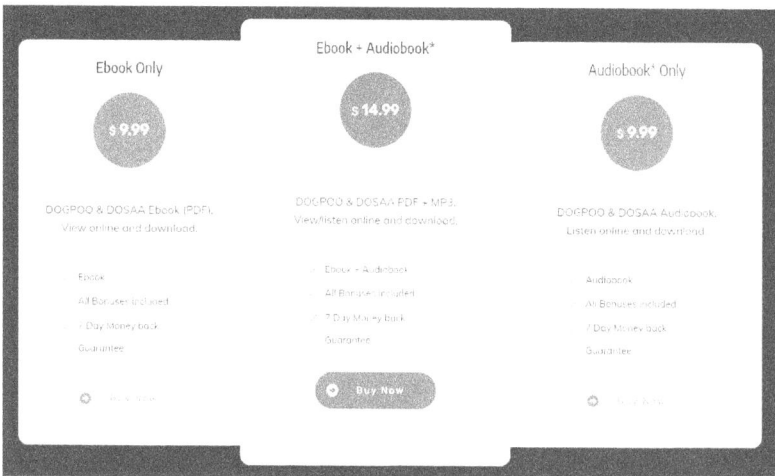

The pricing table is usually the last thing most people think about. They may have some idea about what they want to charge, but creating a pricing table drills it down much deeper than simply having 3 numbers in your head.

Most people will put more thought into what theme and plugins to use, design of the landing page, branding colors, logo design, registering social media accounts (like creating a Twitter account, Facebook page, Instagram account, etc). And then they completely lose track of one critical piece to all of this: the pricing table (which is an integral part of your offer).

You should create the pricing table before the product, before the landing page, and before you even think about features and benefits.

You don't need a fancy tool or theme or WordPress plugin to create a pricing table. You can do it easily with a simple Excel spreadsheet, Google Sheet (free), or OpenOffice Calc (open source and free).

	A	B	C	D
		Gold	Platinum	Inner Circle
1		99/yr	199/yr	499/yr
2				
3	1-on-1 Coaching Calls (1/mo.)			Y
4	1-on-1 Email & Chat Access to Me			Y
5	Group calls (1/mo.)		Y	Y
6	CoolCastPlayer ($199)		1-site	Unlimited
7	S3MediaVault ($199)		1-site	Unlimited
8	Premium Podcasting ($99)	Y	Y	Y
9	Podcasting: Absolute Essentials ($49)	Y	Y	Y
10	99Design Hack ($49)	Y	Y	Y
11	WordPress Security ($199)	Y	Y	Y
12	Behind the scenes of the Academy ($99)	Y	Y	Y
13	Podcasting Confessions Ebook ($10)	Y	Y	Y
14	Podcasting Confessions Audio ($8)	Y	Y	Y
15	SubscribeMe ebook ($5)	Y	Y	Y
16	NBLEB.com Book ($3)	Y	Y	Y
17	eBay Podcast Monetization ($19)	Y	Y	Y
18	Private Community ($99)	Y	Y	Y
19	Private Community ($99)	Y	Y	Y

The screenshot above was the first draft of my pricing table that I first created a few years ago for my Digital Creators Academy at SubscribeMe.fm/academy. At that time, I had not created most of the courses you see above.

And that helped me eventually create my pricing table below, which is what it looks like now.

The image below has been edited because the first column is very long.

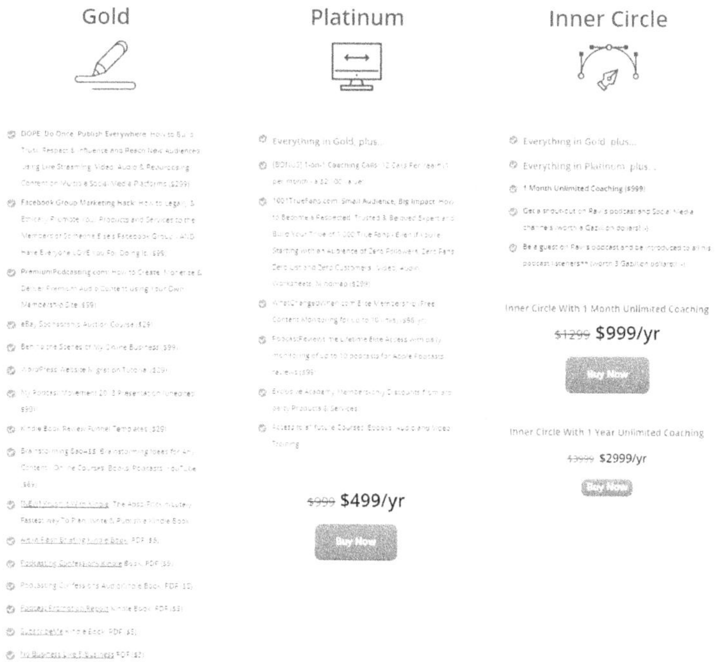

Gold	Platinum	Inner Circle

(pricing table — details largely illegible)

Gold — $999 $499/yr — Buy Now

Platinum — $999 $499/yr — Buy Now

Inner Circle

Inner Circle With 1 Month Unlimited Coaching
$1299 $999/yr — Buy Now

Inner Circle With 1 Year Unlimited Coaching
$3999 $2999/yr — Buy Now

Over the last 25 years, I've developed WordPress plugins and digital info products, creating websites while also working for multiple Fortune 100 and Fortune 10 companies 10 years, as an enterprise software architect (in my previous life before I left all of it and became a full-time entrepreneur).

And during that time, one of the techniques I came up with was to take an idea, and before writing a single line of code or creating even a single page, or even installing WordPress to create a website, I would make a list of all of the software or WordPress plugin's features and benefits.

I would even write out the entire sales page, features, benefits, potential objections, how to overcome them, what were the possible drawbacks, how my product compared to a competitor's, and so on, and I would address them all in the copy and also create the pricing table *before* I did anything else.

When I started working on DAP in 2007 - a year before it was publicly released in 2008 - I followed this very strategy. I used some tool - can't remember what it was, but it wasn't a spreadsheet. I created a features table because DAP is a membership plugin that had to compete with other membership software.

Back then, the only real competitor was this software called Amember. And Amember was not a WordPress plugin - it was a stand-alone PHP script and did not integrate with WordPress. I had just gotten into WordPress plugins and that's when I decided that DAP was going to be the first-ever WordPress membership plugin, which it certainly became when I launched it in 2008.

You may have heard of Mike Filsaime, one of the creators of Webinar Jam. He had released a product called Butterfly Marketing, which was a stand-alone PHP web app, did not work with WordPress, and had a built-in affiliate module. It was a pretty barebones script that you could install on each website you owned, and each of those sites suddenly became like a mini membership site, with its own set of users, and affiliates, and so on. And it could integrate with just Paypal at the time.

So I did some market research, and then made a list of everything I need to be including as part of DAP. I wish I'd known about the mindmap-brainstorming technique that I cover in a different chapter.

And one of the features that I had come up with, which no one had thought of before, was the ability to drip content like you could drip emails. So that's how I invented content dripping, and I called it a ContentResponder - which could drip content that was created previously, just like an Autoresponder could drip emails that were written previously.

So my pricing table items became my list of features and benefits, like...

"Integrates with WordPress: ✓ (green checkmark that says that a feature is included as part of that membership level.

Autoresponder: ✓ . Broadcasts: ✓ . Affiliate Module: ✓ .

By the way, thanks to Mike Filsaime's Butterfly Marketing script, I was insistent on DAP having a built-in affiliate module from day 1. That delayed the launch by probably up to a month, but it was a critical part of DAP's USP.

You can do the same thing when it comes to writing your next book. Instead of a pricing table, when you're writing a book, you start with the Table of Contents (TOC). I call it the "TOC Technique", which is covered in a different chapter.

Similarly, when it comes to a membership site that has a lot of digital products, coaching, community and consulting, with different tiers, you create a pricing table.

Creating the pricing table first helps trigger conscious and subconscious thoughts about not just the pricing of the different tiers, but also the value of your offer. Everything starts and ends with your offer.

If your offer is no good, then even a $10/month membership can feel too expensive. But a great offer can make a $500/month membership feel like a bargain.

And a pricing table also helps you take inventory of all of your assets that you have, what you are capable of creating quickly, and what you can get others to create for you (freelance, guest content, etc).

So first start by making a list of every digital and physical asset that you already own. If you've been online for even a few years, I'm sure you've created digital assets of one form or the other - like articles, ebooks, kindle books, youtube videos, podcasts, blog posts, webinars, interviews, guest posts, and so on. Physical assets could be a physical printed book, paperback or hardcover, printed magazines, tchotchkes, and gifts you have previously created like t-shirts, caps, pens, keychains, etc.

Just write down every single thing that comes to mind. Look around your room. Don't leave anything out. Even if you have a special edition item, like a few limited edition books or short-run t-shirts you got printed with your domain on it, or whatever these items are, it's ok if you have only 5 of them, you can offer them as a fast-action bonus, say only for the first 5 people. Every single asset can be put to great use in your launch.

You can even do a quick video to show off these exclusive bonuses. And put that video on your sales page, right below the pricing table. So doesn't matter if you have just a few of something, write them all down. At this point, all you're doing is a complete brain dump. So take a complete inventory. Useful or not, doesn't matter. You can collate and curate later. Just keep noting down everything you can think of.

Now that you have a full list in your spreadsheet in the first column, call it "Master Library" or "Digital Vault" or something cool like that. Now make a full copy of that entire spreadsheet. Call this copy Phase 1.

Now back to the Master Library spreadsheet. At this point, you've made a note of everything you have previously created.

Insert a blank row at the bottom, and start noting down all of the items that you think you can create in the future. Doesn't have to be right away. It's fine if it's something you can probably get to only a year from now. It's fine if it needs time and research - you can always outsource the research. It's fine if you think you can create a new product along with a joint venture (JV) partner.

Maybe it's something you can pay others to create for you. Maybe you can exchange reports or kindle books or courses with other JV partners - you give them a Kindle book for their library, they give you one for your library. So if you have somebody at the top of your mind who you think you can approach to do this content exchange, make a note of their name. This type of content exchange doesn't have to be limited to just ebooks. You can do it with single audio or video mini-course, a PDF eBook or report, and even an entire audio or video course with multiple files. You could interview other guests and use the audio from that. Or maybe collect written quotes or answers to various questions from several experts in your niche, and put those notes together and BAM! – you have a report.

Try to be creative and think of anything and everything you can add to this library.

And now go into the Phase 1 sheet, and start fine-tuning and rearranging the items in terms of value - highest value at the top, lowest at the bottom. Remember, this is Phase 1. So when you eventually create your actual pricing table on your sales page, it will probably look very similar to Phase 1 items. Don't get overzealous and promise them things that you don't know if you can create by yourself. Only stick to items that you know for sure that you can create, doesn't matter if it's in 3 months or 6 months.

It's ok to include "Coming Soon" items that are not ready yet. And you could have due dates next to those items on your sales page so that the member signing up knows when it's coming, and what's available to them right now.

In my pricing table shown earlier, I included premium items like 1-on-1 coaching, group calls, personal email, and chat access. Then I listed some of my other ready-made assets, like a couple of plugins I've created, like S3MediaVault.com and CoolCastPlayer.com.

I have 4 columns in my spreadsheet. The first column lists all of the assets. Columns 2, 3, and 4 are the Membership Level names. The Level/Tier names are not important at this stage. Whatever you call them, the person seeing the pricing table will get it right away that those are 3 separate membership levels, each one stacking upon the previous level, and adding more value. So don't be wasting 2 hours trying to figure out cool names for your membership levels. That's not what adds real value to your members.

But for what it's worth, here is a quick list of membership tier names to give you some ideas.

Bronze, Silver, Gold, Platinum, Titanium	Basic, Plus, Ultimate
Gold, Platinum, Platinum Elite	Basic, Plus, Platinum Plus
Gold, Platinum, Diamond, Titanium	Basic, Plus, Elite
Beginner, Intermediate, Advanced	Basic, Performance, Ultimate
Beginner, Growth, Performance	Basic, Intermediate, Advanced
Do-it-yourself, Done-with-you, Done-for-you	Basic, Enhanced, Ultimate
DIY, DWY, DFY	Plus, Premium, Platinum
Free, Personal, Professional	Starter, Growth, Skyrocket
Creator, Builder, Entrepreneur	Starter, Growth, Performance
Starter, Professional, Extreme	Elementary, Enterprising, Einstein
Subscriber, Ambassador, Partner	Elementary, Exotic, Exquisite
Star, All-Star, Superstar	Regular, Ultimate, Elite
Developer, Integrator, White Label	Standard, Plus, Premium
Developer, Team, Business	Solo, Basic, Team
User, Developer, Agency	Solo, Team, Enterprise
Standard, Advanced, Enterprise	Solo, Team, Enterprise
Personal, Professional, Premium	Business, Growth, Enterprise
Studio, Agency, Enterprise, White Label	Casual, Easy, Child's Play
Standard, Pro, Business, Business Plus	Hard, Difficult, Tough, Challenging.
Tier 1, Tier 2, Tier 3 (T1, T2, T3)	Insane, Very Hard, Very Difficult, Extreme, Impossible

Level 1, Level 2, Level 3 (L1, L2, L3)	Player, All-Star, Champion
Elementary, Advanced, Premium	Gratis, Ad Hoc, Bona Fide, Carpe Diem, Ad Infinitum
Classic, Unlimited, Infinite	Weekly
Fan, Player, Superstar	Monthly
Ninja, Ronin, Samurai, Shogun	Bi-Monthly
Candle, Bonfire, Blaze	Annual
Sprout, Blossom, Garden, Estate, Forest	Lifetime
Hamlet, Village, Town, City, Metropolis	Unlimited
Founding Member	Partner
Inaugural Member	JV
Alumni	Agcncy
Essentials	Custom
Enterprise Plus	Special

Badass Bonuses

What I'm about to tell you might make you cringe a bit, especially if you're in the business of selling SaaS (software as a service) or other physical products. But in the online marketing niche, especially in the digital info products niche, a critical piece of your launch and your offer is your Bonuses.

It's not enough to have just one or two throw-in types of bonuses. You've got to have some badass bonuses – and hopefully a few of them.

I would recommend having at least 3 bonuses, and if possible even 5 or more.

It's also important that you don't just take some blah report or a short video course that you would normally sell for like $29, and artificially hike it up to some outrageously inflated value, like $299, just to make your bonuses look valuable.

Your bonuses should be legitimate digital products that could sell by themselves at whatever price you're stating is their value. So if a video course bonus has a $99 value, then you must be able to sell it on its own for $99, or at the very least at half that price. Don't simply exaggerate their value, because your buyers will be able to sense the fake value and will be turned off from buying your product, and your reputation will also take a hit.

Let me quickly restate a couple of things I wrote in an earlier chapter about creating your library of content – the same can be said for your bonuses too: Make a list of every digital and physical asset that you already own. If you've been online for even a few years, I'm sure you've created digital assets of one form or the other - like articles, ebooks, kindle books, youtube videos, podcasts, blog posts, webinars, interviews, guest posts, and so on. Physical assets could be a physical printed book, paperback or hardcover, printed magazines, tchotchkes, and gifts you have previously created like t-shirts, caps, pens, keychains, etc.

Just write down every single thing that comes to mind. Look around your room. Don't leave anything out. Even if you have a special edition item, like maybe a few limited edition books or short-run t-shirts you got printed with your domain on it, or whatever these items are, it's ok if you have only 5 of them, now you can offer them as a fast-action bonus, say only for the first 5 people.

Flip the Script

If you have an eBook for $10, and a Video course for $99, offering your eBook as a bonus for the Course may not have high perceived value. But if you flip the offer, and offer your $99 course as a bonus for your $10 eBook, now suddenly, your offer looks a whole lot stronger and more irresistible.

And if you're rather new to selling digital products online, I'm willing to bet that your $10 eBook will sell a lot more with a $99 course as a bonus, than the other way around.

You have to sell 200 copies of your eBook to make the same as selling just 20 copies of your video course. So selling the course (and offering the eBook as a bonus) might seem like the obvious choice.

But just because you have an offer doesn't mean people are going to take you up on it and plunk down their credit card and pay you $99. You have a lot more work to do to sell a $99 course than a $10 eBook. And if you are an experienced marketer and have a decent audience (email list, social followers, know how to run ads, etc), then yes, selling the course is the better choice, because a video course has a much higher perceived value than an eBook, which is why you can charge more for a course than for an eBook.

However, if you're just getting started, or you've not been getting traction, and just want to build a customer list to whom you can sell other stuff later, it's not a bad thing to sell 100 copies of your eBook and get 100 paying customers on your list, and then later sell them other courses, community access and even coaching on the backend.

But my main point here is to show you how critical bonuses are for a digital product launch by showing you how a $10 eBook offer can be elevated by giving away a fantastic $99 video course for free.

Now imagine adding bonuses like multiple video courses and 1-on-1 time with you or free community access all adding up to hundreds, if not thousands, of dollars worth of bonuses.

[Psst… that's exactly what I did with the launch of this very book, at DogpooBook.com]

Badass bonuses can turn a ho-hum launch into a remarkable money-maker. So be sure to put some thought and time into creating some really valuable bonuses, and don't let your bonuses be a "blah" afterthought.

Expiring Bonuses

Once you have a good collection of digital assets to offer as a bonus, you can even increase the urgency and scarcity elements of your offer by giving away the most number of bonuses on Day #1 of your launch and expiring one or more bonuses with each passing day.

TOC Technique

I came up with this idea many years ago but never gave it a proper name that is easy to understand and implement, until a couple of years ago. I now call it the TOC TAC TIC, get it? ;-)

Back in 2007, I published my first book, called "No Business Like E-Business", which at the time, went on to become an Amazon category best-seller for several days in a row with zero marketing. This was a pretty big deal for me because it was a physical book (paperback), and there was no Kindle yet. Social media was not as widely used as it is now, and MySpace (which I somehow never joined) was probably still more popular than Facebook.

I did have a small list of customers in a different niche, but I did not promote this book to that list as I thought my book was not a good match for them (I chickened out, basically). Never even told anyone other than a few of my close friends and relatives, never advertised it anywhere. So the fact that it became a category bestseller, was incredibly gratifying.

I initially wrote most of it in about a year, then life happened; I took a couple of years' break, and when I got back to it, from that point onwards, it then took me another 2 years where I ended up (unnecessarily) rewriting most of it. So it took me about 3 years in total to complete the book, averaging about a couple of pages per day – sometimes 20 pages on a weekend, sometimes nothing at all for weeks.

At the time, I had many other things going on. I had a full-time job, I had my PHP scripts website MyWebMasterInABox.com - which is now defunct, but you can still see what it looked like back then. My second child had just been born, my wife had taken an extended, unpaid leave of absence from her job, and I was the sole earner; I was in a terrible situation at work, with an insanely angry, verbally, mentally abusive boss. I could not quit because I had to keep a job to keep my Green Card application going - it was all a complete mess. Those few years were probably the darkest years of my life, and if not for my amazing wife Veena and my precious kids, I don't know if I would've made it.

I was working in New York City. I would commute to the city by train every day. I had a company-provided laptop, which has some amazing stories attached to it, that I'll talk about on my podcast someday. I had a laptop but I didn't have Internet access on the train. Never occurred to me to get a wifi card. But not having wifi was easily the best thing that happened for my book. It kind of forced me to work offline, so I used to just open up Word, and start working on my book.

Initially, I started writing the book sequentially. Acknowledgment, Introduction, Chapter 1, then Chapter 2, etc. But this sequential process started burning me out pretty quickly. There were some things that I was in no mood to write about - like the stuff you know very well, but you know it's going to take you hours and hours to put them into words, and some of these were boring topics to me, but I believed were essential to the reader.

That's when I came up with a new technique: I decided to create the entire table of contents (TOC) first - start to finish. I was going to think of every single question that someone new to an online business would wonder about, and then create exciting titles for the chapters and sub-chapters, where a potential reader should be able to simply look at the chapter titles alone and get excited about buying my book.

And this is labeled as "TOC Technique".

I was hoping that the exciting chapter titles would also give me added motivation to write the chapters ☺. And they did. I wrote interesting chapter & sub-chapter titles, which covered everything someone needed to know about creating an eBusiness (adding the word "e" to indicate a digital, online product or service was considered cool back then – eBooks, eCommerce, eScholar, eStudent, etc).

Once I had completed the TOC, every time I opened my laptop, I would just scan the titles and sub-titles, just pick one that interested me at that moment, and I would dive right into that section.

If there was something I needed to research, parts that needed additional info (like references, names of authors, website links, book names, etc), or simply sections within that chapter that I was too bored to work on at that very moment, I would just type "xxx" (without the quotes), and continue with the rest of the chapter.

Just permitting myself to do these two things - 1) dive into sections randomly, and 2) type "xxx" to skip sections - massively speeded up my writing because I no longer felt the FOMO (fear of missing out) that I would miss out on something just because I left it incomplete and had to work on everything right away to completion.

So I didn't have to get slowed down or distracted because there was something that I had to research or think more about. I could easily search for "xxx" and quickly figure out all of the gaps that needed filling (Multi-pass strategy > Single-pass).

Movies and documentaries are filmed out of sequence as well. They don't shoot the movie in the sequence that you end up watching - like 1st scene of the movie first, then 2nd scene of the movie next, etc. The scenes are shot in a completely random order, depending on the availability of the actors, location, etc.

So I started writing my book in this controlled chaos. And that's when I started making the most progress.

And I have since followed the model of TOC Technique, Random Order, and Triple-X Skipping, for all of my subsequent books (this is my 8th one). You can see the rest of them here: SubscribeMe.fm/books.

And this technique is so powerful, that it can be used for brainstorming and creating so many other things.

I've used this technique to write documentation for DigitalAccessPass.com, map out an email series, series of blog posts, series of FB posts, etc.

You can use this technique to write the content for your lead magnet. Start with the topic for your lead magnet. Then create your Table of Contents first. You don't want to write a 300-page ebook for your lead magnet. Let's say, a handful of main chapters, each with 2-3 sub-chapters. So you need to be careful about not being too ambitious with the scope. And creating a table of contents will help you keep the scope simple and on-point.

If you wish to write an email autoresponder series for someone who has just signed up for your lead magnet, same thing. Create a table of contents for your email series. The introduction is the first email, Chapter 1 and sub-chapter 1.1 will be the next email, sub-chapter 1.2 is the next one, then comes Chapter 2, and so on.

Wish to create a series of content marketing videos? Talking about the benefits of your product? Start with the TOC first.

Want to create a series of tweets to promote your launch? Or do ongoing content marketing? Start with the TOC first.

Want to create a series of FB posts to educate people about your product or service? How about giving them a lot of value by giving away a lot of information about your niche? How do you decide what each post should be, and what the content within each post should talk about? Start with the TOC first.

Writing blog posts for content marketing? How do you decide what to write about? Use the TOC Technique.

"Dream Book" TOC

I'm going to give you some real-world examples so that you can get an idea of how powerful this technique is for churning out content at will, never getting writer's block ever again, never having to wonder what to blog about or how to do come up with content for your content marketing.

All of this starts by creating what I call your "Dream Book TOC". So you need to create the table of contents of what you would consider your "dream" book. And this Dream Book TOC will not only help with content creation and content marketing, but it will help you research your niche even *before* you ever get started.

Below, I'll show you how to come up with this Dream Book TOC, what you would have as a part of this book, and how to brainstorm ideas for that. And in the process of creating this TOC, you'll end up doing a lot of amazing research and getting great ideas about your niche, and your ideal audience, and what is important to them.

Brainstorming

I define this as a creative process where you choose a particular topic, and then let your mind roam freely and uninhibitedly, fly in any and every direction, without any rules or restrictions, come up with lots of ideas (relevant or tangential), think of problems of varying degrees of urgency, thoughts of varying levels of relevance, and solutions of differing complexities. It is effectively a complete brain dump of every sliver of thought or micro-thought you may have about the target of the brainstorming.

And a Mindmap is the perfect tool that will allow your mind to do exactly that: Fly in all directions, all at once, brainstorm at will, and allow you to capture those thoughts and ideas, at nearly the speed of thought (it also helps if you can type reasonably fast).

The mindmap tool I recommend is XMind.net - it has a free version that offers everything you need for brainstorming.

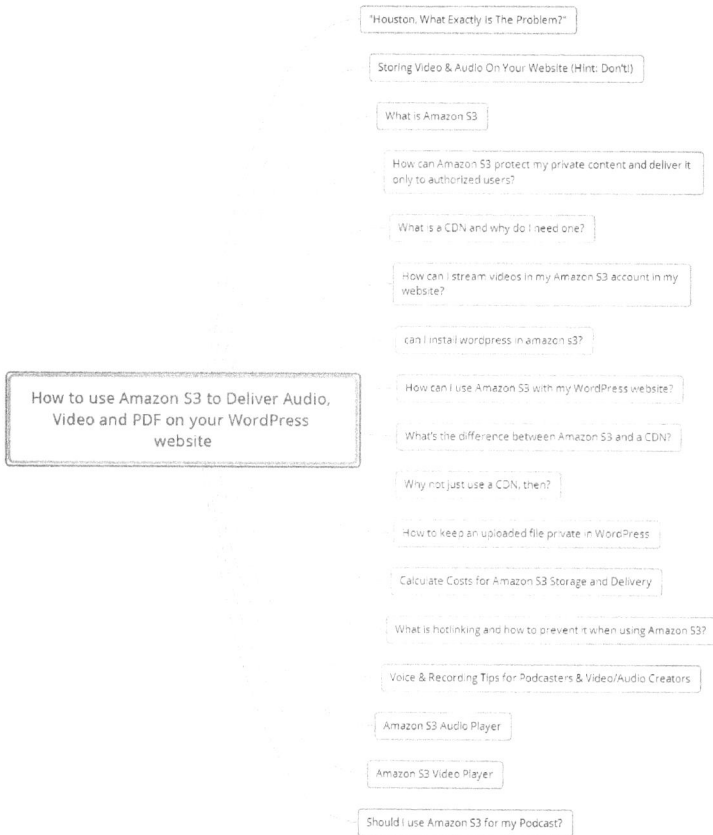

The image above is a screenshot of the first draft of my mindmap that I created when I was getting ready to write a long-form, "skyscraper" post for Search Engine Optimization (SEO). Once I created the topics, I just had to do a Ctrl+A and Ctrl+C (select all & copy) which copies the text from all of the nodes, and then paste it into Word, and bam! - my TOC was ready.

And that mindmap turned into this full post at https://s3mediavault.com/how-why-use-amazon-s3-deliver-audio-video-pdf/

Table Of Contents ⌄

I have an online course called **Brainstorming Badass: The Abso-Frickin-Lutely Fastest way to Brainstorm and Churn out ideas for the next 33 years - for your online courses, podcast, live streaming videos, webinars, Kindle books, YouTube channel, and any imaginable type of Content Marketing**.

It's arguably the best how-to course out there that shows you exactly how to get the best ideas for whatever content it is that you're creating. And I gave away that course for free with every copy of this eBook sold through my website.

Here's how to brainstorm in a nutshell: Search the platforms mentioned below for various keywords from your niche, "look inside" at the table of contents of other Amazon Kindle books in your niche, research competing products & services, online forums, titles of podcasts and YouTube videos, etc.

Here's a list of where you can research what people are talking about, and for ideas about your niche:

iTunes (desktop) Search
Podcast Episode Titles
YouTube.com
Reddit.com
Twitter search
ClickBank.com
Udemy.com
Google Search for Courses
    <keywords> online course
    <keywords> digital course
    <keywords> book (eBook)
    <keywords> audio book (audiobook)
Communities
    Quora.com
    Answers.yahoo.com
    Facebook Groups

Online Forums
Amazon Books

Make a list of all the topics you've found through research. If you use a Mindmap, it will be easier to form the structure right as you're brainstorming ideas. If not, that's ok – you can use a simple text editor too. And then edit your notes and figure out which are the main chapter titles, which are sub-chapters, and which are topics inside those sub-chapters, and so on.

And with a few hours of focused research, as shown above, you can come up with an amazing list of content for your Dream Book TOC.

Are You An Expert?

The Dream Book TOC technique will also help you quickly figure out if you're an expert in your niche, and if not, what it would take for you to get there.

If you come up with the table of contents for a dream book in a niche, you look at that entire TOC, at each chapter and sub-chapter, and your wonder "Oh wow, I have no idea what any of that stuff is, and I don't have any clue how I'm going to even *begin* writing this book", then you know right away that this is not the right market for you.

I'm not talking about partnering with or hiring some other expert in that niche and having them create the content. We're not going that far yet. I'm assuming you're a small business owner, an independent freelancer, and you're trying to carve out a name for yourself in your niche. So I'm presuming that you want to be the expert.

So if your dream book TOC scares you, then you're not an expert in this niche, and you shouldn't be writing a book about it.

On the flip side, if you are an expert in your niche, then your dream book TOC will make you go...

"Heck yeah, I can churn out all of this content for this niche. I can write a book with all of these chapters, I can blog about this, I can do a podcast about this, I can start a YouTube channel about this. If I do a podcast, I know so much about this stuff that I don't need to bring on experts and do interview guests to create the content. I can simply pick any topic, fire up my mic and recording software, and start deep diving into these topics without having to spend days researching this. And I can be a guest on any podcast, YouTube/TV/radio show, and talk for hours on any of these topics! No problem!'

That's how I feel about my knowledge and expertise - which is, all things digital product creation, creating membership sites and online courses and digital marketing.

So if you were in my niche, here's how to go create your dream book TOC.

1) Amazon

Go to Amazon.com. Search for "membership sites". From the list of books that show up, for each one, do a right-click, open in a new tab, so that you keep that browser window open while opening new tabs for each of the results. Go deep into each book. See if they have a label called "Look Inside" near the book image. Amazon usually shows you a bunch of pages from the beginning of the book, and that will almost always include the book's table of contents. So make a list of everything you see there. Now go back to the tab where you had the original list from your search. Do a Right-click, open in a new tab, for the next book. Rinse, repeat. Then search for a different set of keywords. Like "online courses", "digital marketing" and "recurring income". You should now have a pretty good list.

2) Facebook Groups

Go to Facebook, click on "Groups", search for "membership sites", "digital marketing " "online courses", etc. Join 3 groups. Start reading the conversations. Don't immediately start promoting yourself, your website, podcast, etc. Just watch and learn. Pretend to be a coach in your niche, and imagine each person there as your client.

In my niche, the kind of questions I'll usually see people asking are:

- Which is the best membership plugin to use?
- Planning to start a website. Should I use WordPress? Or something like Wix or Squarespace?
- Which web host should I use?
- Which web host do you use?
- I want to sell a book and then an online course. Which plugin is best for me?

Make a note of not just the questions, but also the answers given by others. Add each of these questions to your dream book TOC as chapters.

If someone asks "Which video platform should I use for hosting my online course videos", take the best answers that you see given by others - so people may have said something like Wistia, Vimeo, YouTube, Amazon S3. Now reviewing those platforms can become a chapter.

3) Google

Google "membership sites" and "online courses". Take other keywords from your dream book TOC and search for those keywords. Add the word "reviews" to your searches. This will spawn a whole new bunch of articles, reviews, other people's products, and services and info products that they've created about the same topic. Keep adding to your TOC.

4) Content Marketplaces

Go to digital content marketplaces like SkillShare.com, LinkedIn Learning, ClickBank.com, and Udemy.com. Search for your keywords. Go to the websites of each of the vendors selling an info product in your niche, and these marketers have probably already done most of your work for you. Read the sales copy - they've probably listed the benefits, features, advantages, disadvantages, fears, and apprehensions of the audience. Go ahead and note down the topics. Don't steal the actual copy – that's copyright infringement – just the topics.

And here's the cool thing about this dream book TOC that you're creating: You can write a blog post about this, create a free report, create a podcast episode, a Kindle book, or YouTube channel.

And the next time someone asks about these topics in a Facebook group, you can genuinely post a link to your content - whether that is a blog post, podcast episode, or YouTube video. You would be sending people directly to something that can answer their questions, and that content just happens to belong to you. And this is the most non-spammy way to let people know that you're an authority.

Of course, even there, you have to be smart about it. You must provide some answers in the group first, and not just give out your link. So if someone asks, "Which video platform do you guys use? I'm planning to start an online course". Your answer should be something like... "For sales videos, I would use YouTube, because promoting your YouTube videos and increasing its views helps the ranking of those videos on YouTube.com, which will help your videos be found on YouTube and even on Google. And for private videos, I would recommend Vimeo or Amazon S3. I've created an entire podcast episode about exactly this topic. Check out https://SubscribeMe.fm/23 where I talked about various video options for your membership site or online course."

Boom! No spam, all value. They get their answers upfront without being forced to go to your website. And you get to send them to a link where they can get more details.

And on that page, they should be able to do so without having to give you their email first. Give first, ask later. Of course, you can always promote your lead magnet on that page, and still get them on your list.

1) Amazon
2) Facebook
3) Google
4) Marketplaces like Udemy and Skillshare

You can keep expanding on that if you need more ideas down the line - like YouTube, Audible.com, Spotify, iTunes, etc.

Do not shortcut this process, even if it takes you a week or two. This is especially critical if you're still in the beginning stages of creating your website or digital product. This will help you quickly determine whether you're cut out for this niche. And if you are not, then by this time, you know what to expect when it comes to becoming an expert in any niche. So you'll be more careful in picking a niche, or even a super-niche, where you can shine, have an authoritative voice, create great content, and add tremendous value to your audience.

That's how you build an audience, a growing community, and true fans.

And along the way, that will help you achieve whatever goals you have set out for yourself - whether that is to sell more books, become a celebrity, a speaker, a highly sought-after consultant, coach, sell more products, or whatever your dream goal is.

Video Tips for Online Course Creators

Start by brainstorming ideas using a Mindmap (aka an IdeaMap)

I don't think there's a single more powerful tool for brainstorming ideas, practically at the speed of thought, like using a Mindmap. I love and recommend Xmind.net mind-mapping software. They have a free version which is all you need. I even have a course about this, called **Brainstorming Badass: The Abso-Frickin-Lutely Fastest way to Brainstorm and Churn out ideas for the next 33 years - for your online courses, podcast, live streaming videos, webinars, Kindle books, YouTube channel, and any imaginable type of Content Marketing**. You can get it for free if you're a member of my Digital Creators Academy, at SubscribeMe.fm/academy.

Save the Best For First

You know the saying *Save The Best For Last*. Scratch that. Today, people's attention spans have gotten so short - like the attention span of a goldfish, it is said :-). So do not hold back. You've got to start your content like a Bond movie - cut right to the chase. Get into the core content quickly.

There's no time for a slick 20-second splashy video intro, no time for an elaborate introduction of yourself, background story, history, preamble, no nothing. Quickly tease what's coming up in the video lesson, or even the entire course, so that the person watching has an idea as to what's coming up and can get excited about what they're about to learn. And then dive right in.

Keep the videos short

Ideally, about 5-10 minutes. I'm only talking about course videos here. Not social videos or content marketing videos.

7 Minutes

Udemy.com, which is one of the biggest course marketplaces online, recommends a video length of up to 7 minutes.

I've also talked about it in episode 59 of my podcast, titled **How Long Should Videos In Your Online Course Be?** Check it out at SubscribeMe.fm/59

In that episode, I focused more on the "length" question - how long should my book be, how long should my podcast be, how long should my webinar be, etc. I wanted this chapter to focus entirely on JUST online course videos, and their creation and delivery.

MIT Study

A study conducted by MIT of over 6.9 million video sessions recorded for Massive Open Online Courses (MOOC) found that the optimal video length should be **under 6 minutes**. Shorter videos were found to be much more engaging. Videos longer than 6 minutes had significant viewer drop-off.

By the way, MOOCs (Mooc.org) are "free online courses available for anyone to enroll. MOOCs provide an affordable and flexible way to learn new skills, advance your career and deliver quality educational experiences at scale."

They have free courses from some of the biggest universities, like MIT, Stanford, and so on.

This MIT study "is the largest-scale study of video engagement to date, using data from 6.9 million video watching sessions across four courses on the edX MOOC platform. We measure engagement by how long students are watching each video, and whether they attempt to answer post-video assessment problems."

So here are their main takeaways from the study:

* Shorter videos are much more engaging

* Khan-style tablet drawing tutorials are more engaging than PowerPoint slides or code screencasts

* Informal talking-head videos are more engaging

* Even high quality pre-recorded classroom lectures are not as engaging when chopped up for a MOOC

* Videos that intersperse an instructor's talking head with slides are more engaging than slides alone.

* Videos where instructors speak fairly fast and with high enthusiasm are more engaging

And their recommendations were:

* Invest in pre-production lesson planning to segment videos into chunks shorter than 6 minutes (your IdeaMap will be very helpful for this)

* Display the instructor's head at opportune times in the video

* Try filming in an informal setting; not necessary to invest in big-budget studio productions

* The instructors should bring out their enthusiasm, and do not need to purposely slow down

* Focus more on the first-watch experience; add support for rewatching and skimming

* Students engage differently with lecture and tutorial videos

Another study from Academia.edu found that students engaged the most with videos that were under 15 minutes, and ideally, under 10 minutes.

So overall, for most niches, my recommendation is to keep it between 5-10 minutes - ideally, within 6 minutes.

Video Size

Not all of your members will watch a video all the way through even after they click play. That means, if you're using standard progressive download videos (which I talk about further below), once they click play on your video, the entire video will start downloading to their device, even if they watch just 5 seconds of it. It will download the entire video even if they just click play, and then pause it right away.

And they may do it more than once if they stop watching the video because they got distracted, or had to take care of something, and come back later and hit refresh on the page.

So you're going to pay for a lot of wasted bandwidth regardless, unless you use True Streaming Videos (coming below).

And that's why it is critical that you keep your videos short, because if you have a long video, then you'll waste a LOT MORE bandwidth in the long-run, because of how people watch videos in spurts. So the shorter your videos, the less bandwidth you'll waste, and the smaller the bill will be from your video provider, like Amazon S3 – which is what I recommend for storing all of your media files.

Video Resolution

I've seen some course creators go overboard by creating their videos in 4K. Unless you're in a highly specialized niche - like photography, or art or modeling, or some niche that requires impeccable details in your videos - 4K is overkill.

Also, depending on your audience and where they're geo-located, even 1080p might be too much, and 720p might be more than enough.

So encode your videos in no greater than 1080p. 720p would be just fine as the maximum resolution if you're doing presentations and talking-head videos.

Multiple Resolutions

Make your videos available in multiple resolutions - 1080p at the highest, then going lower with 720p, 360p, 240p and 144p. So if you have viewers in countries where they don't have high-speed internet access, or maybe they have a cap on their bandwidth, or maybe they're watching on a 2G or 3G phone connection with limited bandwidth, they won't care about HD so much.

They may not even be able to watch HD videos without the video sputtering and freezing every few seconds, because they just don't have high-speed internet access. So make it easier for them to watch your videos by offering lower resolutions. And my WordPress plugin S3MediaVault.com will take care of all of this for you, by the way.

Encoding

If your video creation software doesn't give you the ability to encode your video in a web-friendly, bandwidth-friendly format, then use the free software HandBrake.fr that will allow you to properly encode your main video in the right format and compress it so you can keep the quality high, but also make the size of the video smaller. Small video sizes will lead to a smaller bandwidth bill for you.

Ain't No TED Talk!

Keep it simple - no need for elaborate presentations.

You could just have your IdeaMap (your Mindmap with all of your ideas) open on your screen, do a screen recording, and walk them through each node, one by one, expanding each one as you go. A few of my courses were created this way because it just gives you the ability to create content super-fast.

No need to waste hours hunting for fancy photos and images or creating cartoon animations and a "spectacular presentation". No need for overkill.

You're not exactly giving a TED talk ☺. You're also not exactly giving a presentation on stage at Social Media Marketing World or some big conference. So don't get too hung up over the slickness or spiffyness (new word) of the visuals.

Your members just want to learn the content in the best way possible. So instead of all that, use as many real-world screenshots of whatever it is that you're teaching.

Maybe even do a screencast of whatever software program you're using, or any articles that you're referring to, and so on. And if you do need some great images to visually influence or motivate, you can get them at free stock photo websites like Pexels.com or Pixabay.com

Jump Cut Joy: Ditch the Teleprompter

A lot of people give too much value to a teleprompter. I've had one before. I created one in the past using my old iPad and a teleprompter mirror stand with see-through glass that you can put a camera behind and the iPad becomes your teleprompter.

It's way over-hyped, because reading from a teleprompter and still looking natural requires a lot of practice - A LOT! And it means having a script that practically spells out word for word what you're going to say. Because it's not easy to read from a script in front of you, make sure you have enough head and eyes movement so that it's not blatantly obvious that you're reading from a teleprompter, and then also look natural, talk natural, and then also go with the flow and appear casual and say things off the top of your head. It's hard to do all of that at the same time. And the fact that it requires a script ahead of time, makes the preparation a lot harder. And after trying to do that a few times, most people would give up making videos entirely.

And if you're just going to have bullet points on the teleprompter and you're going to speak naturally about each bullet point, and you don't need a word-for-word script, then that's great! That means you don't need a teleprompter at all! But a lot of people will not be able to talk for long without a proper script, and your impromptu videos might have a lot of umms and aahs and breaks. And then suddenly, it takes an insane amount of time to edit those videos.

Plus you probably shouldn't be doing long video lessons as a full talking-head video anyway - not unless you are as dashing and good-looking as me :-). JUST KIDDING! No one can be as dashing as good-looking as me. Kidding! If I can do such videos with this face made for radio, I mean podcasts, anyone can. You get my point.

Instead, here's a middle-ground, a great option that has worked for me VERY well.

What you can do as a talking-head video, is the quick intro video, where you can briefly appear on camera to introduce yourself, tease the course a little bit, give them the lay of the land, and then go back to screen captures. Maybe even include your talking head in the lower left or right corner of the screen. I don't prefer that because being on camera is more work for me, with lighting and shaving and looking half-decent.

But the point is, you can create a short script. And sit in front of your monitor, and your phone camera in between you and the monitor. And then, pull up the script on the monitor. Memorize and rehearse a couple of lines. Hit record, start talking, and then if you get stuck, without moving your head, just give a brief pause, just move your eyes a little bit to look at the script right behind the camera, then talk again, and keep doing that until your script is done.

And then editing is so much simple. Just keep going until you hit a break, cut that part out, and continue with the next segment.

And you might see your head and body movements jump a little bit between the cuts. And that's why it's called a JumpCut. And it's a perfectly fine and accepted way of editing for almost all types of videos, whether it is course videos, sales videos, or documentation videos.

Hey Guys

Don't say "Hey guys". Always talk like you're talking to one person. No "Hey there RaviNation" or "SubscribeMeGang" or any such terms. One of the most powerful aspects of direct response marketing is directly talking to one person - the viewer, the reader, or the listener. So whether it's your podcast, your blog, your YouTube video, or your online course, always remember that only one person is reading, watching, or listening at a time. So talk to that one person. And that one person only. Like I'm doing right now, where I'm talking to you, and not to a group of people.

And every one of your course video viewers will feel like you are talking directly to them, and not grouping them into some anonymous, invisible "group".

Record in Spurts

Record your videos in short segments. Meaning the part of recording, stopping, saving, checking, and then starting the recording again. So even if it's only a 10-minute lesson, you could record it in 2-3 minute segments and save the recording every 2-3 minutes. So that even if something goes wrong, like your computer crashes, or the recording or editing software quits suddenly, or you lose power and your laptop wasn't plugged in, or your phone's battery dies, or someone calls you in the middle of a recording, or whatever. This way you will never lose more than 2 or 3 or 5 minutes of work max.

Anti Perfection

Do NOT strive for perfection. As the saying goes, Perfection is the enemy of progress. Perfectionism takes like 10-times longer, creates a lot of stress because of the unnecessary pressure you've put on yourself to try and make everything just perfect, it won't allow you to take quick action because you have to plan and debate everything in your mind to excruciating detail, you won't be able to look or talk naturally, which means you have to script every word, which means you might end up sounding like a robot.

Refusing perfectionism will allow you to be natural, be yourself, reduce stress and pressure, launch your course sooner, save you tons of time, which you can use on actually promoting the course.

Tone, Tracking, Transcripts, and more

* Explain it like you're talking to a friend, a peer, or even a coaching client, and not like you're talking to your 8-year-old. That will prevent you from coming across as patronizing.

* Make sure your viewer can track progress. So the next time they come back to your video course, they should be able to pick up watching the video right where they left off the last time.

* Create captions for your international viewers who may not be familiar with your language, or may not understand your accent or speed of delivery.

* Offer Transcripts of your videos, in case someone wants to skim through your course. Now, Captions and Transcripts are optional, because it takes time to create those. So I would say they're not a must-have for launching your course. You can always add them after the fact too. So don't let those two items slow you down.

* Cut to the chase: Don't have long, extended intros, too much small talk, or excessive banter. Online Course Videos aren't your live video stream where you feel compelled to engage with those joining the stream.

* If you're using a learning management system (LMS) that allows your members to mark a module or lesson as complete and then move on to the next one, then it's best that you keep the number of videos on a page to between 1 and 5. The more videos you have on a page, the longer it might take for the page to load. I once saw an online course with 20 videos, like 10 or 15 audios, and a bunch of PDFs, all on one page. That's just extreme overkill, and it's going to cause tremendous overwhelm as well.

* Optimize for mobile: Make sure your website is responsive, your member pages are responsive, and your video player is responsive and works on all mobile devices.

Streaming vs. Progressive Downloads

Streaming is a highly misused word. Some use the word "Streaming" to describe any video that's playing in their browser or audio that's playing on their device.

But just because you are watching a video online, doesn't mean it is being "Streamed". This might not be of relevance to regular folks, but it is highly relevant to digital content creators.

Progressive Downloads

Regular videos - aka "progressive download" videos - are progressively (aka continuously) downloaded to the viewer's browser first, even if the video has been paused. And that's why using plugins like Video Downloader and Video Downloader will let you download the video you're watching.

But as a creator, progressive download videos can increase your bandwidth costs to deliver that video. That's because, as soon as the viewer hits "Play" on the video, the video starts to download to their computer (in whatever the "temp" folder of the browser is, where it stores all temporary internet files).

And then, even if the viewer clicked "Pause" right after they clicked "Play", the video will still continue to download all the way until it is completely downloaded. So if it's a big file, then the entire file of tens- or hundreds of MB's of data is downloaded to their device first (whether it's their computer or mobile device). And regardless of whether they end up watching a few seconds video or a few minutes of the video, the video was downloaded in full to their device.

That means, the video creator - aka, YOU - ended up delivering the entire video, even though they may or may not watch it, or only watch it partially.

So that leads to higher bandwidth costs for you, the creator. And for the viewer, their internet bandwidth is used to download the full video, even though they may or may not watch it, or only watch it partially. That means higher bandwidth costs for your viewer as well - especially if they're on a mobile device and are using their data and have a limited data plan.

Streaming Video

And that's where "Streaming Video" is much more beneficial to everyone involved - well, almost to everyone involved. And that's because, with streaming video, the video is delivered as a "download as you watch" stream of data.

There could be tens or hundreds or thousands of such segments depending on how long the video is. And those segments are delivered one by one to the viewer's device, as they continue to watch the video. But if the viewer hits Pause on the video player, then the segments will stop being downloaded.

So only the bare minimum amount of video data is delivered to the viewer, as needed, as they continue to watch. And that ends up saving you - the provider - money in terms of bandwidth costs; and also reduces the viewer's data usage as the consumer.

So both Streaming and Progressive Download videos are secure. But even between those two, Streaming Videos are THE MOST secure - because they are streamed in real-time, in bits and pieces, to the viewer's browser. That means plugins like Video Downloader, Video DownloadHelper, and even the most popular video downloading software Internet Download Manager won't be able to download your video (their only option is to record their screen to make a copy).

To allow or not to allow (downloads)

There is one main downside to streaming: If some in your audience are from countries where they have slow or poor internet access, streaming videos will be almost unwatchable to them, because their internet access will never be fast enough to download the video "segments" fast enough for them to continue watching normally. And may result in the video freezing up every few seconds while the downloading of the segments catches up to their viewing. But with progressive downloads, those who have poor internet access speeds, will be able to hit Play on the video, then hit Pause, and come back in however long, and the video would continue to download the whole time they're away from their device because that's what progressively downloading means. But you can't do that with streaming where you can Play, Pause and come back later to a fully downloaded video, because the video doesn't download full with streaming.

Also, the best membership sites allow people to consume the content they've paid for in multiple ways - view the video, download the video, download the mp3 audio version of the video, download the presentation as a PowerPoint, download the transcripts as a PDF, and so on.

So you should focus on making it easy for your paying members to download the content that they've actually paid for. Don't make it harder for 99% of your paying members just to secure your content from the 1% of pirates, who will steal and share your content no matter what.

So forget about the 1%, and focus on the 99%.

* Try to create evergreen content by avoiding dating your videos by mentioning current dates and events as much as possible, unless it's highly relevant to your course material.

If you can't create evergreen content because your show is about current events, then that's ok. If you can't, you can't. But if CAN, then evergreen is the way to go.

Also, don't mention any specific offers or pricing or phone numbers, or specific long links in your videos, because those things can change in the future. This is why, if you notice, in the direct response ads on TV, they'll say "Call the number on your screen right now, and you'll get" - and the voice changes and reads out the current offer, and they give out a different number based on the TV show or geo-location because that's how they track the performance of the ads.

Media Hosting

DO NOT store videos or audio on your website. You might wonder, why not just upload these files to your website via FTP or through the WordPress Media page and just store them on your own website? After all, you have "Unlimited Hosting" and "Unlimited Bandwidth" from your web host, so why not take advantage of it, right? That's a great question asked by a lot of WordPress users. And here's why.

Regular web hosts (think Godaddy, Dreamhost, Hostgator, etc - which are terrible web hosts, by the way - I highly recommend SiteGround and LiquidWeb) are not suited for media hosting, not even if you have a VPS or Dedicated Server.

If you're an Online Course Creator and you have Audio, Video, and PDF, and other files (like mindmaps, PowerPoints, docs, zips, etc) in your courses, and you release a new course or do a launch, then when an even reasonably large number of your members - like under 50, for eg., - try to access your online course and download those files, that means potentially hundreds (or thousands) of requests to your video, audio, and PDF.

And that could cause a big spike in server utilization on your web host. Don't forget - when a file is downloaded from your website, it's not just your server's "bandwidth" that is being used. Your server has to allocate server resources to stay connected with that person downloading the file and has to make sure the file gets delivered fully. And that's even without any kind of security on the file.

So if you try to protect the file with some kind of a plain PHP script, now that means any request to the file is intercepted by your PHP download protector script, and that script has to be running the entire time that the file is being downloaded. That's not a big deal for smaller files, but when it comes to audio or more specifically video, we're talking about potentially tens or hundreds of MB's in file size. And that's just for one file. If you have an online course, then you now have tens of such videos, audio, and PDF. Then add tens of different members who bought your online course trying to access them at or around the same time.

All of this could cause a massive spike in your actual server resources - like memory, several concurrent PHP threads running, etc. So long technical story short, that kind of load increase on your website could cause problems for your members: Website being too slow, errors when trying to log in and navigate through your membership site, videos and audio loading very slowly (or not at all), your website crashing and your members can't even get to your member's area, etc

And the cool thing is, I've been aware of all of these challenges since 2009, when I first launched my video player WordPress plugin, called S3MediaVault, at S3MediaVault.com, which allows you to implement all the key points I talked about - like having a responsive video player, ability to add captions, create transcripts, allowing your members to track progress, so that if they watch 3:35 seconds of a video, and come back another day, it will pick up right from 3:36 seconds, right where they left off previously. And it lets you see how long each of your videos was watched overall, how LONG each member watched it, how many TIMES did they watch it, and so on. It allows you to create videos that are super secure and load super fast, making sure the links to the videos cannot be shared with their friends or other unauthorized users.

Sale Before Scale

I think I might be pretty decent at coming up with acronyms and catchphrases ;-).

King of Akron

4x NBA Champion
4x Finals MVP
4x NBA MVP
Laker
Extracted max $$$ from
my wallet
Basically my fam

King of Acronyms
& Catchphrases

DOPE (Do Once, Publish Everywhere)
DOGPOO (Do Once, Get Paid Only Once)
DOSAA (Do Once, Sell Again & Again)
DAP (Digital Access Pass)
MOMMY (More Offers = More Money for You)
WMD (Web Marketer's Dream Kit)
TOC-T (Table of Contents Technique)
B5, B95 (Brilliant 5, Blah 95)
USE (Urgency, Scarcity, Exclusivity)
WTRMI ("water me" = What That Really Means Is)
Show The Last Thing First
Start With the Last Thing First
Create Less, Promote More
Sell First, Create Later
Go Deep, Then Wide
Sale Before Scale
Outbox Marketing
Native Content Marketing

I'm a business coach - I help those who are new to an online business and have never sold anything online before, as well as those who are currently already selling something.

One thing in common between both of those types of clients is that they both want more sales (of course, who doesn't?).

But the problem with those who are new to selling online is that they haven't sold much of anything online, if at all made they've even a single sale. That means they don't yet have an answer to "What has worked well for you previously?".

They have not yet had any success selling anything, but they do want to sell a *lot* of that one thing, whatever their core product or service is.

People worry about scale before they've made a single sale. It's the classic case of counting the chickens before they hatch.

And that's how I came up with "Sale Before Scale".

Here's the main takeaway:

Try to sell ONE SINGLE thing.
For a ONE-TIME fee.
To ONE SINGLE person.
Do it ONE SINGLE time.

Notice the pattern?

After you've done it once, now see if you can do it again.

And again. And again.

As Paul Graham said, "do things that don't scale".

I say, focus on your first few sales before you start thinking about how to scale it.

That's how you validate your niche, validate your product, your pricing, and develop your sales process.

And only then do you try to scale it.

The best way to validate your product is not just asking people if they would buy it *if* you were to offer them that. Just go out and make an offer first.

If you simply ask people "Would you buy this?", they'll probably say yes, because talk is cheap. I discussed this in another chapter as well.

But if they have to pull out their card and put their money where their mouth is? That's where the rubber meets the road and things get real.

So you have to commit and make an offer - even if you haven't created the product yet.

That leads to one of the other phrases that I coined: Sell First, Create Later (separate chapter about this).

That leads to another one of my catch-phrases: MOMMY!

More Offers = More Money for You.

If you want to make more money, you've got to sell more stuff. You've got to make more offers.

But of course, you can't always be pitching and selling like an obnoxious spam-caller (who have, by the way, surpassed the sleazeball-ness (new word) of the proverbial "car salesman"), or you'll burn your list and alienate your audience.

You have to find the right balance and nuanced position between providing value and pitching your products.

I write about this in the chapter "Jab-Hook, Jab-Hook, Jab-Hook".

Fans in the Pudding

Know the saying "proof is in the pudding"? I wanted to give you first-hand proof of making a full-time living from your 1,000 true fans.

Back in 2007, I had a full-time job. I had started developing DigitalAccessPass (DAP) on the side, working nights and weekends. I eventually launched it in October 2008 to a list of 1300+ mostly-inactive list that I had built over many years of selling "PHP Scripts" from one of my earlier websites, MyWebmasterInABox.com. With that small list, I was able to get about 5 sales the first weekend that it launched.

We reached close to 100 buyers over the next few months. Fast-forward to mid-2009, I was still working at my full-time job in New York City. I was waking up at 5 AM, driving to the train station (rain or snow), after first shoveling my driveway of about 10 inches of snow before driving to the station during winter, go through an entire day at work, subway train to Grand Central, Metro from GC to Ossining, NY (where my house was at the time), drive back from the station to my home. Kids, homework, NBA basketball, catching up with my wife - by the time I was done with my duties, it was usually around 10 PM. I would then go to the basement and start working on DAP and all of the support tickets that had accumulated during the day. And it would be around 2 AM before I could go to bed. I would have to wake up in about 3 hours. I would sometimes catch a snooze on the train, but usually, I would work on my book that I was writing back then, or work on new features for DAP.

This went on for many years. I had been doing my online business as a side-hustle to my main job, since 2000. So I probably averaged about 5 hours of sleep a night for about 9 years straight. But in 2009, it all came to a head. DAP was just starting to find some traction, but I had a full-time job, my wife had a full-time job, little kids at home, daycare, babysitters, long commutes, bad weather for about 6 months a year. Things got real bad for a while. I was experiencing tremendous burn- out. I was anxious all the time, I couldn't sleep, even went into a depression.

That was around the time my wife Veena Prashanth was looking for a change at her job, as she had hit the proverbial "glass ceiling" for women. I begged her to come and join me so we could work together on DAP. Long story short, she agreed! She dove right in with both feet into the business, and DAP sales immediately grew like over 1000% the next few months, because she took control of the business like a superstar takes over a game when it gets close. She was developing new features, fixing bugs, and helping customers super fast. And about 8 months later, I quit my job. Encouraged by DAP's growth, we sold our house in Ossining, NY, and moved to San Diego. And the rest, as they say, is history!

My wife and I quit really lucrative, high-paying, high-powered, high-influence jobs, and DAP had well short of 1,000 paid users at the time. But we were able to afford a nice living with less than 1,000 paying customers. And we weren't even charging a subscription fee at the time – it was all from one-time sales.

That why I continue to harp on one point: You don't need "millions" of *anything* in life – you don't need millions of customers, millions of downloads, millions of listeners, millions of website visits, or millions of Facebook page likes, or millions of email subscribers.

You can do really, *really* well with 1,000 fans in pretty much all of those groups.

One. Thousand. True. Fans. Who will buy whatever you publish.

But you've got to sell stuff for them to buy! You can't survive on Facebook likes or Instagram followers and Cute-GIF posts and time-wasting questions and like-baits. You can't use social currency to buy groceries or pay for gas.

You've got to build a business. And for that, you've got to create, sell and deliver products.

That's what I've written about in the rest of this book, and talk about on my podcast at SubscribeMe.fm.

Go Deep, Then Wide

And the Biggest Secret to Success I Learned From My Father, Google, and Miley Cyrus.

"Every father should remember one day his son will follow his example, not his advice." - Charles Kettering

"Go Deep, Then Wide": This was the biggest thing I learned from my late father R.N. Jayagopal, song and story writer extraordinaire, rest in peace.

He actually taught me the opposite: Go wide, and enjoy the multiple sources of income.

And that's OK because he wasn't trying to mislead me. He meant it sincerely. It's just that he didn't fully quite understand his own mega-success in life. Many years later, I realized that I have to do what he *did*, not what he *said*.

And it is an immutable law to learning from successful people, is to *do as they do, not as they say*. Usually, that quote is said in a negative context, because a lot of people will be doing one thing but then teaching another thing, sometimes intentionally. That is why a lot of online courses about making money don't work because they're not teaching you what they're doing.

I'm an entrepreneur today because of my father. He was so ahead of time that he had figured out the concept of multiple streams of income back in the 60s.

He always told me that I should set up different streams of income from different sources, even if they're not very big sources because there would always be money coming in, so that I'll never have to worry about having enough to pay the bills, and that would allow me to freely pursue my dreams and ambitions and goals, whatever they were.

What a beautifully simple concept: set up multiple streams, never worry about your living expenses, then go after your dreams.

Except, there was one little problem: That exact formula never worked for me, and probably won't work for you either, certainly not in that exact form.

So what was that small flaw in his advice?

He did not start thinking about diversifying his income until he had been well established as a superstar in his career. He didn't realize that he was able to go wide, because he had already gone deep first.

If you try to create multiple smaller streams first (so you can go after your big dream later), it's probably not going to work, because you're too busy postponing your main dream, not working on your one big thing, and too worried about creating plan B, C, and D first before you ever get to plan A.

But if you simply switched it around just a little bit - where you went after Plan A first, and went deep, really deep, into your core niche, into your core passion, your core expertise, then you have just exponentially increased your chance for success. Because you're only working on plan A the whole time.

Your time, effort, energy, and money can all be focused primarily on making Plan A work. That means you are not focusing on 10 other side projects, the smaller fish, you're not distracted, and you're not juggling too many things and spreading yourself too thin. When you zero in on something like a laser, you are bound to break through at some point.

So the key is to go deep first. It's like drilling for oil. You can only strike oil if you dig deep enough in one place. You have more chances of striking oil if you start with one single hole that is 100 feet deep, than digging 10 holes that are each 10 feet deep. If you do the math, in both cases, you've dug 100 feet in total. So the amount of work you did is the same. But you have a much higher chance of striking oil in the single, 100-foot hole than in any of the other 10 holes.

Of course, this is just an example of going deep first. So we're going to assume that you've done your homework on where to dig, whether there is any oil there, do you have permission to dig there, etc, etc – aka Market Research. So don't get too technical on me, ok? ☺

Let me give you some examples of people and companies who went deep first, and only then went wide.

Let's start with Google. What has always been their superpower? It's Search. As a sidebar, I owe my entire career as a web developer and WordPress developer, to Google, because without the ability to search for just about every little error and issue and troubleshooting problem, something that was impossible to do with Yahoo or Altavista or Ask Jeeves, if you're old enough, you'll remember those names - so without Google, I would have *never, ever* made it from India to America in the year 2000.

So Google was, and still is, the greatest at search. And then, from a little company that existed back in the day called Goto.com (if I'm not mistaken), Google borrowed the idea of allowing companies and marketers to pay for ads that appeared on a page along with results for the main search. And then, if you automated the process of buying an online ad, and on top of that also turn that into an auction where marketers could bid for a spot on a page, that should make you a lot of money.

So they started showing ads on their search results pages. And that turned out into a massive success, made them billions of dollars, and when they went on to become one of the biggest companies in the world, almost all of their income came from online ads. And I remember that being a problem at the time of their IPO - a lot of investors were concerned that Google relied too much on one source of income.

Their original superpower was Search. Then they figured out how to monetize that. And a lot of their other products came later, like Gmail, AdSense, Google Plus, and YouTube – all of them were basically an excuse to show you more ads.

AdSense was a revolutionary product that allowed regular website owners like me to be able to display ads on their websites. The same thing with YouTube - anyone with a few dollars can buy an ad on a YouTube video or show it on millions of websites using AdWords. And then they realized that mobile phones were going to be the future of search, so they bought Android, started making phones, created a smart assistant, and so on.

Everything is tied back to search - their superpower, their core expertise - and the ability to display ads.

Now, think about their products that failed or probably will fail or just not be that big of a success: Google Plus, Google Glass, Boston Robotics (where the robots look like scary monster dogs straight from sci-fi movie hell - later sold off), the self-driving car division, going to space, etc.

They made a lot of money first with their core competency and expertise. And they used the profits to later experiment with a lot of different things – aka, go wide - and work on a ton of new products and services, some of them completely unrelated because they were making money hand-over-fist with online advertising.

They went, really, *really* deep with search. They didn't just stop with cataloging websites, they created Google maps that let us tour the world, even under the sea, see the world from a satellite, map out continents and countries.

You get the idea. They went deep into their superpower, and only later, went wide and experimented with other things. Guess what? To this day, they've found the most success in products and services that complement their core offering, and many of their completely unrelated, non-core-competency, pie-in-the-sky ideas have unsurprisingly failed.

I'm not telling you not to have big dreams or gigantic ambitions. I'm just saying that you've got to start with one thing, and go deep first, and see if you can get that to work when it comes to your core niche, core passion, and core expertise.

Back to my father, he was the most gifted writer and poet that India has ever produced. He won awards at both the National and International levels. One of the movies he directed won the best picture award at the Tashkent Film Festival in Russia. I was only a few years old when I remember him going to Russia with a delegate of Indian artists. He was invited to the Kremlin, had dinner with the Russian President, one time he was even invited to a Black Tie dinner at the white house with President Bill Clinton, and he sat at the same table as the President of the United States, along with really big celebrities from around the world!

He went *really* deep into his core expertise - which was songwriting, screenplay, and direction. And then, he was able to parlay that success into a whole bunch of side projects: he built a school for the poor, he donated countless hours and money to charity, he was a very high dignitary in the Lions Club, an international charity organization. He wrote, produced, and directed TV shows (even cast me as the lead in a few of them!), took on a whole bunch of little side gigs with good pay, and later in his life, he ended up creating about 50 different revenue streams.

Of course, he advised me to do the same, because it had worked for him. Or so he thought. Except, he got it just a bit backward, not out of malice, but out of ignorance. He was a self-made man, but he wasn't good at reverse engineering his own success.

So for many years, I tried to do the same - tried to go wide first and create several income streams that would "one day" allow me to go after my BIG DREAM, which was to be an actor and singer. Unfortunately, I failed at almost all of those things, and turns out, I wasn't good enough at acting or singing to do it at the highest of the highest levels.

It wasn't until I figured out what my superpower was, or what it *could* be, that I started getting traction. That's when I started seeing little gains. Little successes. Tiny steps, all towards the same direction. Digging deeper into the same hole, rather than futzing around with a bunch of shallow holes.

And that's the same thing that's going to help you today in your life and business.

If what you're doing is not working in achieving your goals of financial freedom, then you've got to dig deeper.

Instead of trying to create 10 different products – like a plugin, an eBook, a course, a coaching program, a Facebook group, etc - how about creating just one product first, and then go deep down that niche?

So if you started with a simple product – like an eBook - you could turn that into an online course. Then later start a podcast on the same topic. Then start a community around that same niche.

And that's exactly what I've done. Every single one of my products has been created for Entrepreneurs and Digital Creators.

And it all started with Software because that was my core competency, my superpower, at least for the longest time. I found success with PHP scripts. Based on that, I created Digital Access Pass, a WordPress plugin. Then came more plugins like S3MediaVault and CoolCastPlayer.

I started a podcast SubscribeMe.fm in the same niche, wrote 7 books (this one is my 8th) for the same niche, started my Digital Creators Academy for the same audience, and so on.

The whole time, I've been digging deeper and deeper. And my audience and customer base have been consistently growing the whole time. And because I've been focused on primarily the same niche, I get a lot of feedback and ideas from my existing customers for new products. And when I launch a new product, I have an existing audience to launch it to.

Consistently moving in the same direction has brought me quite far. To get to your destination, you not only have to start driving in the right direction, but you have to *continue* driving in the same direction. You can't go a few miles in one direction, a few miles in another direction, and so on.

When was the last time you thought about being the best at something in the world?

Let's say you have a course about Dog Training, what if you decided, that your course is going to be the absolute best dog training course in the world?

The absolute best guitar learning course in the world?

Or the absolute best photography course in this world?

What if you even just started thinking about what it would take to be "the best" at literally anything in this world?

It's ok if you don't become the absolute GOAT (Greatest Of All Time), but imagine what it would do for you in terms of name, fame, and money if you could even just be in even the top 10 in this world at something? Heck, even a top 100 in a world of 8 billion people? What if you were in the top 100 in just your country? That means not 7.2 billion, but maybe just 370 million (like in the US)? What if you were the best in your state? Or just your city?

As Miley Cyrus would say, sometimes, it's the climb. Sometimes just what the journey itself does for you, what it helps you achieve, is already worth more than actually reaching your destination.

But for that to happen, first, of course, you must want it, with your entire being. And then, you have to discard everything that's not in alignment with that. Stop trying to teach stuff that you're not good at or things that you don't think you're the best at.

Cut out distractions, side projects, shiny objects, and laser focus on just one thing.

Trust me, there will be time for those 20 other things too. For now, just focus on one thing. One big thing. And go deep, and keep doing deeper and deeper and deeper, until you strike oil. Or maybe you'll strike gold.

And along the way, you'll learn so much about digging, about tools and techniques and tactics of digging, that worst comes to worst, if you don't strike oil or gold, you are practically guaranteed to become one of the world's biggest experts on digging, and you'll be able to create a whole bunch of books and courses and coaching about digging, and make yourself fame and fortune, all just from that one superpower: digging a deeper hole.

I've been doing that, and I'm going to continue doing that.

Find your superpower, and then squeeze it for everything you've got.

As Robert Frost wrote...

The woods are lovely, dark and deep,
But I have promises to keep,
And miles to go before I sleep,
And miles to go before I sleep.

And I'm going to make sure I walk all those miles in the same direction ☺

Judging You By Your TOC

Not everyone will judge your book by its cover. Many will give you a second shot and take a quick peek inside.

But they absolutely will judge your book by its Table of Contents (TOC).

The TOC for who you are, is your online presence.

Your website is critical. But it's not the best indication of who someone is. Most people's websites are like the person going out on a first date: All cleaned up, well dressed, smelling good, and on their best behavior.

But their social posts are an indication of what they're like when hanging out with friends, wearing home clothes, not having showered in a day (or three), drinking a cold beverage or maybe smoking something, being loud and carefree while "letting their hair down".

Your tweets, Facebook posts, Instagram posts, YouTube comments, Reddit posts and comments, your "Likes" on all these platforms –says a lot more about who you are, than your perfectly polished website.

So be sure to put your best foot forward on social media. Be authentic, share a lot, but don't over-share, keep some of your inner thoughts inside if they don't truly represent who you are, share your best ideas, thoughts, and content, and leave the best kind of breadcrumbs that can lead a complete stranger to the most authentic you.

A Tale of Two Timers

A Tale of Two Timers: A Simple Productivity Hack

Here's a simple hack to keep you focused on your writing (or whatever it is that you're creating, like videos or blogging).

1) Set up a cool-looking visual "Count Up" timer that tracks your overall progress. Every time you start writing, start the timer and turn it off as soon as you're done. I use the iOS app MultiTimer.

(Actual screenshot of my timer while writing this very book).

2) Now start a regular "Count Down" timer on your phone for 10-20 minutes. You can do this by saying "<voice assistant>, set a timer for 10 minutes".

This timer is to get you to keep writing for that specified period.

Here's how these two timers help:

* Timer #1 (Count Up) will help you keep track of how much time you've spent working on your book, and will give you tangible visual feedback and a sense of satisfaction, and maybe even a sense of urgency, every time you look at the timer and see how many hours you've already spent.

It's also really cool for posting screenshots on social media to show your progress as well as for self-accountability.

* Timer #2 is just to keep you focused on one thing for some time. It's cool how we can trick our minds to really lock in when there's a clock ticking.

A deadline plus some pressure works wonders for getting things done.

And since it's a short timer, you don't have to worry about whether you can sustain it, and you get to look forward to it being over rather quickly, plus the sense of accomplishment and satisfaction of having "beasted" for that short period, and you got stuff done!

This is way simpler and less intimidating than the Pomodoro. That means you'll actually implement it. Two timers for the same task. One keeps overall progress, another one for immediate focus.

Both Word and Google Docs have a way to get the total document editing time. However, that doesn't track the research time that goes into your book, the Google searches, watching videos or reading documents & blog posts, creating images, finding data, searching through your own content to find relevant information, etc.

It's also less "monitorable" in real-time, and also less cool and less shareable.

Don't Go For the Blonde

When it comes to finding a joint venture (JV) partner or an influencer or an affiliate to help you promote your product, you would be making a big mistake if all you did was try to go after just the biggest names in your market.

And I'm calling this the "Don't Go For the Blonde" technique.

Of course, I mean no disrespect to brunettes, or blondes, or whatever color your hair may be.

What I'm referring to here, is a scene from the movie "A Beautiful Mind" where actor Russell Crowe plays famous mathematician John Nash, widely regarded as one of the great mathematicians of the 20th century, who won a shared Nobel Prize in 1994.

Here's the video, but let me set up the scene:

Russell Crowe's John Nash is in a bar with his friends. And in walks an attractive blonde woman, with 4 brunette friends. And when all of his friends start just ogling at the blonde and ignore her friends, John Nash comes up with a suggestion, which went on to become the basis of his Nobel Prize-winning "Equilibrium Game Theory".

The idea is that if everyone went after the blonde, she would ignore all of them because she's feeling way too important. And *after* the rejection, if they now approached her friends, they would now be insulted that they weren't approached first and would shun the guys. And everyone "loses".

So Nash says, instead, ignore the blonde and go straight for the brunettes, and that way everyone his 4 friends and the 4 brunettes – can all get a date.

This is what tends to happen in the real world as well. I've seen a lot of newbies and inexperienced marketers, looking at all the big-name marketers in their industry, and lusting after their big lists and audiences, and thinking "All I have to do is do a JV with Mr. Big-name-marketer and I'll have them blast my product to hundreds of thousands of people on their list, and I'll hit big time soon thereafter."

That's a flawed way to look at it and it has a few problems:

1) The biggest names may have thousands or hundreds of thousands of subscribers on their lists. They worked very hard to build this list, probably over many years. And most of them won't endlessly spam their lists with offers. OK, some of them do, but they usually lose subscribers pretty fast. So Spam Karma is usually quick to take effect.

So they have to be judicious in emailing their list, as these marketers usually have their own products to promote. There may be favors that they have to return - maybe a friend of theirs mailed their list for this person's launch, and now they have to email their list for that friend's next promotion. And then every so often comes along an insanely great product - like Dropbox when it first came out, or a new Membership Plugin like DigitalAccessPass.com, or Quiz Builder like SmartQuizBuilder.com - and they are compelled to participate in it because the product itself is so new and noteworthy.

So by the time they're done with promoting their own products, returning-the-favor mailings, and the occasional remarkable-new-kid-on-the-block mailings, they're already at risk of burning out their lists. So they're probably not going to mail out for your product launch - unless you're launching something spectacular.

It's got to be spectacular in other people's minds, not just yours because I'm sure you will always think your new book or plugin or product is always going to be spectacular.

So if you're thinking people will email their lists on your behalf just because you came out with a new product, or just because you joined their mastermind group, or because you bought this marketer's products, or because you joined their Facebook group, or because they appeared as a guest on your show, then stop right now, because it's most probably not happening.

I'll give you a small example of my own. At DAP, we have almost 30,000 DAP users. And we have so many other lists outside of DAP. If you came to us and said that, you have, say, a new WordPress plugin launching, and you want us to promote it to our lists of tens of thousands of users - most of them buyers - which we have built with lots of hard work over the years, then guess what? It's not going to happen.

So don't waste your time following a marketer, buying their products, their books, joining their expensive mastermind or coaching program, just because you think they will one day turn around and promote your product to their lists. You are in for a big disappointment if you do that. It just doesn't work that way, and you may not even understand the full extent of it, until you've built your own list, and only then will you realize the true value of having that list, using it more to deliver value than to sell products. And on the occasions that you do wish to promote something, you want to save that for your own products or to return the favor of someone who has helped you, or to gain the favor of someone who might soon help you.

And the crazy thing, do you want to know of a guaranteed way to get the attention of a big-name marketer? It is to promote *their* product as an affiliate, get them a bunch of sales, and get a big commission check from them. And if you help them sell a lot, that's when you can reasonably expect them to reciprocate.

But if you had a big list already and had the brand recognition and respect to get people on your list to buy stuff, why sell use that to sell other people's products? Why not save that to promote your own book, podcast, online course, or membership site?

Always buy, don't rent. Build your own business. Not someone else's.

It's like when someone is a tennis newbie yet wants to play against Rafael Nadal - not gonna happen unless you have a relationship with Rafa or people who are connected to him. When you are first getting started with Tennis, you won't be able to get the top players in the league to play with you. In the same way, as you get good at tennis, you won't want to play with someone who is several levels below you in terms of skill. I mean, you might play with your kids, but you know what I'm talking about.

You have to find someone just *above* your level to play tennis with. Not even someone at your level. Someone slightly better. And that applies to real-world marketing too.

Don't go after the A-listers right off the bat. Go for the B, C, D players. Like me. I consider myself a C or D-lister if you consider the overall scheme of things. I'm not ashamed to tell you that.

I'm not at an A-lister level, like Richard Branson or Bill Gates. I'm not at a Chris Saaca or Tim Ferris Level. So yeah, I would say C-lister, in terms of the money I make. But in terms of actual popularity, I might even be a D-lister. And that's ok.

So, find the D-list Superstars in your niche. These are the people who might take the time and the inclination to help you, and of course, you need to bring them some value too. But they'll be more open to doing a mutually beneficial joint venture. And I have lots and lots of ideas about how to find such D-list Super Stars, how to approach them without being obnoxious, how to enter a community and establish a name for yourself, and lots of other stuff that I will talk about in another book or course, or probably on my podcast.

So ignore the blonde, and go for her friends, and you are most likely to get a date.

The Flip Side

The other side of this is just going for the home run right from the get-go – to shoot for the stars and at least land on the moon, as I like to say.

(Leslie Calvin "Les" Brown said, "Shoot for the moon. Even if you miss, you'll land among the stars". Sounds cool, but maybe he didn't realize that the moon is so much closer than the nearest star? Moon: 240,250 miles away. Sun: 92.9 million miles away.)

So sure, do that too.

Ask Seth Godin to be your guest on your first-ever podcast even if you have almost no listeners. Or ask to be the lead in the movie that you've written yourself, even if you're a complete nobody (example in next chapter).

Be sure to bet on yourself and swing for the fences. But don't give up if you happen to miss the first time.

There are other ways to win even if you don't hit a home run every single time.

The Bayonne Bleeder

"He was called the Bayonne Bleeder for the punishment he took during his fights. Chuck Wepner must have felt that the heavyweight championship was his as he saw Muhammad Ali go down as a result of a right hand to the chest. It was not to be as Ali staggered back to his feet and continued to batter the "Bayonne Bleeder" and eventually stopping Wepner with but 19 seconds left in the fight", writes Tom Denelson of Inside Boxing.

Wepner never won a major championship, but he did become immortalized in history in a way that no one could have imagined.

On that fateful night, as Chuck Wepner came back to take blow after brutal blow from Muhammed Ali, a young, impressionable, and unknown Philadelphia resident was watching on closed-circuit TV.

Inspired by Wepner's relentless comebacks, this young man went home that night and wrote the screenplay for what would become not only one of the greatest movies of all time but also gave birth to arguably the greatest American icon.

Because the movie was based on him, Wepner was offered a choice by this young man – receive $70,000 upfront or 1% of the profits of a movie that was not yet made.

Wepner - who had never heard of the young man - opted for cash upfront instead of unseen profits.

And because of that one mistake, he lost over $8,000,000 (8 million) as the movie went on to make over $800,000,000 (800 million) in profits the world over.

If you haven't already guessed by now, the young man was Sylvester Stallone and the name of the movie was Rocky.

Chuck Wepner is believed to have retired a rather poor, liquor salesman in Bayonne, while Stallone would go on to become famous around the world as the Italian Stallion.

Stallone had an idea after watching Wepner that night. He could have gone home that night, knocked down a couple of cold ones, watched a sitcom on TV, and gone to bed.

Instead, he was inspired and motivated enough to go beyond 32 previously rejected scripts, to write this script in just three days – his 33rd script.

Rocky was close to never getting made, as producers went running when Stallone insisted that he play "Rocky Balboa" himself.

But Stallone persisted, and of course, he won.

When opportunity strikes, what will you do?

Will you be a Wepner? Or a Stallone?

Chuck Wepner

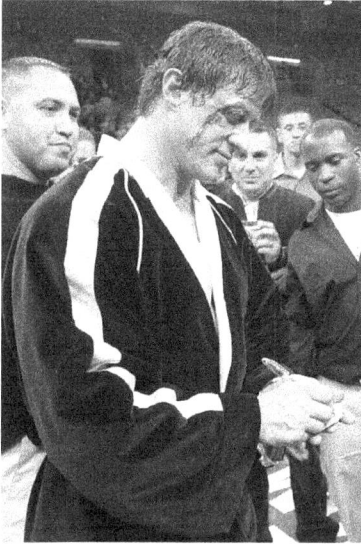

Sylvester Stallone

Consistently Mediocre or Inconsistently Epic

It is hard enough to create — even just one time - content, products, or services that are epic. And it becomes 100x harder to do that consistently over and over again.

We don't watch a Leonardo Di Caprio-, James Cameron- or Meryl Streep movie because they *consistently* release a movie every year. We watch them because even if they release a movie inconsistently (time-wise), the one thing we can expect is that whatever they release, they tried to make it Epic (quality-wise).

We don't listen to a Podcast because they religiously release an episode every week. We listen because they put out great content.

We don't buy a book from Seth Godin because he releases a book every year. We do it because his books are epic, even if he has no schedule or consistency for how often to release them.

 "Consistency" should be measured based on "Quality", not "Timing".

It's better to be Inconsistently (time-wise) Epic, than Consistently (time-wise) Mediocre.

Should you strive for consistency in both timing and quality? Of course.

But if you can't do both, better to prioritize Quality over Timing.

Use USE

Every offer should end in a call to action (CTA) – like "Buy this", "Click here", "Sign up" or "Call us".

Every piece of content you publish should also have some kind of a CTA, but we'll only address CTAs on your offer page in this chapter.

A CTA alone isn't always enough to get your audience to take action. There need to be some additional motivations to push them towards taking action *now*.

Without that added motivation, your offer will probably get set aside for "I'll get back to this later". And "later" usually means "never", because you may not get another chance to get them back to your website.

Urgency

Every student in school is aware of how urgency can get a lot of things done fast – like, only a few days remaining before an exam, or a deadline to turn in that homework or project.

Like it or not, even in other aspects of life, without any kind of urgency or deadline, a lot of things won't get done - at least not on time.

3 days left to pay this bill, or a $35 late fee.
Finals in 4 days.
Flight leaves in 45 minutes.
Last day to send in your proposal.
Client needs this by tomorrow.
Boss needs the report in 1 hour.

Urgency is also about importance. Make your product or service important to your audience, and that will help increase the urgency. If it's not important, urgency won't work.

"Price goes up at midnight tonight"
"Enrollment ends tonight and will reopen again only after 3 months"
"Coupon expires tomorrow"

Scarcity

Scarcity is another major trigger that gets people to take action fast. If there's too much of something, fewer will want it, because there's so much anyway, I can always get it whenever I want.

But put a limitation on the number and make only a limited number available (even if it's an artificial restriction), and be sure to make them aware that only a few are left, and suddenly more people will want it. Just basic human psychology: We want what we can't have (or what we may never be able to have because it ran out).

In dating, the "hard to get" person appears seemingly more attractive than someone who is "available any time", even if it's a fake manipulation.

That "clingy" friend who's always there is less fun than that friend who appears elusive and busy.

The fear of scarcity is why people started hoarding - of all things, toilet paper! - in early 2020 as the pandemic was starting to get worse.

And that's why there are massive lines to buy an iPhone every time a new model is launched because there are so few of them. And a few months after the launch, when there's way more supply than demand, phone companies have to make up special discounted and bonus offers just to get people to upgrade to those same phones that had a line for a mile around the block just a few months earlier.

Changingminds puts it well:

> Scarcity is the lack of something. When we realize that we do not have something, we desire it.
>
> If something is not scarce, then it is not desired or valued that much. Praises from a teacher who seldom praises are valued more than praises from a teacher who is liberal with his or her praise.

"Only 5 left in stock"
"Are you coming to the concert? I only have 2 tickets left"
"Last 3 left at this price"

You can easily add scarcity to any offer, without making it look fake.

 "Only 3 copies left" will work for a physical book or widget. But you can't say that about a digital product like a PDF or software, because everyone knows that you can't run out of digital copies of PDFs or Zip files.

Instead, you could add a more sensible limitation:

"Special early-bird free bonus course for the first 50 buyers".
"Free 1 hour Coaching by me when you buy during the launch"
"Free T-shirt with your purchase today"
"Premium Support + Setup Call if you become a Platinum Member"
"Exclusive In-Person Bootcamp for all Founding Members"
"Get 1 ticket for free (a $99 value) to our Seminar when you buy VIP access"
"I can only take on Five new 1-on-1 Coaching Clients at this".

Urgency and scarcity trigger FOMO - Fear of Missing Out. "What if I miss out on this deal? I'll probably never get this price/product/version again, so I better get it now".

Exclusivity is another important trigger that can get people to take action.

"Special Collection"
"Collector's / Limited Edition"
"Personally Autographed"
"A signed Photo with me"
"VIP Access"
"Access to After Party"
"Front of Line access" (skip the lines)
"Spend 1 full day with me at my home"
"Private Mastermind Group with 20 incredibly successful entrepreneurs"
"You have to apply and be approved before you can be accepted into the Mastermind"

USE Abuse

If you don't use USE triggers properly, or if you try to fake them, they can backfire.

* Having a "Lowest Price Ever" sale multiple times a year
* Products are discounted all the time
* Increasing the price to then offer it at a lower price
* When they try to leave your website, showing an exit popup that gives them a discount "Only if you buy now"
* Showing a count-down timer after which offer is supposed to expire "tonight", but the offer is still there and the timer always resets every time you visit the page, even after a week.

Sticking to an expiring offer is going to be very hard. If you're doing a 3-day sale, you'll probably get the most sales on the last day, and probably the most per-hour sales in the last few hours.

As tempting as it is to keep the offer open for another day or two, you shouldn't.

And that's because when people know that you have a strict deadline and won't easily budge to make a few extra bucks, it will increase the credibility of your USE triggers. And the next time you say the offer expires tonight, they know you really mean tonight. And that will get you much better results the next time you send out an offer.

Why (Most) Webinars & Live Videos Suck

What do bad Karaoke singers and many live video creators have in common? They both suck and they don't even know it!

Do you remember the last time you signed up for a webinar, showed up at the pre-scheduled time, and then watched it start to finish in one sitting? If you have, then congratulations - you're in the minuscule minority.

Most people are getting jaded by so-called "webinars", which are nothing but a pre-recorded video, with a long, drawn-out intro, where the presenter usually starts slow, welcomes users as if real users are tuning in live in real-time. Maybe it was a real live webinar at some point in the past when real people were listening in real-time. But it's most probably not live when *you* get to watch it.

These webinars usually take about 10 minutes to get to the main content. It starts with the obligatory self-praise, warm-and-cuddly family pictures with kids and pets, vacation shots, and a "check out how awesome I am" list of accomplishments.

Honestly, most webinars are a waste of time because there's way too much fluff.

And most webinars send you a replay link later, so if it's important enough, you can always watch the replay. And hopefully, they don't do that stupid thing of disabling all video controls, which means you can't fast forward and skip the fluff. If they do, then just open the video on a mobile device, where those gimmicks won't work, and all of the controls will be available for you.

Have you ever been to a Karaoke party? I've been at many, especially holiday and New Year's parties. *Everyone* thinks that they're a rockstar, *everybody* thinks they've got an amazing voice. And the *massive* gap between their imagination and reality is just mind-numbing.

So when I say mind-numbing, I don't mean that as a figure of speech. My mind has actually gone numb listening to some of these folks "sing". Like the prisoner in a horror movie, where the bad guys are doing something horrible to them, and the prisoner's mind just becomes numb to the pain and torture and goes wandering somewhere far and away to a much happier place.

That's how a lot of live videos feel. Especially the Facebook lives. I wouldn't be offended if you told me that some of my live videos sucked too.

For the most part, it takes people a few seconds to realize that the recording is already on - that first 5 seconds can be super-annoying as the person is looking into the phone and not saying anything because the Facebook app is not giving them a proper indication that they're already live and on the air. That's a problem with the app, of course, but still annoying.

<sidebar> Once you're done with the live video, you can go back into that post and edit out the first few seconds of awkward silence or the fumbling start.</sidebar>

Sometimes it could just be a spotty internet connection. A lot of rambling, periods of dead-air, distractions and noise from the surroundings, distractions from the Facebook friends who're starting to watch the video and leaving comments, it takes time to get used to looking at the actual camera - which is a tiny black hole on one end of your phone, rather than looking at your own image on the screen.

Because if you look at your on the phone screen when recording instead of directly at the little black dot that is the camera, then to your viewer, it will seem like you're looking slightly off-camera, and not directly at them. And that can look unprofessional, annoying, and your viewers can't connect with you just like you wouldn't be able to connect with someone you're talking to and looking at, but they're not looking back at you and are instead always looking at someone sitting behind you.

One thing Facebook live videos have going for them is that Facebook aggressively promotes live videos. Sometimes when I'm on Facebook, I get annoyed by all of the many live video notifications. If you're using Facebook on the desktop, you'll get a little notification on the left bottom corner. And these days, you will even see a small, thumbnail size of the actual live video show up in the bottom left corner. It is muted, but it's still the actual live feed. So yes, Facebook live videos are great for getting noticed. But as the creator, what you do with that attention is an altogether different matter.

The big problem with Facebook live videos is that most people think that they can just hit "go live" and start winging it. For the average person, doing a great live video that is interesting, fast-paced, and offers value to their target audience, is hard. And what's worse, like the karaoke night, they don't know that their live performance sucks, that they may not have the talent, training, or technique to pull off a live video; maybe they don't have the right equipment - like using the built-in phone mic gives you decent audio, but not for regular use, or maybe they don't have great content, or they are not entertaining, or they are not good at winging it, and sometimes, let's admit it - some people are just not that interesting.

You might look at the video view numbers that some live videos get and think that those folks are killing it. But the reality is, it only takes 3 seconds of viewing a video for Facebook to count it as an actual "View". At least it is 30 seconds on YouTube to be counted as a view. So on Facebook, as you're scrolling through your feed, if you see that someone is live, and just out of curiosity, you pause for *literally* 3 seconds, and bam, they've now got an extra "View". So they now have more encouragement to create more such videos. It's like the fake, courteous applause that the bad Karaoke singer gets at the end of a terrible performance. And now they think they're good, and want to go at it one more time!

So does that mean webinars are dead? No.

Does it mean that you shouldn't ever do a live video again? No.

My goal is to just make you consider all these factors so that you can step it up when it comes to your live videos and webinars.

A webinar can be a terrific lead magnet. You give them great value, and in return, they give you their email id. And of course, you can also pitch a special offer at the end of the webinar.

Video is great at building rapport, communicating much more effectively than the written word, and way more fun than a simple PDF report.

So that's really what your webinar should be: Packed with great value, very little fluff, and an offer at the end. The offer doesn't necessarily have to be a sales pitch, but there needs to be some kind of a call to action (CTA).

There needs to be a CTA that's a part of everything you do - whether that's an email that you send to your list, YouTube video, podcast, webinar, report, Kindle book, or even your online course.

Breaking this down further, if the goal of your webinar is to provide great content, with almost no fluff, no distractions, no tangents, and the maximum value in the minimum possible time, then you know that you cannot wing it.

Social content needs to be short and to the point. It's a world of bite-sized content - TikTok, Tweets, YouTube shorts, and Instagram Reels. People are listening to their podcasts at 2x speed I've gotten so used to listening to podcasts at about 1.8x speed, that if I listen to any podcast at normal speed, it sounds like everyone's talking drunk and slurring their speech. I even listen to my own podcast episodes at 1.8x as I can't stand even my own voice at normal speed anymore!

I can't remember the last time I watched a full episode of Saturday Night Live - a hugely popular comedy show in the US - live when it aired. It's a live show but incredible the amount of preparation that goes into creating this live show is incredible, and I write about this in the chapter "Put your pen down, script it and rehearse it".

Live videos are hard, at least if you want to do it well. It takes a lot of prep work, from lighting to clothes, makeup, and script. And most people doing live videos and live audio today are putting in very little preparation, and it shows.

So instead of a live webinar where you're just rambling, making small talk during the intro, and showing an extended resume of yours, to begin with, how about creating a crisp, short, tightly edited, well-produced, great piece of content?

Everyone wants everything now, with the least fluff, fewest (or no) ads, and no distractions. I have ad blockers in all my browsers (Firefox, Chrome, and Opera which has it built-in). I have another browser plugin that blocks all auto-play videos on web pages. Popup ads? Gone. Never see them. People record live shows on their DVR and watch them later so that they can fast-forward through the ads.

Shows like Tim Ferris that have about 5 minutes of ads upfront? I fast-forward through all of it. The podcast app I use has a skip setting for each podcast. More about that in a different chapter.

If it's a mid-roll ad that's not too long, I'll probably continue listening to it. But on shows that I listen to frequently, I know that in the middle of a show there's a long ad break of 3-5 minutes. So I'll actually stop whatever I'm doing, even if I'm doing the dishes, dry my hand, pull out my phone, and fast forward through the ads. I watch how-to videos on YouTube on 2x speed. People are doing speed-reading so they can read more.

See where I'm going with this?

You need to provide value fast. You cannot be like...

"Umm… hello? Is this thing on? Oh yes, hi. Welcome to my Facebook live video. I'm sitting here today in my home office, the weather is great outside, and I've been thinking about this for quite some time. Oh, I see that Jim has just joined. Hi Jim! Thanks for joining. Jim says the lighting looks good, Ravi. Thanks, Jim. I'm in my home office, sitting by the window. I like natural lighting. How's your day going, Jim?"

Sorry, I had to bore you for a minute there, to show you how boring live videos can sometimes be. The same thing goes for webinars too.

Scripted, Rehearsed, Edited, Produced, Max Value in Min Time.

That should be the goal for all of your content. Sure, you can let your personality shine here and there, throw in a few jokes, some random stuff. But never stray too far from the core message.

Instead of one long video, how about you break it out into segments, and create 5 different videos, each of them 5 minutes long? Each of them teaches one specific thing only. One core message, one big takeaway, one call to action. The power of one. Short and simple.

If you already know that the webinar is not a real, live webinar, and a pre-recorded video, why can't you take an hour and edit out all of the nonsense and fluff? Like... "Alright guys, we're going to get started in a minute here. People are just starting to log in. Let me welcome you all to the call. Post a comment in the sidebar if this is the first time you've been on a webinar with me".

Really? Just so many things wrong with webinars these days. All of those audience-engaging things might work on a real, live webinar. Engaging with the early comers, making sure they stay engaged, maybe even get some feedback from them while you wait for the call to start. I've done this myself many times.

Early in the DAP days, I used to do a *lot* of webinars for DAP users. We used to get at least 50 attendees, and sometimes over 200 plus people on the calls. And I always used to log in 10 minutes early, do audio and visual checks, ask people if they could hear me and see my screen, and so on. And I even used to un-mute the early comers one by one, ask them to introduce themselves, give out their website name, and then have a quick chat for about 30 seconds. It did wonders for audience retention, and it made people want to show up early just so they could get some exposure for their website.

But guess what? All of that stuff sucks to listen to if you're listening to a replay, where you are not as interested or engaged as a live attendee, you were not part of that call, and you want to get to the core content fast and want to soak it all in as quickly as possible.

If it's a pre-recorded video and not a live webinar, why not edit all that fluff out? And on top of that, why make them wait to watch it? Nobody cares about coming back and watching it only during scheduled time, hours, or days into the future. People have way too much stuff to do. Deliver your video right away. If I sign up for something, it already shows you I'm interested in it. So I want to watch it now, and I don't care if you think I should come back an hour later or a day later to watch it. I'm literally wasting my time right now on Facebook, and I just gave you my email - show me the dang video already! ☺

Would you ever do the same with a PDF report? "Hey Ravi, thank you for signing up for my Podcast Promotion Report. Now that I have your email, select the time via the calendar below, when you can read this report. And then come back 6 hours later to read the report. And you can only read this report if you come back at the scheduled time."

Can you imagine anyone doing that to their fresh new email subscriber?

If you had a podcast, would you tell your listeners, hey, come back only during this particular time, and only then can you listen to my podcast episode? Of course not.

Podcasts are popular because people can listen to them on their own time, because they don't have to sit in front of a computer to do it, they can pause, rewind and fast-forward and even skip entire episodes if they wish to. "On-demand" has never been truer than right now.

Netflix shows you a "Skip Intro" button at the beginning of a new episode. So if you're binge-watching episodes, you don't want to keep seeing the same intros and end-titles over and over again. And just as the episode is ending, it will show you a "Play next episode" section. And if you don't do anything for like 5 seconds, it will automatically play the next episode. Perfect for binge-watchers! And if it automatically goes to the next episode, it will even automatically skip the intro of the next episode, and land you right at the actual start of the next episode. So you go from the end of one episode right into the core of the next one.

It's all about keeping your attention. Audience retention, stickiness, and making sure you don't get distracted by the real task at hand - which is to keep you watching.

So, deliver value *right now*. And do it in short bursts, unless you're building a strong story, and you have great content to deliver, that all fit together, and can't be split into parts - like, say, a sales video. If you go to PremiumPodcasting.com, the sales video on that page is 20 minutes long. And there's a strong reason for that.

If it hadn't been scripted, rehearsed, tightly edited, and well-produced, that same video could've easily been 30 or 40 minutes long. But I shaved it down to the shortest length possible that I needed to tell the story. And I have 3 case studies in the video, plus audio and video clips that all convey a very strong message about how to monetize your podcast.

So the big takeaway here is this:

Scripted, Rehearsed, Edited, Produced, and Max Value in Min Time.

Use that to rethink and plan all of your content - whether that is a podcast episode, YouTube video, Facebook live video, online course video, a sales video, social video, or documentation video.

Put Your Pen Down, Script it, and Rehearse It

A few months ago, I started writing an article about how starting with a script is critical to your entire content creation process. And I also wanted to emphasize why even a little bit of practice (or rehearsal) can help with creating great audio/visual content - whether it is for podcasts, live videos, or social media videos, etc.

So I started by writing the title: Script it and Rehearse it. And then suddenly, ta-da... a light bulb came on in my head because guess what "script it and rehearse it" sounded like ... yup, "flip it and reverse it". So of course, me being cringey dad and all, I had to create this unbelievably cringey Missy Elliott clip ☺ that you can hear on my podcast episode.

I truly believe that the greatest performances you've ever seen on TV, in movies, or real-life - have almost all been scripted and rehearsed - usually a lot.

A lot of people seem to think there's no real need to practice many of the things they do in their daily life.

If you were starting a podcast, a YouTube channel, or recording a live video, most people won't realize the need for a script, or practice. They might come up with some basic bullet points and think about things for a minute before they hit record, but that's not what I'm talking about. I'm talking about an actual script and an actual rehearsal.

If you find someone just crushing it on a podcast, or stage, or a live video, or with any kind of performance, remember that even if they haven't practiced that specific segment that you're watching or listening to, the way they make it look easy is because they've probably put in the work for years leading up to that moment.

A.k.a "The 10,000 Hour Rule" they've put into their craft, as coined by author Malcolm Gladwell in his book Outliers: The Story of Success.

Many people feel that practicing what you're going to say (e.g., on your podcast) will make you sound too robotic. They think the term "sounds too rehearsed" is a bad thing. In fact, for most things, that's not a negative.

So I wanted to emphasize that there's absolutely nothing wrong with having a script or practicing it.

Whether it's the nightly news, a stand-up routine by Dave Chappelle, a state of the union address by a President, or Saturday Night Live - all of it involves scripting and rehearsing.

There's this incredible sequence in the movie Reservoir Dogs, directed by Quentin Tarantino. In the movie, Mr. Orange (Tim Roth) is an undercover cop and needs to infiltrate a gang. And their plan to do that is for him to casually run into the gang at a bar and start a conversation, and in the process tell a fake story that would endear himself to them, which would give him a foot in the door to join the gang.

But Mr. Orange has to say the story so convincingly that the gang needs to believe it is true. And if they even get a hint that he's lying, that could blow his cover and get him killed.

So a fellow cop gives Tim Roth's character - Mr. Orange, the undercover cop - the script of that story where he walks into a bathroom with a bag full of drugs and runs into 4 cops and a drug-sniffing dog. Roth's job is to memorize it, live it, feel it, and make it his own, and be able to say it with such authenticity and conviction, that when he narrates that story to the gang members, they should believe the story and develop a connection with him.

This clip is so good that you need to watch the video clip, as reading about it, and worse, me trying to explain it, doesn't do it any justice. So watch "The Commode Story" scene here.

Next stop: Saturday Night Live (SNL).

SNL is a live TV show, that airs Saturday Nights here in the US, taped live in the studio in front of a live audience. Except for the occasional pre-produced segments that require them to be in a different location, it's live all the way through.

There was this one time when singer Ashlee Simpson, the younger sister of singer and actress Jessica Simpson, was supposed to do a live performance of a song, and someone screwed up something somewhere, and her vocals came out blaring on the speakers, but it wasn't her singing – it was her pre-recorded voice in the background, probably from the original soundtrack. Her lips weren't even moving. And that's when they realized that she had just lip-synced an entire song without telling her audience. It was a very embarrassing thing for the singer and SNL because lip-syncing goes against the live nature of SNL. You can read more about it here (with video).

In the article titled The untold truth of Saturday Night Live, the author writes about what a week behind the scenes at Saturday Night Live looks like and how an episode of SNL is produced:

"Monday: The guest host arrives at 30 Rockefeller Center in New York City, where SNL is shot. They go to Michaels' office, where they talk to writers and cast members about their comedic strengths, impressions they can do, and other suggestions. Writers then pitch their ideas.

Tuesday: As a holdover from the show's cocaine-fueled days in the '70s, writers spend all day and night writing their sketches. The host and a cast member also shoot the short commercials to promote the episode. They're edited and put on the air within hours of being shot.

Wednesday: The table read is at 4 p.m. Every proposed sketch is included, so it usually takes at least three hours. Then producers and the head writers determine which sketches are good enough.

Thursday: At 6 a.m., set builders begin constructing sets at a shop in the Brooklyn Navy Yard. At 30 Rock, the crew firms up plans for costumes, wigs, and makeup. Any pre-taped video bits are recorded.

Friday: Rehearsals and rewrites.

Saturday: The sketch order is set and presented to a live audience at 8 p.m. Any last-minute changes (or sketches that are cut) happen by 11:30 p.m. when the show goes live.

While many of the show's performers come from an improv comedy background, it's forbidden to improvise on SNL. The show has to be planned down to the second to account for each sketch, musical performance, and a commercial break."

Ok, back to me...

How cool is that? *One entire week* of practice, following a tight script, no improv allowed (or at the very least not encouraged and is frowned upon), and despite all that, you can still see the actors reading off of big signs off-camera, and they know that you can see that, and that's OK with them.

My point is, so much rehearsal for something where the actors can still read the script, and the audience knows that they're reading from a script.

If you've watched behind the scenes footage of any concert, from Beyonce to Prince to the Eagles to U2, you've probably seen the hundreds of people working behind the scenes, planning every move of every performer, where the mics go, where the props go, who enters where, how, at which point and on and on.

Have you seen stand-up comedians performing a 10-minute set? They've usually practiced that hundreds, if not thousands of times.

Wondering about spontaneity? Practice is required even more so because you've got to practice a lot just so you can appear unpracticed and spontaneous.

You might wonder, what about all those awesome spontaneous and live conversations between 2 or more people on a podcast or a video interview?

Sure, live conversations aren't fully scripted, but the format and structure and even some of the questions are partly, if not fully, scripted, even if you can't always tell.

There's a whole lot of practice that goes into becoming one of the greats. Whether it's LeBron and Michael Jordan practicing their jump shots in the gym, or Tiger Woods golfing in the rain, or Rihanna, Madonna, or Tiffany Haddish performing live, most of it is scripted and rehearsed.

There's a famous quote from musician Jascha Heifetz, who once said: "If I don't practice one day, I know it; two days, the critics know it; three days, the public knows it."

So it's all about putting in the work when no one is watching. Being in the proverbial gym, all by yourself, for long hours, and putting in the work ahead of time, so that when the time to perform arrives, you make it look oh-so-easy and natural and unrehearsed and spontaneous.

Even your practice needs a structure - you can't just wing it and do whatever, whenever. And that's what I mean by the script.

So keeping it to just digital creators, whether you're creating a podcast episode, or a YouTube content marketing video, or a live video, or a sales video, or a documentation video, always start with the script.

And I promise you, everything else will flow beautifully from there.

Here are a few more interesting quotes about practice:

"The difference between ordinary and extraordinary is practice." - Vladimir Horowitz on The Violin Channel

"There is no glory in practice, but without practice, there is no glory." - Anonymous

"Practice isn't the thing you do once you're good. It's the thing you do that makes you good." - Malcolm Gladwell, Outliers: The Story of Success

"Put your pen down, script it and rehearse it." – Ravi Jayagopal ;-)

Reverse Spiderman

I came up with the idea for this as I was preparing for a presentation that I gave at Podcast Movement, Philadelphia, back in 2018.

And my session was titled "How to Create a Premium Podcast & Deliver Patrons-Only Content Using a WordPress Membership Site".

You can watch parts 1, 2 & 3 of my presentation for free, at SubscribeMe.fm/academy/pm18/

In the presentation, I talked about how to deliver Audio in 4 Different Formats:

- Player on a Page
- Downloadable Files
- Members-Only Podcast RSS
- and a Mobile App

As I was creating the slides for my presentation, I had a section in there where I talk about building your own platform, owning that platform, owning your domain, building everything on your own website, vs. building it all on a third-party platform.

As I was doing a comparison table comparing third-party platforms versus your own WordPress site, I came up with the idea for this chapter.

Remember Uncle Ben from Spider-Man? He is Peter Parker's uncle who gets killed by a burglar as he is trying to escape after a robbery. In the movie, Peter Parker, a.k.a Spider-Man, lets a burglar getaway moments earlier, and that same burglar ends up shooting and killing his Uncle Ben a few minutes later. A dying Uncle Ben tells Peter, what has now become one of the most famous movie quotes ever: "With great power, comes great responsibility."

It's an amazing quote, no doubt.

But Uncle Ravi has a quote for you today, that's going to put Uncle Ben's quote to shame ☺.

My take on this is to flip the Spider-Man quote. This is why I call it the "Reverse Spiderman" quote – or Man-Spider.

The original quote from Uncle Ben, "With Great Power comes great responsibility" doesn't make much sense for most people.

So, when I have great power, it comes with great responsibility. Got it. It's kind of like a warning that great power is to be wielded carefully.

But guess what? Most people listening to that quote may not identify with that, because most of us are not at the point of wielding great power, great influence, great fame, or great fortune.

We're all aspiring to get there, including me. I'm on my way, for sure. But I'm not where I had hoped I would be by this point in my life. But that's ok. Every day I'm hustlin', hustlin' ☺

That is why my version of the quote below will make sense for more people:

To have great power, you need to take on great responsibility.

Makes sense right? If you want to be among the best at what you do, you need to go the extra mile, you need to do more, you need to be better, you need to do things that most others won't do, you need to work harder, work smarter, be more responsible, take on more responsibility, be a leader, and be remarkable.

And you have to do all of that first and take on a great deal of responsibility *before* you can get great power.

If you're the class clown, you're never going to be selected to be the class leader.

If you just want to work 9 to 5 and do your tasks and get out, you're not going to get a good enough promotion or a raise.

Trying to be the world's greatest basketball player, like Michael Jordan or LeBron James is probably 100 times harder than even just becoming an NBA player, which by itself is ridiculously hard because out of hundreds of millions of people around the world, only about 450 players make it to the NBA each year.

So, if you want to get to the point of having great power, great influence, or great fame, you need to take on a great deal of responsibility first, in everything you do.

Tying that back to creating an online business, if you want a great deal of power, control, and flexibility in building your website and your online business, you need to use WordPress.

Yes, there are hosted platforms and services like Udemy, ClickFunnels, Teachable, Patreon, and Kajabi, etc.

But all of them have their limits.

The only platform without limits is WordPress.

At this time, according to W3Techs, WordPress powers 42.5% of all sites across the web.

Some of the biggest brands using WordPress are, eBay, Sony, GM, UPS, Forbes, CNN, Samsung, IBM, Tech Crunch, New York Times, Beyonce, Microsoft, Disney, Tim Ferriss, Seth Godin, even Facebook uses it for their newsroom.

There's a reason why all of these companies didn't go for some convenient hosted platform like ClickFunnels.

There's a reason why the biggest companies are not building their businesses on a third-party platform.

They want to control the look and feel, user experience, be able to implement the features they want, how they want them.

From the weekend blogger to the solopreneur to the 10-, 100- or 10,000 people company, they want to accept payments and store those payment profiles within their own Paypal or Stripe or merchant accounts, and not have them be locked up in a third-party company's payment processor - like with Patreon or Udemy.

I discuss this further in the chapter "Digital Sharecropping".

There are so many things you need to consider when building your online business:

- Ability to control the look & feel of your website.
- Include different media like Video, Audio, and PDF.
- Have a podcast player, if it's a podcast website.

- Create a sales video.
- Create a landing page with various conversion elements, like social proof, scarcity, contemporary design, text, video, images, add Facebook and Google pixels and be able to track visits, movement, conversion, and cart abandonment.
- An easy-to-use but powerful shopping cart - like SmartPayCart.com - which lets you do 1-click upsells and downsells and order bumps and multi-pricing and accept payments via different payment processors like Paypal, Stripe, ClickBank, or even BitCoin.
- Be able to recruit affiliates who will promote *your* products and services for a commission.
- Offer 2-tier commissions if you wanted to, or just a single-tier.

And that's just scratching the surface.

There are just so many different components that go into building a long-term, profitable online business.

And if you go with WordPress, then there's a plugin for pretty much anything and everything you can imagine.

DigitalAccessPass.com and SmartPayCart.com are arguably the world's best combination of membership platform plus shopping cart, with Veena Prashanth, who is my lovely wife and Co-founder & co-developer of DAP and creator of SPC and a whole bunch of other plugins like SmartQuizBuilder.com, at the helm.

We already offer you the best combination of tools that you need to create and run your online business. And then there are plugins for everything else.

Your smartphone wouldn't be very smart if there was no app store and you couldn't install apps from third-party companies that let you enhance the features of your phone and apps that you let you do more than just your phone's built-in apps.

Imagine if you had to just wait for Apple or Google to release every new app on their own, and there was no way to install any third-party apps or any additional software. If they don't make it a part of the system, and there were no apps other than those released by Apple or Google, the world would be way behind right now.

Similarly, when you host with a proprietary third-party system, you are completely and utterly reliant on them for all functionality.

But with WordPress, you have the equivalent of an app store - which is the WordPress plugin repository as well as all the commercial themes and plugins - which let you greatly enhance what you want from your website.

So when some of the biggest brands, companies, and celebrities are using WordPress, why consider a third-party platform?

Whether it is to create a membership site, or an online course, and accept payments and be able to offer upsells and downsells and order bumps, and do email marketing with email autoresponders and broadcasts, allow every new member to become an instant affiliate to promote your products and even services, or to create a premium podcast, it would be a mistake to not use WordPress for your business now and in the future.

Yes, building a WordPress-based ecommerce website can take a little bit of work. But what great thing has ever happened without putting in the work?

You have to install plugins and themes. Then configure them. And make sure they play well with each other. And apply updates, install security plugins, and so on.

And anytime you start wondering if the other side - the non-WordPress platform side - is greener, and you think you might be better off with a third-party system where you *think* that they take care of everything and you *think* that it will be easier than WordPress, just re-read this chapter as well as "Digital Sharecropping".

And remember the Reverse Spiderman Quote from Uncle Ravi:

To have great power, you need to take on great responsibility.

99Designs hack

99Designs.com is a great website to run a design contest for your website logo, book cover, or podcast artwork, but it can be a bit expensive.

So, instead of running a regular contest and paying up to $1300, I have a clever tactic for paying the least amount, for possibly the best design.

E.g., let's say you are writing a book about Dog Training.

* Do a search on Google for "dog training site:99designs.com" (use the full search term as-is, without the quotes, of course).

What this does is to search just the website 99designs.com for the words "dog training". You'll get a bunch of results as seen above.

* Go to each of those links (open results in a new tab so you don't lose the search screen).

* Those are the links to various contests that have already been completed (rarely will you get one that's still in progress).

* Here's the screenshot of an old contest in that niche.

Dog Training logo needed! Make us millionaires. Image examples and clear description provided.

—

thedogcollege needed a new logo design and created a contest on 99designs.

A winner was selected from 92 designs submitted by 17 freelance designers.

92	17	1
entries	designers	winner

Winning design by Bossall691

* You'll see that the above contest was completed and a winning design has already been chosen.

* Further below on that same page, you'll see that 92127 other entries were submitted that did not win.

Entries from this contest ↓

by Karl paran

by Alambaba

THE DOG COLLEGE

by DonMare

by MattyC

by Alambaba

by Alambaba

by Alambaba

THE DOG COLLEGE

by Haris 3Dmodeling

* Check out the remaining entries that did not win and see if you like any of them. Imagine those designs with your own twist and words on them.

* If you find something that resonates with you, contact the designer who created that design directly via the website itself, and ask them if they will customize it for you for a small fee. Ask them specifically how much they would charge.

Before I came up with this hack, I had paid $399 for my podcast artwork. You can still see the contest here. Here's the winning design from that contest.

I've been using the same image for my show since 2016 when the podcast was launched.

* A few months after my podcast launch, when I was about to launch my book "SubscribeMe", I wanted to use 99Designs again but did not want to pay yet another $399 or more.

And that's when I came up with this idea: My wife Veena Prashanth had run a contest for her book "Upsells Unleashed" a few months earlier. So using the same tactic I mentioned above, I chose one of the many designs that were submitted but hadn't won (see below).

You can see her picture on the image, and the title is that of her book.

* Of the many discarded designs on 99Designs.com using the search technique I mentioned earlier, this is the one that I liked the most.

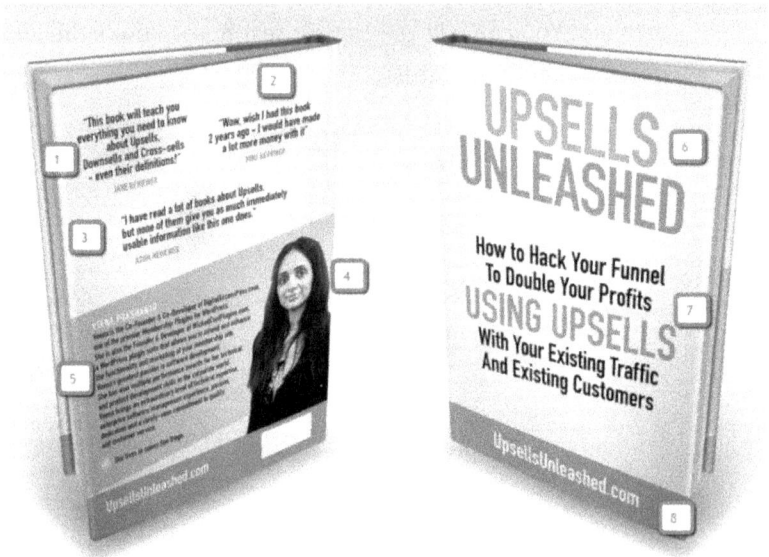

* So I directly messaged the designer of this cover (it had not won) and asked if they would customize it for me. They agreed to do it for $50. After a few messages back and forth (see the markings above which I used to explain what I wanted to be changed), the image below is what I ended up with.

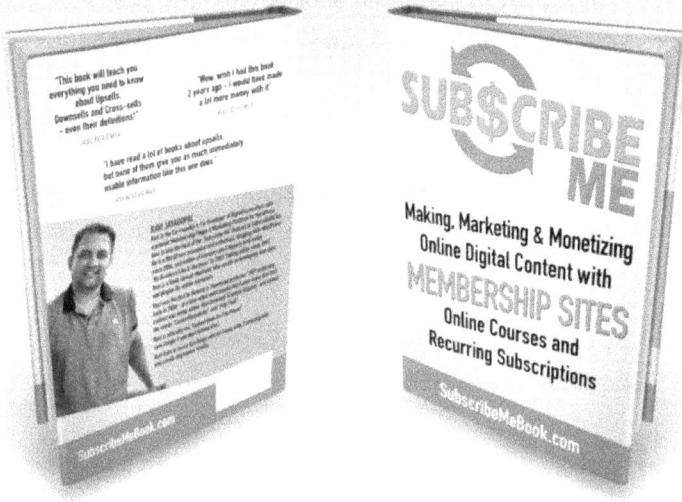

* My wife spent $800 on her contest. I took advantage of that and paid $50 for an unused design for my book. Pretty, pretty, pretty cool! ;-)

* I was so thrilled with the designer's work and also that I was able to save on an $800 package (which is what I was considering strongly at the time), that I gave them a $50 tip. So my total cost was still $100, compared to the $800 it might've been. I saved $700 just like that.

You too can take advantage of other people's contests and use their discarded designs to save possibly hundreds on your book cover, podcast artwork, logo, or other design.

* Most designers will not refuse your request to modify a past design for you (unless they've already used it elsewhere – make sure of that), because they have already put in the work and created the design, and they didn't win the contest. So it's already a wasted effort and sunk cost for them. They'll probably be happy to get paid a few extra dollars for a few additional minutes of their time customizing the words and a bit of the design for you.

* Obviously, if you need a lot of changes, they'll probably charge you more. But at least you won't have to pay $400 - $1300 to run a brand new contest!

* So for your podcast artwork, just search for "podcast artwork" and "podcast logo" on Google.com, but restrict your search to just 99designs.com. So do the 2 searches below on Google, separately:

podcast artwork site:99designs.com
podcast logo site:99designs.com

Look at all of the results. Open each link in a new tab. Go through all of the resulting designs. See the ones that did not win. Shortlist a few that you love after you imagine your podcast title's text in that image. Then contact the designer. See if they can modify it for you for a fee. Tell them you prefer to do it via 99Designs.com itself (so that neither of you violates the company's terms, and it's a safer bet for you as there's accountability for them as well). That's it! Within a few days, you can end up with something awesome.

And don't try to get it "perfect" the first time around. If it's 80% close, just go with it. Speed is critical. You can always tweak it later in a year. Who knows, you may even want to change it for the 1st anniversary of your show. So don't get too bogged down by trying to get it "absolutely perfect".

99designs.com › … › Illustration or graphics contests ▼

Podcast artwork | Illustration or graphics contest | 99designs

We need **artwork** for our new **Podcast**. Dimensions: It needs to be 3000 x 3000 pixels, 72 dpi, in JPEG or PNG format with... appropriate file extensions (.jpg, ...

99designs.com › Poster › Poster contests ▼

Podcast cover art | Poster contest | 99designs

nataliechoufani got their new poster by running a design contest. Winner. "**Podcast cover art**" winning Poster by ISShaikh007. by ISShaikh007. **Podcast cover art**.

99designs.com › Other design › Other design contests ▼

Podcast cover art | Other design contest | 99designs

acremades created a custom other design on 99designs. They got dozens of unique ideas from professional designers and picked their favorite.

99designs.com › Other design › Other design contests ▼

Design podcast artwork for a coffee podcast | Other design ...

Roast and Reason will be a weekly podcast and blog focused on all things coffee. This design is for the **podcast artwork**. If the design also... works as a logo for ...

99designs.com › Poster › Poster contests ▼

Podcast artwork | Poster contest | 99designs

sbrody80 got their new poster by running a design contest: Winner. "**Podcast Artwork**" winning Poster by ag16. by ag16. **Podcast Artwork**. Get your own design.

99designs.com › Logo design › Logo design contests ▼

Podcast Artwork for Women Entrepreneurs | Logo design contest

Podcast Artwork for Women Entrepreneurs. nataliem2 needed a new logo design and created a contest on 99designs. A winner was selected from 86 designs ...

Results Roadmap

Results Roadmap

| 0 | Your Target Buyer | 1 | 2 | 3 | | N |

Before getting started — Your Target Buyer — Different milestones for your Buyer to get from where they are now to where they wish to be — Desired Results — Next steps

The illustration above shows what I call the "Results Roadmap".

It starts with your target buyer - where they are currently with their need/want/problem.

The green destination icon shows where they wish to get to – this is the point where their need/want/problem has been solved or satisfied.

The numbers 1, 2 & 3 illustrate the different milestones (tracking points) along their journey.

0 could be where they are before they realize the need or the problem.

N depicts the point where they are after they've achieved their initial goal.

You can create amazing Lead Magnets using this.

If you can figure out the Results Roadmap for your target buyer and what your product/service helps them with, your lead magnet could be something that helps them get from point 0-to-1, or 1-to-2, or 2-3, etc. I call each mini step a "Milestone Journey" (MJ).

And once you figure out these MJs, you can create amazing content free based on them. You can get content ideas from them for your content marketing – like live videos, free webinars, your own podcast, podcast interviews where you are a guest on other shows, newsletter emails, launch email sequences, etc.

The reason for using these Milestone Journeys as free content is something I elaborate on in the next chapter "Jab-Hook, Jab-Hook, Jab-Hook".

The idea is to make the free content you're creating and the value you are adding to your audience, closely related to your core product.

So if you can teach your audience about getting from 0-to-1, or 1-to-2, or 2-3, etc, you can also be promoting your core product at the same time, saying, these are the milestone journeys, but if you want the whole roadmap, I have created that for you as well.

And my Results Roadmap will not also help you with your product development, by allowing you to focus on the key components/features/benefits that your target buyer is looking for.

And it also allows you to create free content or paid features that help them from before they're even ready to get started, to after they've gotten the desired results.

And N could also be the beginning of a new Results Roadmap with new milestones and destinations.

Jab-Hook, Jab-Hook, Jab-Hook

The basic premise of Gary Vaynerchuk's "Jab, Jab, Jab, Right Hook" was that you give, give, give, and only then ask.

It's a fantastic concept, no doubt. That's what I practice and preach as well.

But I have a slightly different take on it.

The separate and solo "ask" at the end, might alienate some of your audience.

So if you have a product or service, then there's a way to give as well as make a subtle ask in the same piece of content – whether that's an email, a podcast episode, a YouTube video, or a blog post.

See the chapter "I came home and the dog was bald", where I show you how to take a crazy, catchy headline, tell a story, and then finally tie it back to your main call to action.

Similarly, your content can also be giving and promoting at the same time.

There are 2 ways to Jab (Give) and Hook (Ask) at the same time (hence my term, "Jab-Hook"):

1. "Milestone Journey" Content:

In the last chapter, I wrote about what this is. And how you can create content based on these MJs. And after teaching your target buyer how to get from one milestone to the next for free, your subtle pitch at the end could be something like:

"I hope this lesson/trick/hack/tactic/strategy was helpful. If you liked what I just showed you, you're going to love my new course "My Awesome Course" which goes into a lot more detail about how you can <insert desired results>. In fact, what I just taught you was just one piece of the puzzle. And I've put the rest of the pieces into my course that has <state features/benefits>. Check it out at MyAwesomeCourse<dot>com. Use coupon code <platform> to get 25% off".

2. "Benefit Showcase" Content:

Make a note of all your product's features.
Turn each one into an actual benefit.
Create a separate piece of content for each benefit.

So in your content, talk about what the benefit is, how it will "benefit" your reader/listener/viewer, why they need that benefit, what's in it for them, what they lose out on by not having it (lose time/money/effort/energy/happiness).

Show them how they can achieve it without mentioning your product or service – i.e., you should show them how they can achieve it without having to buy your stuff first.

This is the "Give" part where you show them a better way to achieve their goals for free. This is critical because if you can tell them why they need to do something that will help them, and then tell them that they have to buy your stuff first, it suddenly turns into a sleazy bait-and-switch.

After you've shown them the benefits of doing something, and also showed them how they can do it without ever mentioning your product, then at the end, you can now tell them how you have a product that you've created that solves this exact problem, and how your product can help them do the same thing in a much better/faster/cheaper/hands-off way.

And this will be your "Ask".

But you've already given first before asking.

Every bit you give is about showing them how to improve their lives with tips, tricks, tactics, hacks, strategies, and ideas.

And the ask is about telling them that you have already figured out exactly how to do the exact things you just convinced them that they need to do and that there is a solution waiting for them if they ever wish to act on it.

And that's why I call my tactic "Jab-Hook, Jab-Hook, Jab-Hook" as you're giving and asking at the same time, with the giving coming first, and the asking coming later, and neither one interfering with or taking away from the other.

Here's an example:

Product: Content Repurposing software

- Create a content series showing people how to repurpose their content.
- And in each piece, you talk about starting with audio, or with a blog post, or with video.
- Show them how they can do it manually, with existing free tools, all by themselves.
- And at the end of each piece, tell them about your automation platform, software, or service that does it, and how it can do a much better job, how it can be automated, and save them time/effort/money/energy, which they can then use for something more productive.

Product: WordPress Video & Audio Plugin S3MediaVault

- Create a content series with educational content about creating video, audio, PDF's
- What is the difference between Streaming video and Standard (Progressive) video and what are each of their benefits
- Why and When you should or should not stream video and audio
- Where to store your video, audio, pdf's, zip, doc files if you have an online course
- Why you shouldn't store it on your own website and what are the issues it can create for your members, for you, and your website, and where you should store it instead
- Benefits of using Captions, Watermarks, Securing your media files, to allow or to not allow downloading of files
- The ask at the end of each content piece: "I have a WordPress plugin that can help you do all of this with just a few clicks".

Hobbyists vs. Wantrepreneurs

There are two main differences between a Wantrepreneur (someone who aspires to be an Entrepreneur) and a Hobbyist.

1. Return on Investment (ROI)
2. Urgency

Most who have a hobby usually don't care about getting a return on investment from their hobby. They're also not in it to make money.

They are in it for the love of it, maybe for entertainment, for self-fulfillment, time-pass, or even as a distraction. But the last thing on their mind is about earning a few dollars on the side using their hobby.

There is also no sense of urgency about getting great at it either. Sure, someone learning tennis might have an upcoming local club tournament, and if they're the competitive type, they might take some lessons or practice harder so they can have a shot at winning it. But there's no existential urgency about making it all work before a certain week or month or year, because even if they don't get better, they're not going to be upset about it, and it won't affect their life in any way.

But when you're a Wantrepreneur, to be successful, you should want to build towards an ROI, because you're putting so much blood, sweat, and tears, and energy, effort, and sleepless nights and weekends into it. And your family (especially your significant other) is also probably sacrificing for you - time away from you, money for your expenses especially when you're not earning it back, taking on additional chores so that you get to work on your project, etc. Those are all the more reasons for you to want to be rewarded with some form of monetary returns, which would be the ultimate validation of all that hard work and sacrifice.

As a hobbyist, you can quit one hobby literally overnight and pick another one up tomorrow, with no consequences – no one is going to miss a beat about it.

But as a Wantrepreneur, you can't just quit on the project that you've been working on for the last 6 months, spending countless hours and nights and weekends, and switch to another project entirely, just because you got bored of it.

There's more to this, but you get the idea.

If you ever start doing something that you love so much, but you don't care about making money with it, you don't even think you can make money with it, and you actually don't have any desire to make money with it, and you also don't have any kind of sense of urgency that you need to achieve some milestones by certain dates, and if it's like you would rather do it whenever, however, and don't want to be bothered by how much time, effort and energy and money it's costing you, and you don't care about how long it takes to get better at it, whether it's weeks or months or years, then you, my friend, are looking at a hobby.

And that's OK. I have several hobbies too – one of them an outsized, obnoxiously time-consuming hobby: Playing Chess online. Nothing wrong with hobbies.

But if you want to become an entrepreneur, you have to know how to differentiate between something that is a hobby and something that has the potential to make money and maybe even help you earn a living.

And whether you are a Wantrepreneur or you have an existing business and are already an entrepreneur and are looking at starting something new, how badly you feel the need for an ROI, and how much urgency you feel in your bones, will give you some hints as to whether your hobby has the potential to ever grow into a business.

How You Can Be Better Than Disneyland

I live in San Diego, which is less than a 2-hour drive from Disneyland. So I've been to Disneyland many times.

In December 2016, during the holiday break, my family and I went to Universal Studios, which is in Los Angeles, a 3-hour drive from home. We hadn't been there in a few years, so we ended up choosing Universal over Disney.

Universal has something called "Front of Line" access. It costs $100 extra on top of the price of a regular ticket.

When you have a Front of Line pass, you get to go to the front of the line for every single ride, regardless of how long the regular line is. Even though they officially say that you can do this only once per ride, no one's watching, and the attendants don't' care, so you could do this multiple times for each ride if you wanted to.

Even on a regular weekday, the lines are really long – about 1 to 2 hours of waiting for each ride. That's even worse on a major holiday or a long weekend. But because we paid extra for Front of Line access, we were able to go straight to the front of the line for every single ride.

So paying $400 extra for 4 Front of Line passes was *totally* worth it, considering we saved at least 4-6 hours in total of standing in line for the various rides. Go to each ride, go straight to the front by-passing the long lines, get on the ride within minutes, and you're done. And go back again if you loved it. That's a real win-win deal.

Universal wins because it gets to squeeze out an extra $100 per ticket for the front-of-line access, and it was a win for us because we saved so much time, effort, and energy, it made the whole trip so much more enjoyable, we were able to get to all of the rides, many of them multiple times, back-to-back with zero waiting time, and it completely changed the experience.

However, when it comes to Disney, I don't know why, but they don't sell such Front of Line access.

Now, they do have a rather convoluted, confusing version of it, called "Fast Pass".

Fast Pass is free - there's no extra charge for it unlike Universal's Front of Line pass. But you have to physically arrive at the location of each ride, look for the "Fast Pass" vending machines, which by itself has a big line, wait in line, and get the fast pass ticket for that ride from the machine.

Here's the kicker: you cannot use this Fast Pass right away – you get a time slot for later in the day - usually about 2-3 hours from the time you got the pass. So you can't get on the ride now. And even when you come back hours later, you still have to stand in line with all of the other Fast Pass wielding folks because anyone and everyone can get a Fast Pass, because it's free.

So that could still mean a wait of about 1/2 hour – 1 hour at the minimum, depending on how crowded it is that day.

Ok, so what's the big deal? Just go to all of the rides first, get a fast-pass for each one, and then start back at the beginning and start redeeming your fast passes. Right?

Nope. That's not how it works. You only get *one* Fast Pass token every two hours. To get the next fast pass for a different ride, you have to wait for 2 hours.

That means, in those 2 hours, you have to go to another ride and stand in line, and it's probably going to take you at least 1-2 hours to get on that ride. And by the time you come out, you are still not eligible to get another fast pass, because the 2 hours are not up yet. Then you go back to the first ride for which you got a fast pass. And by the time you come out, it's the same thing all over again - get another fast pass for another ride, which you can only redeem in 2 hours or more from that point.

If your head is spinning just from reading that, imagine the plight of people trying to strategize and figure it out just to stand in line for only 6 hours instead of for 8 hours.

So every time we've gone to Disneyland, we've ended up not going to as many rides as we would have if only Disney had sold us something similar to Universal's Front of Line access.

Now, don't tell me Disney is doing this out of the goodness of heart, that they're somehow against making more money, or have suddenly had this anti-capitalistic urge, or this socialistic urge to make the playing field even for everyone. Don't forget - *everything* Disney does, is with an eye towards monetization: their movies turn into toys and t-shirts and merchandising and video games and theme park rides and online games and TV shows and on and on. *Nobody* monetizes end-to-end like Disney.

And given how incredible the Disney marketing machine is, it's not like no one at Disney has thought of it. They probably must have thought about it at some point but decided against it after figuring out that there were better ways to monetize it - like, the gap between rides that forces people to go and spend more money buying a Churro from a food cart, or walking into an expensive restaurant and waiting for an hour just to eat.

I'm sure they have their reasons, but the result is that the Disney experience just sucks for its customers when it comes to the insanely long lines and endless waiting.

So when it comes to your business, be like Universal Studios - not like Disney.

Make sure you're not making the same mistake and failing to provide additional premium products to customers who literally *want* to throw more money at you so that they can get more from whatever it is that you're selling: faster service, Done For You, more handholding, exclusive content, no ads, special treatment, premium access, more access to you, etc.

We faced this same dilemma with DAP many years ago. There were about 3-4 years in the early years of DAP when we had stiff competition from a lot of free membership plugins. Yes, *free*!

Here we were, charging $167 for a 1-site license of DAP, and people were telling us that they would rather go with a free membership plugin rather than pay $167 for DAP. And with those free plugins, they could install the plugin on an unlimited number of websites, and still not pay a single penny. But with DAP, if you purchased an Unlimited-site license, you paid $297.

But as the famous cliche goes, there's no such thing as a free lunch. "Free" actually has a cost associated with it, especially when it comes to a membership plugin. As the developer(s), there is so much support and development involved, and even more so with a WordPress plugin because everyone is installing it on their own website, and every website is different.

You have to constantly keep updating your plugin because of everything else that keeps changing - like new WordPress releases, changes to Paypal or Stripe APIs, changes to hosting software changes, server and database changes, other plugins and themes that can cause a conflict, etc.

Now imagine creating this massive piece of software like a membership plugin, which is essentially the operating system of your ecommerce operations - because it processes payments, protects content, allows you to do upsells, recruit affiliates and pay affiliate commissions, sends out autoresponder and broadcast emails, etc. Now imagine also having to keep it updated constantly, to support everything else that's changing out there, and also having to support hundreds or thousands of plugin users. And as the cherry on top, now imagine having to do *all of that for free*! That's insane.

But guess what? Most of those free plugins are gone, or have introduced premium upsells for the critical add-ons, like a recurring payment processing module, for eg. That's because they couldn't afford to do all of that for free, not for long. Even if you kept the software for free and charged only for support, you're still not going to take home make, because the software is still free, and is going to attract some groups of people with a different mindset. "Hey, it's free, so I shouldn't have to pay for anything. I don't need support, and even if I need it, I would rather post it in Facebook groups and forums and anywhere else I can and see if I can get my questions answered for free, rather than paying a few bucks for support."

Yes, that's what you have to deal with when your product is free, and there are no big monetization opportunities, like how Facebook and Google, and YouTube and Gmail are all essentially free, but they have solid revenue opportunities with advertising.

If the product is free, then *you* are the product. And that doesn't translate so well to the software industry.

So we were able to weather the storm of competitors who were offering their plugin for free, and here we are, humming along just fine, and most of our free competitors are gone.

Around that time, we were hesitant to introduce new tiers for DAP. For the longest time, we just had one-site and multi-site licenses, and both were available for one-time payments with just one year of Upgrades & Support, and you could optionally renew after a year if and only if you needed Upgrades or Support. The problem there was that our software was so stable at one point, that most people didn't need new releases or support after the first year. And since renewal was optional, they never renewed until something stopped working. And the average DAP user was renewing only once every 3 years. That meant we only got a fraction of renewals after a year, compared to how many new users we were signing up a year earlier. So we had to constantly keep looking for new DAP users and new ways to monetize.

So we developed a whole bunch of new and complementary WordPress plugins. This has the same terms, so same issue: one-time fee, 1 Year of Upgrades & Support, then optional renewal for one more year, after a year.

We introduced something called Membership Site In A Box (MSIAB) where we offered DAP and a couple of our other plugins, along with 3-hour setup service. We were initially apprehensive about whether anyone would buy this $500 done-for-you package when there were still free plugins out there. But it turned out to be a huge success because people didn't mind paying for some 1-on-1 consultation and brainstorming and some setup and training on how to use DAP, and cut short the learning curve.

Then we introduced an even higher tier called Membership Site In A Box Pro, and charge $1,000. Some people signed up for that too. Then a few years ago, we removed MSIAB pro, and in its place, introduced a new Platinum membership, which is a monthly subscription, also available as a yearly subscription, and also available as a one-time, lifetime payment.

But we had to package it in such a way that paying $40 a month, or $400 a year, had to become a no-brainer decision (the "Offer"). So we said, ok, we'll give you every single plugin we have ever developed, and every single plugin we will ever develop, plus another 2 hours of setup help, for a monthly fee.

"But wait, there's more!" ☺

We added a 1-hour per month free troubleshooting package, where if you had any issues on your website, we would log in to your site and troubleshoot it and fix it for no extra charge.

Once we added all of that, $40 per month suddenly started looking like a bargain.

We have other subscription tiers now, and we no longer offer one-time purchases. And over the years, many people who had purchased our one-off licenses, have gradually converted over to a monthly subscription, even though we gave them the same renewal terms that we had when they originally signed up.

If we had simply thought who's going to pay for this stuff, who's going to pay $167, or $297, or $497, or $997, or $50 per month for a membership plugin, that too when there are free plugins out there, we would've had to shutter our doors, and we wouldn't be in business today.

We have to give people a lot more credit because they are willing to pay more as long as they get a lot more "value" from the deal.

So it all comes back to your "Offer". And how you package it, position it, and present it. And of course, also in how you deliver it, deliver on the promises, and keep delivering month after month, if you want them to keep paying you month after month.

And don't be afraid to create bigger, more expensive packages, that give people faster service, better access, direct access to you or your team, better training, 1-on-1 calls, faster set up, more hand-holding, that will help them implement your products and services faster, with less headache, with a shorter learning curve, better support, or faster support.

Create more "Front of Line" addons. Don't be like Disney, treating everyone the same and not allowing anyone to pay extra to get extra. When it comes to business, people will pay more so they can do less work, to be helped, to reduce the hassle, to be pampered.

That's what leads to a bigger bottom-line and more profits for you, and also the happiest, easy-to-please, and lowest-overhead customers, who will happily pay extra, to get extra, and they just might also be the ones to praise you and recommend you the most.

Podcasting is Not a Reliable Business Model

It is a "Door Creator"

Podcasting - like Blogging - at its core, is an audience-building platform - a.k.a Content Marketing tool. Just like it is ridiculously hard to create a full-time living with a blog that only generates income via ads alone, creating a Podcast to make money solely via sponsors, is just as hard - probably way harder.

But Podcasting is still one of the greatest things ever invented.

When it comes to the ability to connect with people on a deeper, personal level, Audio is second only to Video. And with all the existing technology that already interrupts, annoys, and distracts us - TV, Netflix, YouTube, Facebook, Twitter, TikTok, Snapchat, Whatsapp, etc - and more ways being created to interrupt every day, Podcasting, in some ways, has become one of the most powerful, relationship- and fan-building tool there is, even more so than video, especially in some age groups and niches.

You cannot listen to the radio show that you want to when you want to. Whatever is playing when you get into your car is what you have to listen to. Even with Satellite radio that has a monthly subscription fee, you get more channels, but you don't get the channels on-demand. You can't get a show on satellite radio to start when you're ready for it - you still have to listen to the shows on their schedule, not on yours.

You can't be driving and watching a YouTube video (I guess you could, but if you did, then you probably wouldn't be well enough to be reading this now, would you? :-). You can't read an online article or a book or a blog post or a PDF report when you're driving to work, or walking your dog, or at the gym, or doing the dishes, etc.

Podcasts can "go where no other media has gone before". The hosts talking on the show - whether they are making you think, laugh, cry or learn - they're in your ears, talking directly to you, they have your fullest attention (or almost), you are kind of locked-in on their voice, even if you're performing a chore.

You chose the podcast yourself. No one spammed you with that podcast. No one signed you up for it without your permission. No popup or malware forced a podcast episode into your ears. There was no Nigerian Prince who asked you for your iTunes id so that they could auto-subscribe you to junk shows. There were no fake billing department calls from Dell asking you for your credit card so that they can charge you for a podcast... Oh wait, that's right - podcasts are free! Most of them, anyway.

YOU chose to search for a podcast. YOU went out and looked for it. YOU voluntarily listened to it, maybe multiple episodes, maybe you even subscribed to it and have it automatically downloaded every week. YOU did all that yourself. And YOU got to listen to the show of your choice, with the topics of your choice, when and where you wanted to listen to it, listening to it when you simply had no other way to entertain yourself, or learn something, or become a part of a movement.

But as powerful as podcasting is, it's still not a dependable business model for most people – i.e., it's not necessarily built for directly making money from your podcast itself, as in ads on your show.

Yes, a lot of people may have been able to reach that rarified air where they can make enough money from sponsors alone. But don't just look at their results and mistakenly think that if you do exactly what they did, then you too will have the same kind of success. That's how there are now a hundred crappy "On Fire" shows (IYKYK).

It depends on a lot of things, but a basic one is how good you are at your craft (skill). Copying their techniques and strategies is not going to duplicate their results. There are also other factors like talent, topic, guests, your influence, and authority in your niche, do you already have an existing audience on other platforms or is your podcast your first ever attempt at building an asset and an audience, and not to forget, timing and some luck too.

Passion, persistence, patience, etc. are must-haves as well. But those can only take you to the next level if you already have a great product to begin with - and that's a great show.

Instead, where Podcasting shines, is its ability to indirectly impact other areas of your business - like developing more Authority, Credibility, Expertise, all of which can be used to get speaking gigs, coaching clients, consulting jobs, drive awareness and traffic to your other products and services, sell more books, build a list, etc.

Only a tiny percentage of podcasters will end up making a successful, full-time living just off of sponsorships and premium subscriptions. So if your goal is to make a living with just a podcast, you are probably going to be disappointed.

So stop lusting after other people's numbers. And instead, think of the outliers' success as them trailblazing a difficult path for all podcasters to follow.

You are better off using your podcast to build an audience, build your brand, and market yourself, your products, and services.

Podcasting is a long-term play – it could be *very* long for most people.

But a Podcast is the world's most powerful "Door Opener".

But I believe so strongly in the medium, that I would take that description even further, and say, that...

A Podcast is the World's Most Powerful Door "CREATOR".

Podcasting doesn't just OPEN doors, it CREATES Doors Where None Existed Before.

And it's also the most impactful "Fan-Building Media" format available to us today, second only to video, but in many ways more powerful, only because we can take audio with us to places where video or websites cannot go.

Here's to hoping that you can find your voice. Your style. And your own story to tell.

Donations Are Not a Reliable Business Model

Building your business on the generosity of strangers - aka Donations - is not a reliable business model.

Maybe for a non-profit, but not so much for a business.

One of the common myths that a lot of content creators have, especially in this day and age of crowdfunding, is that if you have a large enough audience, then you can earn a decent income using donations from your audience.

Let's say you have a podcast.

What would you consider to be a "decent income" from your show?

Is it $50 a month? Or $50 per episode? Maybe a couple of hundred dollars a month?

Sure, if that's your idea of a decent side-income because you consider podcasting your hobby, then maybe you can get into the small percentage of content creators who can earn a few hundred per month with your show. Maybe hit a thousand or two.

But for the most part, a majority of creators will not be able to make even a few hundred dollars a month from their show, and here's why...

A few years ago, I used to listen to a podcast called RadioLab - a popular radio show and podcast with millions of listeners. While listening to the episode published on September 21, 2017, I was shocked to learn about the show's inability to raise funds through donations even though they had a super-successful podcast, which, according to their media kit at the time, had 1.6 million *weekly* radio listeners. I believe their radio show was being repurposed as a podcast as well.

In that episode, the host was practically begging his listeners: (paraphrasing), "Please, can we at least get 1% of our listeners to donate? It's at 0.76% right now".

This was a show where they've always repeatedly mentioned that they intentionally did not have ads on the show just so they can create a better experience for their listeners and that they are solely listener-supported.

They had a rabid fan base of 1.6 million listeners, 57 million annual streaming sessions, 7.7 million annual YouTube views, 5.5 million weekly listeners on 4 nationally broadcast programs. And they couldn't even get 1% of their listeners to donate.

That is exactly my point: the donation model is overrated, and not as great as many people make it out to be.

With donations, you are literally at the mercy of your audience. You could hear the desperation in the host's voice, pleading for donations.

That's the kind of business model that makes me extremely uncomfortable because I would much rather come from a place of authority and subject matter expertise and say that here's this product I have created, or here's this service I'm offering, here's what it is worth, here's how my knowledge and expertise and experience can help you, and I've packaged it all into this online course or membership site, and when you buy it, you will get all these benefits, and you'll save time, money, energy, or be entertained, and so on.

I would rather try to build a business and sell products and services, rather than ask for help to support what I'm doing.

You cannot rely on donations to support a long-term, profitable, online business that you need to be able to count on to pay your bills, fund your lifestyle, your kids' education, and maybe even pay for retirement.

I've been seeing more and more results from podcasters and creators who accept donations. You could say that only a tiny fraction of podcasters can get their audience to donate enough to be able to earn a living.

The remaining majority either get some nice pocket change, or usually close to nothing, and my unscientific polling and research show that the average creator gets less than 1% of their audience to donate - something that Radiolab was also experiencing.

1% of 5 million listeners is 50,000 listeners. And if each person donates 8 dollars a month, that's 400,000 dollars a month. That's a lot of money because their audience is so massive.

Crowdfunding won't work if there's no crowd.

If you listen to "The Feed" podcast from Libsyn, the average podcast gets about 150 downloads per episode (it has gone up and down over the years). Even if you're doing pretty well, that's probably about 2000 downloads per episode.

1% of 2000 is 20 listeners. If 20 listeners donate $5 a month, that's $100 a month. For a lot of people, $100 is nothing to sneeze at. It's certainly better than $0. It can pay for your hosting, software, web services, and t-shirts and tchotchkes that you may want to give away to your listeners.

However, the amount of work it would take to get to 2000 downloads per episode, and then repeatedly keep hammering on every episode asking your listeners to "donate", to help you support the show, to tell them that if they want you to keep going, then they're going to have to raise their hand and help you, that is not something I can rely on to help me make a living.

So if you want real, consistent income, and not just some side-income "hobby" money, then you've *got* to sell products and/or services.

You've got to be able to build a business "behind" your podcast from day 1. You can't just sit around waiting to build a large enough audience just so that one day you *might* make money selling ads.

Here's another thing to consider if you're accepting donations via a 3rd-party platform like Patreon.

With Patreon-like systems, all of the one-time donations, as well as the recurring monthly or episode-based donations from your patrons, are all going into their payment systems.

Patreon doesn't allow you to use your own PayPal or Stripe account. So all of the payment data is in their proprietary system.

If you ever decide to leave Patreon, maybe because they changed their terms and you don't like it anymore, or their politics or their positioning or pricing has changed, they got bought out by a big company and that big company decided to shut them down, maybe they ran out of capital and decided to shut down - whatever the case may be if you wish to leave Patreon, then you will lose *all* of your recurring donations.

You have to basically ask your patrons to cancel their subscription over at Patreon, and come follow you to your new platform, and then sign up again at this new platform.

And any time you ask people to cancel at one location and rejoin at another location, you'll probably lose a majority of your patrons, because people are busy, they may change their mind because they may no longer want to continue supporting your show, or maybe they had forgotten that they were donating to you and this notification might serve as a reminder for them to cancel their donations.

There are so many things that can go wrong and practically overnight, your income could go from a few thousand dollars to close to zero, all because you couldn't take your patrons' payment profiles with you to your new platform.

Now, if a coaching client came to me and said, "I have a podcast. I have zero technical skills, and I don't want the headache of building a website or managing it. I just want an easy way to take payments from my fans who want to support me and send some donations my way", I'm probably going to tell them to check out Patreon.com, which is one of the best fan-funding platforms there is.

They seem to be well funded and are making the right moves in improving their platform. So as much as I would hate sending someone to a third-party hosted platform, I would still do it, because of "horses for courses".

So as a business coach, my job is to educate you about the potential flaws and pitfalls of building your business on a third-party platform. And warn you about how your best option for building a long-term, profitable online business, is to own your platform - OYP, as I call it.

But if you still tell me that you have limitations because of which you're ok with taking the risk of not heeding my advice, I'm going to help you do what you feel is best for you, even if it's not always the perfect solution.

So while Patreon and other similar platforms may be a great way to quickly get going to accept donations and content subscriptions, I don't recommend building your business on a third-party platform.

And finally, here's a fascinating true story that shows how donations are not a reliable business model.

Positioning

On a cold morning in January 2007, a violinist wearing a baseball cap was playing some beautiful music in a Washington DC subway train station.

1,097 people passed him by, but only 7 of them stopped to listen to him. He had a mat spread out in front of him to collect donations.

For his 43-minute performance, he collected a whopping $32.17 from a total of 27 passersby.

He had started the morning at the station, playing Bach's 14-minute Chaconne, generally considered to be the single greatest solo violin work and one of the greatest musical compositions ever created.

And he had played it on one of the finest instruments ever made - a 300-year-old "Gibson ex Huberman" Stradivarius, made in 1713 - which he had purchased for just under 4 million dollars.

Just 3 days earlier, this violinist had performed at a completely sold-out Boston Symphony Hall, where even a half-decent seat cost $100.

The musician was none other than the internationally acclaimed violinist, Joshua Bell.

It was the same artist, the same $4,000,000 violin, the same enchanting music - yet when he put himself in a position of asking, and relied on the generosity of strangers, he earned a pathetic $32.

When his positioning changed, and it became, hey, I'm playing at this fancy, prestigious theater, tickets are in short supply, you'll be paying premium ticket prices and expensive parking and overpriced popcorn and beer, and you get to see me come out on stage wearing nice clothes, and play you the exact same music, most people were entirely happy to do so.

Sometimes, your fans may not know your true worth until you forcefully announce it, and make them aware of it and the value of what they're getting.

Just putting your best content out there, putting your heart and soul into your craft, and hoping for the generosity of strangers, hoping that your audience will notice all of the blood, sweat, and tears you've put into your work, and hoping they'll help you make a living because of their sheer appreciation, is a business model that is destined to fail more often than not.

They're not just going to show up one day and drop money in your PayPal account. And even if they do, it may not earn you enough other than to maybe pay for some gear, and some toys and maybe a dinner at a fine restaurant.

So if you wish to do what you love, and you love it enough to do it all the time and not just on nights and weekends, if you want it to pay your bills, and maybe even pay for your lifestyle, a few vacations, and if you have even grander ambitions then maybe you want it to pay your mortgage, your children's college education and fund your retirement too; If you want to make any meaningful money with your craft and your knowledge and your skills and your experience, you've got to create value, and then build an audience and a community, and charge them for that value that you're providing.

All you need is, as Kevin Kelly wrote, "1000 true fans". You don't need hundreds of thousands of customers, or hundreds of thousands of video views, or downloads, or email subscribers.

Just find your 1,000 true fans, and you can create a great business behind your craft that can support you, your family, and your lifestyle.

Ad Revenue is Not a Reliable Business Model

The ad-revenue and sponsorship models are also unreliable. They're great for supplemental income, but not as your main business.

That is why companies like Twitter, Snapchat, and Yahoo! - despite having hundreds of millions of users using their service - are always struggling to earn big profits, and sometimes are teetering on the edge of going bankrupt, or being bought out, or their shares are tanking and laying off thousands of employees.

Let's talk about ads: Most people dislike ads and I don't even think I'm generalizing it too much. I have mixed feelings about ads. As an entrepreneur at heart, I want creators who are putting their blood, sweat, and tears into creating great content, to be able to pay their bills. I want them to be able to monetize all that hard work. But on the other hand, I also dislike ads, and I try to do everything I can to skip or avoid ads altogether whenever possible.

E.g., I have an ad-blocker plugin in all web browsers (Chrome, Firefox, and Opera), that blocks ads on most websites. Some websites won't let me view the page if I don't disable the ad-blocker. Unless it's a big authority site or the information is exclusive to the site, I'm probably not going to disable the ad-blocker, and usually end up leaving that website altogether because if it's just news I'm looking for, there are any number of other websites covering the same story (see chapter "Seth Godin Ruined The Internet" where I discuss why your Perspective and Opinion are valued far more than just reporting the news).

I'd rather go elsewhere than have obnoxious ads forced on me (not saying all websites do this, but many media websites do). I also have a browser plugin that stops videos from auto-playing on websites (one big reason why you should never, ever auto-play your videos or audio, which can be super-annoying to your visitors – also, browsers block most such videos already, but this plugin also blocks their sneaky workarounds).

But if a quality website displays ads responsibly, doesn't slide big images from all over the place, doesn't block or distract from the content with large flashing gifs, doesn't keep popping up ads that try to trick me into downloading malware, and doesn't auto-play videos, then I'll selectively disable the ad blocker on those sites, as a gesture of my support.

When it comes to ads on TV, the only thing I watch on TV these days is NBA Basketball. Everything else is streaming. Everyone in my family is a huge LeBron James fan. And we buffer all games on our DVR and start watching the games after the buffer hits about 60 minutes (which is the max limit of my DVR).

That way, I can fast-forward all ads, watch just the game, and sometimes even skip the half-time shows, the timeouts, the endless replays, etc. So I watch what would normally be a 3-hour telecast that includes about 45 minutes of ads and a 15-minute half-time show, in just over 2 hours. I save about 1 hour of watching time for every game I watch. And when you're watching around 150 games a year like me, that's at least 150 hours saved – that's like getting a free, bonus half-hour extra, every day, every year!

When I listen to Tim Ferriss' podcast or Marc Maron's WTF podcast (don't anymore) and a few other shows that have the first 5 minutes of the show filled entirely with ads, I completely skip the first section. Tim Ferriss has even said that he uses pre-roll ads for that reason, so his listeners can have a chance to fast-forward through all of it if they don't want to. Now, that's nice of Tim to do, and I've taken full advantage of it before.

I don't mind mid-roll ads that appear in the middle of the show, as long as they're not too long. And more importantly, I love in-context ads that are nicely woven into the show's content. So, mid-roll ads make more sense for your listeners because you get to give them some value first before making them sit through one or more ads.

Give first, ask later. That is a more generous content strategy, than just hitting them on the head with non-stop ads right from the get-go. Sometimes, a podcast will end and there'll be a whole bunch of ads, and I won't even know which show this is – whether it's the ads at the end of the show or ads at the beginning of the next show, because the ads come on even before the actual intro of the show, even before the name is announced!

There is a cool hack I talk about in the chapter "MidRoll Message" that is useful for skipping ads. But more on that later.

Also, as smart-watches become more prevalent, how long do you think it will be before I can say "Hey Siri, fast-forward 30 seconds" in my OverCast app (which is my favorite podcast app for iOS). Yeah, sponsors will not be happy when that day comes. And I believe a couple of quick taps on the Apple AirPods can already do that.

That means coupon-code usage, conversion rates, and ad engagement will all probably drop. And if sponsorship rates drop, so will your income.

Ads are not a great strategy for a successful, long-term profitable business - unless you're already a celebrity or brand with a big audience. But it's not feasible for most independent podcasters, small businesses, and side-hustlers like you and me.

I present to you, exhibit #1: My own, now-defunct website, BabyNamesIndia.com.

At the peak of its powers from 2001-2007, I was getting between 3000 - 5000 visitors per day. And my highest was 6,312 visitors in one single day, on 26th July 2007.

At the time, I was earning about $1,500 per month from AdSense ads on my website. That was with me focusing 100% on the website, creating new content every day, working furiously on updates, adding stuff, tweaking stuff, moving things around as I kept learning and experimenting with SEO. So it was the peak of my attention to this website as well.

There's a large community of Indians all over the world because a lot of people have been migrating away from India for many years now, in search of better opportunities, which includes me as well, which is why I moved to the US in 2000.

Some months, my AdSense earnings would fluctuate between $500 to $1,500 each. But I could never get past $1,500 a month with AdSense, despite being the #1 website on Google for about 7 years straight for most keywords related to Indian baby names, including "Indian baby names"), despite a massive target audience, super-high search rankings on multiple search engines, tons of targeted traffic (almost all of it was Indians), buying every course on AdSense and SEO and list-building and optimizing every darn part of my website, constantly generating more traffic from new sources, and on and on.

The work to stay at the top of Google was relentless, but all of that work didn't pay off as much as I had hoped it would, even though I did reach #1 on Google for a ton of different keywords, and built a list of more than half a million email subscribers at one point.

I couldn't monetize the emails much either, because at that point, Indians in India hardly had credit cards, and even the few who did weren't used to using them online.

So the main reason the website failed when it came to my goals (of making a living online) was that despite the enormous numbers of users and attention, ad revenue just wasn't going to cut it. It was not, and it still cannot be a consistent source of revenue, and can't be scaled as much as you want it to.

At the time, a few websites were doing pretty well with ad monetization, like a popular dating site at the time called Plenty Of Fish. The owner was making about $10,000 a day and was being interviewed on all kinds of shows, speaking at events, and achieved an online marketing rock star status because of how well his AdSense ads were doing.

Turns out, he was an Outlier. He ran into a perfect storm (in a good way) of being early in the online dating website business, his audience was mostly from the US, which means US advertisers paid more to reach US-based audiences (compared to the non-existent Indian online advertisers advertising to Indians). That meant he got a bigger cut from those clicks from Google, he made more money for Google, so Google promoted his website even more, and thus grew his revenue snowball.

But unfortunately, my website BabyNamesIndia.com was the exact opposite: It was attracting 99% Indians, most of them from India. Poor country, Internet use wasn't very widespread at the time, ecommerce was practically non-existent because most Indians in India did not have credit cards back then. And even the tiny percentage that did, did not use it online. So it was a perfect storm of the worst kind for me.

As much as I tried to get out of the ad revenue game, I couldn't. I created my own eBook about Indian baby names and sold it for a couple of dollars, sold a physical book, and sometimes my eBook and book sales would make more than the ads. The ad revenue simply wasn't consistent.

If you started a website or a blog today, it doesn't matter how much great content you write, how much SEO you do on your website, you are probably not going to be able to drive 5,000 unique visitors per day to your website any time soon using just organic traffic.

It won't matter how Ad-clickbaity your content is, even if you're targeting an expensive keyword niche like weight loss or supplements or health and fitness, you will probably not be able to make more than a good chunk of side-income which will probably pay for some toys, dinners, and movies. But it's probably not going to help you replace your income from your day job any time soon.

Also, the amount of work you would have to put in doing SEO and churning out content and tweaking and testing, to maybe make a few hundred dollars a month, just won't be worth it.

So forget monetizing using just ads - you have to think of something that can grow and scale and can be repeated over time, whether it's your blog, podcast, or videos.

The same can be said about monetizing a podcast with sponsorship (earlier chapter). If you want to go the traditional route of signing up with an ad service like MidRoll, the minimum downloads you'll need is apparently about 5,000 per episode. For the amount of work, creativity, dedication, marketing, passion, and persistence it would take to grow a podcast to at least 5,000 downloads - only to get $10 CPM (Cost Per Mille, aka cost per thousand downloads/views/etc)? You would be making $50 an episode, which means $200 a month if you release 4 episodes.

Sure, $200 is more than $0. But it's not day-job-quitting money either. Double it or even triple the CPM's, it's still $600 a month - nowhere nearly enough for a full-time living.

And the crazier part is, even if you do hit the 5K mark after 1-2 years of putting in crazy work and great content, and you get a $10 CPM from a few advertisers, and they ask you to give out a special coupon code to your listeners so they can see if your listeners are engaging and whether it's worth advertising on your show – and your listeners don't respond at all even after hearing the ad a few times, the advertisers will simply stop sponsoring your podcast because they're not even getting a reasonable ROI from your show.

It's the same with YouTube too: 1,000 subscribers and 4,000 hours of watch time just to even be eligible for monetization.

Grow with YouTube

As a YouTube partner, you'll be eligible to earn money from your videos, get creator support and more. Learn more

To get into the YouTube Partner Programme, your channel needs 4,000 public watch hours in the last 12 months, and 1,000 subscribers. Your channel will also get reviewed to make sure that it follows YouTube monetisation policies

What if I already started the application? ⑦

19 subscribers   228 public watch hours
1,000 needed   4,000 needed

⊘ We'll send you an email when you're eligible to apply

Potentially hundreds of videos created, all of which have to be thoroughly optimized, from the thumbnails to titles and descriptions, keep viewers watching for as long as possible, etc. And after many years of finally getting to a point where you are just about to break through, YouTube could just change their rules overnight, make it harder to make money, or suspend your videos or your channel for some infraction, and everything could disappear overnight.

Even using affiliate marketing and trying to link to affiliate products to get back a commission if someone goes on to buy something from the vendor, is not a great long-term model. It's great for the vendor because you're sending them tons of traffic on your dime, you're working hard to send people to their website, where the visitors will be exposed to the product owner's brand, the site owner gets to cookie them, put them on a list, get to know who they are, send them emails, market to them, sell to them. From all that traffic you're sending them, *if and only if* someone goes on to buy something from the seller, then you get paid a commission. And sure, it can be a big check if the product being sold is a high-ticket item.

But which of these is better: Earning (say) 30% of the sale and no access to the customer you just sent them, or 70% of the sale and also owning the customer's contact info so you can engage with them again in the future?

Also if it's a non-affiliate sale, or the buyer gets cookied on the desktop but buys on their mobile phone, then the vendor gets to keep 100% of the profits. And as browsers block more and more cookies, there's a chance that even a legit sale might not be tracked, and you lose out on potential commissions. Even tracking affiliate referrals using IP is getting harder because of privacy laws concerning geolocation data.

But Affiliate marketing does have its benefits: You don't have to worry about building an entire product from scratch, figuring out what people will pay for, building a website and a sales page, a funnel, processing the sale, refunds, customer service, or tech support.

But what you get as an affiliate is usually going to be much smaller compared to what the product owner gets to keep even after they've paid you for the few sales you sent them - unless you're a super promoter like AppSumo (who keep up to 75% of the sale depending on the type of promo, because they own the traffic, the funnel, as well as the payments).

And because the product owner owns the user experience, brand experience, gets to know their email id and put them on a list and turn them into a customer, they can keep sending them emails, keep selling more stuff, tell them about their podcast, YouTube channel, Kindle eBook, live events, and more.

So as an affiliate, in the short term, you can quickly start making money online because you don't have to build an entire business first. And it's also great as supplemental income to your core business, where you can refer great third-party products and services that align with your audience's needs. I myself do a lot of affiliate marketing where I promote products and services I use and would recommend anyway to my audience even if they didn't have an affiliate program.

But in the long term, you're helping build someone else's audience, somebody else's list, somebody else's business - instead of growing your own audience, your own list, your own customers, and building your own long-term, profitable online business.

So, monetizing your audience with sponsors or affiliate marketing works fine in some situations, but it's not the best core business model for the long term.

That is why you've got to create your own products and services.

Mid-roll Message

The mid-roll ad (somewhere near the middle of the show) is the most powerful slot for attention in a podcast.

I use the iOS app Overcast. And its feature of being able to skip intros and outros makes the mid-roll message that much more important (other apps probably have something similar).

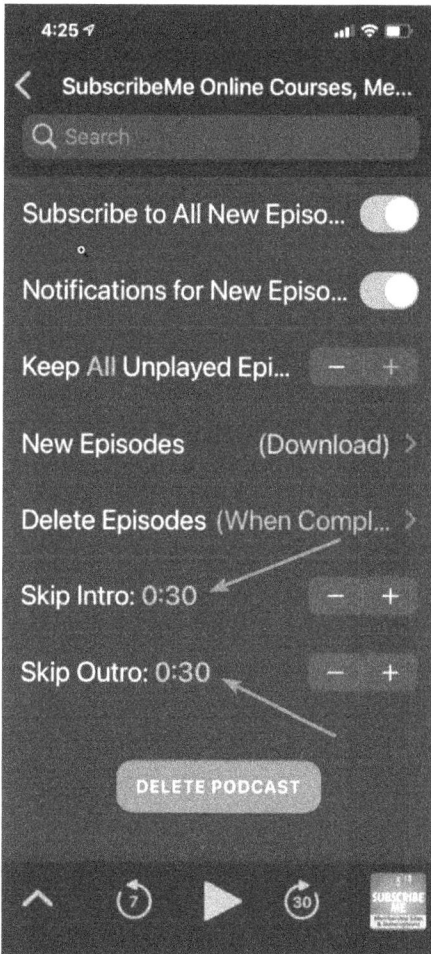

Unfortunately, many of us podcasters have inadvertently trained listeners into thinking Intros and Outros are skippable.

A bunch of ads right from the get-go, extended music, exaggerated intro, "Housekeeping" like asking for ratings & reviews right at the beginning before providing an ounce of value first, taking too long to get to the interesting part promised in the title, etc.

I'm sure all of that works for many shows, more so *after* the host has built a relationship with the listener, but sometimes that can turn off new listeners.

Plus most regular listeners of a podcast know exactly how many seconds to skip at the beginning to get to the core content. And most skip the end anyway.

And that brings us to the precious Mid-roll Message.

There are multiple ways to do this:

1) Uggh: Abrupt cutting to an ad with no warning whatsoever - usually stitched ads that programmatically look for a pause, and not for context. Not a fan of this.

2) Yawn: "We'll be right back after these messages". Yawn! Skip!!

3) Neat: Product Placement: "Yeah, it's funny you mention that. I did go to their website for the offer, and their site was down! By the way, the best web hosting service I use and recommend, is...".

4) LOVE IT: In-context or In-Conversation ad: "I was talking to my coaching client the other day... and by the way, I do have a coaching program where I ....".

The bottom line is that the Mid-roll is where you can get the most attention, because it's within the flow, and not easily skipped like a Pre-roll or Post-roll message. Most people are doing their dishes or driving and won't care about stopping what they're doing to hit fast forward. Many will just listen through, as long as it's interesting and well presented.

If I were an advertiser, I would insist on a Mid-roll ad - or pay less for a Pre- or Post-roll (least for the post-roll).

If you're a podcaster, be sure to use the middle section of your show for your most important and impactful messages. And weave it into the content in such a way that it doesn't sound like an abrupt interruption.

Put Your Money Where Your Mouth Is And Pay to Play

You've probably heard of the saying "Put your money where your mouth is".

Most of us probably use it without even realizing the astounding depth and practicality behind that statement.

No other one-liner even comes close to what I've always been preaching.

And that is, to say, stop only talking about your passion project, and start putting in some money into whatever you're trying to accomplish.

That's what it means when they say "get some skin in the game".

If you've seen Shark Tank, you'll frequently see the Sharks, who are the investors, ask how much of their own money that an entrepreneur has invested in the business. The less money they have invested, the less impressed the sharks are, and the less they want to make a deal with you.

If all you do is simply talk the big talk about how passionate you are about something, about how much you care about something, but then you have nothing invested in it financially, then it makes it that much easier for you to just walk away from all of it.

Don't just TELL me, SHOW me.

Show me that you care - about your online business, your online course, audio course, Kindle book, your podcast, your YouTube channel.

In another episode, Mark Cuban talks about why it's not a great idea to take a loan for your fledgling business. His point is that if you're using other people's money to fund your business, and you don't have any of your own money in it, that means you don't have *your* skin in the game - it's other people's skin.

If you take a small business loan without offering any collateral, and your business goes down the tubes, you can declare bankruptcy. Or if you raise a lot of funds from angel investors and venture capitalists, you will have less to lose, compared to say, taking out a line of credit on your only home where your spouse and kids live. Or maybe your parent took out a line of credit for your sake, and if you don't take earn back the investment, then either of you could lose your home!

Some might say it's smart to use other people's money. But that transference of risk to others can also be a sign for potential investors and partners, like the folks from Shark Tank.

This is the same thing that happened during the dotcom boom of the early 2000s. They were getting so much investment despite not having a real product, no sales, no business model, absolutely *nothing* in many cases except registered users and email accounts.

That's why they spent like crazy on super-bowl ads, spending millions of dollars throwing lavish parties, private planes for their executives, and lived a Wolf of Wall Street type lifestyle. And probably the only difference was that the Wolf was at least making money, illegally or not. And these dotcoms were making near zero dollars in revenue, and all of their capital-raising was based on showing how many new user accounts they had gained and how fast that number was growing.

You can't tell me that your podcast, your blog, kindle book, or YouTube channel is "just a hobby" and that is the reason why you're not investing in marketing and promotion. Because there are millions of people, and you are probably already one of them, who spend hundreds of dollars, if not thousands, on their favorite hobby.

We're not talking about just casual hobbies - we're talking serious, passionate hobbies that almost cross the line and qualify as an overgrown hobby that could be a borderline money-maker on the side.

If you currently get into trouble for overdoing a hobby, spending too much time or money on it, and you get into trouble with your parent, spouse, or relative, and they're telling you to tone it down a notch, then *that* is your favorite hobby.

Let me give you some quick examples of hobbies where people spend crazy amounts of time, money, and effort:

Sports: Sports fans - and I'm one of the crazy fans - spend insane amounts of money on game tickets, hats, t-shirts, betting on our teams (just lost $500 this year betting on the LA Lakers), playing fantasy sports, etc. Sports fans are among the most passionate hobbyists in the world.

Next, people who play a sport themselves: Spending on Golf club memberships and buying actual golf clubs and paying for everything at the club and paying for your caddy, or if you play tennis, or any other sport, then club memberships, league fees, sports equipment, coaching, physical trainers, dieticians, and on and on.

If you see the way some people spend money on their game, you'll think they're training to be the next superstar in the sports league. But most of them have no intention of ever doing that. And they don't care about becoming a professional athlete or earning money from the sport. They just want to spend a few times a week playing their favorite sport, and because they're competitive, they will spend a lot of time on fitness and equipment and coaching, to get better.

A lot of people spend thousands of dollars over their lifetime learning a musical instrument, or vocal lessons, buying gear, etc.

You probably have a crazy passion of your own and you probably spend a lot of money feeding that passion.

So saying that you don't have money to spend on promoting your Kindle book, or podcast, or your lead magnet, is not good enough. It's not that you can't afford it, it's just that you don't *want* to afford it.

It's like when I was about 50 pounds overweight a few years ago (I still am about 20 pounds overweight). For many years, my excuse was that I didn't have the time. Between getting up at 5 AM, shoveling the driveway of my Ossining home in New York state, driving to the station in dangerously slippy, slidey roads, taking the Metro to Manhattan Grand Central, taking another 2 subway trains, then walking for another 10 minutes - all just to get to work!

And then in the evening, replay that whole process all over again, in reverse. Then I reach home, spend some time with the family, watch maybe the second half of a LeBron James Basketball game, and *then* get to work on my side-business at the time (DigitalAccessPass.com - DAP) writing my book, and so on. I would sleep for 4-5 hours a night just so I could work on DAP and my book and my other websites at the time, like BabyNamesIndia.com. And I would tell myself that I didn't have the time to take care of my health – which was in some ways, very true.

So was I crazy busy? Yes. Was I doing so many things that I didn't even have time to get a decent 7 hours of sleep? Yes. Had I already cut down every single additional non-trivial thing out of my life just so I could focus on just the things I most wanted to? Yes.

I had cut it right to the bone. But I know that I could have still made time for a 20-minute workout every day. Or worst case, every other day. Or at least on the weekends. So I didn't *have* the time (technically true) because I didn't *make* the time – probably because working out had the lowest priority for me among everything else at the time. And that bad decision affected my health at the time.

So the same way, it's not like you *can't* afford to invest money into promoting your product. It's just that you don't *want* to afford it. Because putting your money where your mouth is, can be scary.

What do we humans do when we're terrified of change? We just go back to our old ways and stay in our comfort zone. So for content creators and creative people, do you know what our comfort zone is? Do you know when we're performing at our peak and creating great content? That's our comfort zone.

As podcasters, what do we do when nothing seems to be working? CREATE MORE PODCAST EPISODES!

If you are a book writer, and you're not selling enough books, what do we do? WE WRITE MORE BOOKS!

If you have a membership site, and no one is signing up, what do we do? WE CREATE MORE VIDEOS!

You get the idea. Spending real, hard-earned cash on ads is a scary concept for a lot of us. There are so many things we're afraid of: What if I screw up the ad? Do I have to figure out Facebook advertising now? What if my ad sucks and I don't get results and I just end up wasting $50 for nothing?

And the minute you stop *talking* about how important your website is, or your blog is, or your podcast is, or your Kindle book is - and you put your money where your mouth is - as in, start spending some money on advertising that all-important thing, *that's* when you'll start to think about your business in a whole new light.

Because you now know that there's a cost to every click, every visitor, every view, and you already know you don't like wasting any money. So those two things combined - that every visitor has a cost, and you don't want to waste money - are guaranteed to light a fire inside you like nothing else.

Let's say you've been dragging your feet about creating a great lead magnet and putting up an email sign-up form on your home page so that you can build a list. You might be putting off the project using so many different excuses.

But what if you found out that one of your affiliates has decided to email their list about your product or service in two days, and they're going to send you a few thousand visitors to your website over the next week?

Suddenly, you sit up, eyes wide open, heart racing with excitement. There's a new sense of urgency that wasn't there before. Because now you know, that it would be such a criminal waste of precious attention, and such a huge lost opportunity to build your list, if you don't get your email signup form and lead magnet in order quickly before the affiliate promotes your website.

So what might've normally taken you weeks, will now probably get done in 2 hours.

In the same way, if you're going to be getting a lot of traffic to your site over the next 2 days because you've just launched this Facebook ad campaign, you know that it would be a waste of money to drive clicks to a landing page that doesn't have a way of turning those visitors into email subscribers. And if you can't get their email before they leave your website, then there's no way to know who they were, so you could send them great value, get them to come back, and buy your stuff.

Of course, you used to have the ability to re-targeting our visitors by embedding a retargeting pixel on your site, so you can re-target them later via Facebook or Google ads because you know they already visited your website. But with a lot of browsers blocking tracking pixels by default, and all the laws being passed about cookies and user tracking, retargeting using pixels is dying and will be obsolete soon. I'm sure something else will take its place, but it won't be as accurate as retargeting pixels were.

Also, retargeting is much less effective compared to being able to send your potential buyer an email. So it's like a potential customer walking into your shop, you don't offer them any kind of gift or coupon in exchange for their phone number or email. You let them walk out the door without getting their contact information, and now you go spend money on display advertising in the mall or ads on the radio to get their attention, all so you can let them know that you have a gift or coupon for them if they come back and give you their contact information.

They *just* walked into your shop - you could've easily gotten their information for no extra charge - just the cost of your gift, or a discount. You didn't. And you lost out on possibly an immediate sale, and also on any potential future sales because now you have no way of contacting them even if you have the biggest blow-out sale of the year!

So you must be willing to pay to play.

There are so many ways to come up with a quick $50-$200 each month just so you can use that to promote your product or services, or even your podcast or YouTube channel. If you Google it, you can find tons of websites dedicated to making a few extra dollars on the side. But here are a few quick ones:

1) Start with your online subscriptions. Revisit all of your monthly payments. Like Netflix, HBO, Hulu, Cable TV subscription, Phone service, Spotify, Showtime. Anything you can cancel for a few months? You don't even have to cancel any of them permanently - just for a few short months. Well, at least that's what I want you to tell yourself, just a few short months, so you kind of trick your mind into believing that it's not permanent, just a tiny temporary change.

And then a few months go by without it, and you just might realize that you never really needed it after all.

Anyway, do you need ALL of those movie and TV show subscriptions? Can you cancel a few of them? Or downgrade any of them to a lower tier for a short while? E.g., you may not have checked your Cable TV lineup in a while, and you might realize that you don't watch most of those channels anyway and you're paying for a lot of channels that never watch, or only watch once in a great while. Get rid of them. Switch to a lower package that has fewer channels.

You can always re-sign up for any subscriptions that you need after a few months. It's not the end of the world. So revisit your content subscriptions. It will help a great deal if you just sit down and note down everything you're paying for currently, and maybe get rid of the bottom half of your list. Again, only temporarily (*wink *wink). And this could easily save you between $20 - $50 bucks a month.

2) Shiny Domain Syndrome: Start with your currently registered domain names. Over time, most online entrepreneurs tend to accumulate a whole bunch of domain names. That's because we are constantly getting ideas, and what's the first thing many of us

do when we're the most excited about a new idea? We go and register a domain name.

I've easily registered over 500 domain names in my lifetime. And I never end up doing anything with the majority of them. Every year, I go into my Godaddy account and if there's a domain that I don't think I'll ever do anything with, or if it's an idea I've outgrown, or am no longer excited about even though it may have sounded like the next big thing a year ago when I registered it, I'll go in and I'll just turn off the auto-renewal feature for that domain – but I won't cancel it just yet. So what that does is pushes the burden of deciding whether that one is worth keeping, to down the road, a few months from now.

A friend posted this on Facebook recently: "I'm so happy. As part of 2018, I took a look at all the old half-baked ideas that were still around, podcasts that had podfaded, and memberships to resources I never visited. By the end of this month, I will be put close to $150 a month back in my pocket."

3) Revisit online services: Do you host websites with more than one web host? You may have signed up with multiple hosts over time, so revisit that. Maybe get rid of websites that are no longer a part of your vision and roadmap going forward. Consolidate those web hosts into one solid web host. At this point, I only recommend SiteGround and Liquid Web.

4) One person's junk is another person's treasure: Here's another way for most people to make a quick few hundred over the next 2 months: Put everything you're not using on sale - books, CD's, gaming consoles, games, furniture, toys, etc. There are so many marketplaces out there. Start with eBay. A few years ago, my then-14-yr-old son made over $1,000 in a single summer, selling off stuff that he didn't use anymore - or in some cases, never did.

5) Barter for Promos: Approach Facebook group owners in your niche and offer them a small payment to do a sponsored post. Or

approach other podcasters and do a promo swap or just pay them to do a host-read ad about your product.

You can take that one step further and do this with other Podcasters, Email List Owners, and anyone who looks like they may have built up an audience. Don't just focus on the big-name influencers, because if they're worth it, then you will either have to have previously a relationship with them, or someone they know - or you may simply have to outright pay them a lot. In many cases, influencers may want an upfront fee as well as an affiliate commission, which you may not be able to do when you're just getting started.

6) UserTesting.com: You can sign up with them and get paid for testing of products for other companies, and sometimes simply offering feedback. Most tests take under 10 minutes, and you get paid $10 for that. That's the same as making $60 per hour. And you can easily make a few hundred dollars a month like my son has been doing for over a year now.

There are entire websites dedicated to helping you with earning on the side, but you get the idea. If you even do just a few of the things I mentioned above, you could make anywhere between $50 to $200 a month.

And if you start bartering, you can easily get a bunch of free ads without any actual cash spent. Of course, the downside of not spending cash is that you have to instead spend time and energy. But if you're just getting started, then you probably have more time than money. Just cut down on watching Netflix and you can get back some time to do other things.

The key is, whatever money you end up making, or saving, don't go out and blow all of that on Amazon buying some cool electronic toys. It should be reserved only for promoting your stuff.

You've got to turn into that 10-year-old, who wants to save up to buy their favorite toy or shoes or game. And they suddenly start calculating everything. My son has always been like that. If he knows he has to save up to buy a $100 video game, he suddenly wants to put a tag on everything. "Dad, remember you told me a while ago that I can do chores around the house and earn money, I want to start doing that now. How much will you pay me for doing this, or doing that?"

And then we're all outside, and I ask him if he wants me to bring take-out food, he'll be like, I'm not hungry right now, I already ate. But whatever you were going to spend on buying me food, give me that as cash ☺.

I've seen other kids do this too. Once they set their mind on something, they're going to figure out 100 different ways to achieve that goal, and they're not going to stop until they've gotten that thing.

I want you to go back to that same level of innocence, but the same level of stubbornness and doggedness, and single-mindedness in finding ways to save $50 - $200 a month. And then it'll be fun to be able to spend that money on promoting your podcast, or lead magnet, or for gifts and giveaways for your listeners or subscribers in exchange for maybe sharing your website or link on their Facebook feed, or for joining your group, or joining your list, and so on.

And don't forget to build a list, from day 1.

If you spent all of your ad dollars on promoting your lead magnet so you can build a list, that would probably be the best way to spend your money. Once you have a list, as long as you're providing them value and keeping them engaged, you can promote multiple things over time.

Killer Lead Magnet

AKA Free Bonus, Freebie, Bribe, Lead Magnet - they all mean the same thing.

You promise your visitor something of value, in exchange for their email.

And for best results, it has *got* to be something *really* good. Something you could easily charge for and people would be willing to pay for.

It's even worth paying someone to create it for you – either entirely, or parts of it. It should be *that* good.

But first, you should have a really good idea of who your exact target audience is for your podcast. It doesn't matter if they're a podcast listener, YouTube subscriber, blog reader, social media follower, email subscriber, or future buyer of your digital products like eBooks and online courses.

You've probably heard about creating an audience "avatar" to identify your target audience: Who is this person? What do they want? What benefit will they get from your lead magnet? What's different about your content? Why should they follow you? What makes you different/special/an expert? There's plenty of articles about that if you just Google it.

But once you've already done that, you have to make sure your lead magnet is super-relevant, useful, exciting, and targeted towards your ideal target audience.

Your target prospect is looking to get from point A (where they are now) to point B (where they're hoping to be or where you're promising they'll be if they buy your product).

And let's say there are several steps in getting from point A to B. Your lead magnet should help them with one or more of those steps and help solve part of the problem they're looking to solve. And then give it away for free.

I have a whole bunch of lead magnets I've created and given away for free over the years, including premium Kindle eBooks and mini-video courses. I've given away the 7 books that I've written for free, as a PDF, at one point or the other (this is my 8th book).

If your target audience is on Facebook, then start with Facebook ads. It's easier to figure out compared to Google ads. If they're not on Facebook, then advertise wherever they are – like on Instagram (which is owned by Facebook, just so you know), LinkedIn, other podcasts, etc.

I've personally not had much success with Twitter ads in the past, plus it could quickly become expensive. But be sure to test Twitter ads for your niche.

1. Ads on other people's email lists (targeted lists, of course)
2. Ads on other people's podcasts – pay for it, barter products or services, or exchange ads
3. Do a joint 2-part episode with another podcaster in your niche: 1st part is published on one podcast, the 2nd part is on the other one. And both of you get to promote your shows on both episodes (and use the mid-roll to promote your lead magnet).
4. Facebook ads
5. Promote (with permission) in Facebook groups. Just contact the admin of the group and ask them if they will post a "sponsored post" in the group for you, recommending your lead magnet. Of course, you've got to have already joined the group first, determined that it has high-quality members who post high-quality content, build a relationship with the admin, etc.
6. QuuuPromote.co

7. Ads on OverCast.fm (which is my favorite podcast app, and they have a great ad network where they will promote your ad to those who are still using their free version of their app, which is ad-supported). Of course, you can't promote your lead magnet, but you can directly promote your podcast.
8. Google Display Network
9. Twitter ads
10. LinkedIn ads
11. Instagram ads
12. Joint Ventures
13. Sell a low-cost digital product, offer tons of bonuses, create an affiliate program and give away 50% - 75% commissions to your affiliates.
14. If you use something like DigitalAccessPass.com (DAP), every buyer can instantly become an affiliate as well, and they can start promoting it to their audience.

Ads on third-party email lists and **Ads in Facebook groups** will take time and effort and connections to research, talk to the owners, figure out a payment, etc. So in the beginning, you could just start with Facebook ads.

I've done **Sponsored Posts in Facebook groups** with a few different groups for my paid products. Once you have contributed to the group and earned the group's / admin's trust and respect, you can approach the Facebook admin, offer them a free copy of your product or service, make them an affiliate, and ask if they would recommend your product with a sponsored post linking to their affiliate link for your product. So that way, you can pay them commissions on any resulting sales from the group. A membership plugin like DAP comes with a built-in affiliate module that you can use to recruit affiliates and create accounts for them, set affiliate commissions for different products, and so on. And you can also offer the Facebook admin additional commissions compared to other regular affiliates – and be sure to let them know that as well. So between creating a good relationship, earning their trust and respect, offering them a free copy, and also offering a good commission on any potential sales, you can get many Facebook admins to work with you on figuring out some offer that they're willing to put their name behind.

This can happen when you get your lead magnet right, your audience right, and your offer right.

You get a whole bunch of email sign-ups in a short amount of time.

Of course, building a list of emails is only the beginning. You will still have to nurture your list, send them great content that is of great value to them, and only then will they stay on your list.

Once you figure that part out, that's when you can promote other things like your podcast, your latest (related and relevant) paid and free offers, and convert them into your true fans (see chapter "Jab Hook, Jab Hook, Jab Hook".

And the image below is a screenshot of just one of over 50 such pages of notifications. And this didn't happen because I told people to sign-up for an email list just so I can send them "updates about my podcast". No - this happened because of a Killer Lead Magnet, promoted to the right audience.

AWeber Notifications	@yahoo.com) was added to "PodcastPromotionReport FREE"	12:52 AM
AWeber Notifications	@outlook.com) was added to "PodcastPromotionReport FREE"	1:38 AM
AWeber Notifications	o "PodcastPromotionReport FREE"	2:31 AM
AWeber Notifications	d to "PoccastPromotionReport FREE"	2:46 AM
AWeber Notifications	to "Podcast Promotion Report - Free"	2:54 AM
AWeber Notifications	ed to "PodcastPromotionReport FREE"	3:16 AM
AWeber Notifications	d to "PodcastPromotionReport FREE"	3:23 AM
AWeber Notifications	castPromotionReport FREE"	3:35 AM
AWeber Notifications	stPromotionReport FREE"	3:39 AM
AWeber Notifications	tPromotionReport FREE"	3:40 AM
AWeber Notifications	"PodcastPromotionReport FREE"	3:47 AM
AWeber Notifications	"PodcastPromotionReport FREE"	3:56 AM
AWeber Notifications	stPromotionReport FREE"	4:07 AM
AWeber Notifications	PromotionReport FREE"	4:08 AM
AWeber Notifications	ded to "PodcastPromotionReport FREE"	4:36 AM
AWeber Notifications	PodcastPromotionReport FREE"	4:39 AM
AWeber Notifications	ided to "PodcastPromotionReport FREE"	5:19 AM
AWeber Notifications	to "PodcastPromotionReport FREE"	5:31 AM
AWeber Notifications	PodcastPromotionReport FREE"	5:43 AM
AWeber Notifications	d to "PodcastPromotionReport FREE"	6:06 AM
AWeber Notifications	omotionReport FREE"	6:08 AM
AWeber Notifications	"PodcastPromotionReport FREE"	6:55 AM
AWeber Notifications	dcastPromotionReport FREE"	7:03 AM
AWeber Notifications	o "PodcastPromotionReport FREE"	7:05 AM
AWeber Notifications	"PodcastPromotionReport FREE"	7:18 AM
AWeber Notifications	d to "PodcastPromotionReport FREE"	8:41 AM
AWeber Notifications	ed to "PodcastPromotionReport FREE"	8:52 AM
AWeber Notifications	astPromotionReport FREE"	8:57 AM
AWeber Notifications	d to "PodcastPromotionReport FREE"	9:02 AM
AWeber Notifications	to "PodcastPromotionReport FREE"	9:10 AM
AWeber Notifications	lcastPromotionReport FREE"	9:28 AM
AWeber Notifications	added to "PodcastPromotionReport FREE"	9:33 AM
AWeber Notifications	o "PodcastPromotionReport FREE"	10:16 AM
AWeber Notifications	ocastPromotionReport FREE"	10:41 AM

Krush it With Kindle

It should be ILLEGAL to so easily publish a book and become an author, using just FREE tools (everything below is free).

* Brainstorming ideas and your Table of Contents: XMind Mindmapping software

* Composing & Editing: MS Word, Google Docs, Open Office

* Grammar & Improving Copy: Grammarly

* Cover image: Canva, Gimp, Photopea (web-based)

* Kindle converter or 7-zip

* Stock photos: Pexels, Pixabay

* Print Paperback: KDP

* My Kindle book "Krush it With Kindle: The Abso-Frickin-Lutely Fastest way To Plan, Write & Publish a Kindle Book" - also free at OneDayOneTime.com for a limited time.

End-to-end, you can now write, publish and launch a real book, for free.

There are simply no more excuses left - at least when it comes to tools, tech, or training - for NOT writing a book.

You can even create a Kindle book using your existing content, like blog posts, Twitter threads, cleaned-up transcriptions of your Podcast episodes and YouTube videos, etc.

Create fantastic reports, and give them away for free. But **publish them as a Kindle book first**.

Don't get too hung up about actually making sales from your Kindle book. Yes, making some money is important too. But that is not your primary focus here because you're going to be using it to build your email list.

Offer your Kindle eBook to them for free (as a PDF). A real, paid Kindle eBook with a few good reviews will vastly increase the perceived value of your "Report".

So, publish it on Kindle primarily to establish a tangible value for your report. Try to get 10-20 reviews, and then give it away for free.

And wherever you promote this – on your website, podcast, YouTube channel, Twitter feed - be sure to let your audience know that what you're giving away is an actual, real, paid Kindle book that is selling for $X, and has Y reviews, and maybe even highlight a few.

For most regular folks just getting started and don't have an existing audience, you can reap way greater benefits in the long run by giving away your eBooks and reports in exchange for their email than you ever will just selling them on Kindle.

Publish a few paid Kindle eBooks that you can use as a bonus – for joining your list, for sending you an email, for sharing your podcast or YouTube channel on Facebook or Twitter, etc. Revisit your past content – podcast episodes, blog posts, social media posts, etc. Then create short reports or eBooks from those. It doesn't even have to be very long. A well-written 30-50 page eBook is good enough as long as it helps the reader accomplish at least one thing really well.

Give those these "Kindle eBooks" (PDF, basically) in Facebook groups (get permission first), including groups that you are the admin of, run ads against them, and build an email list.

Make sure you use scarcity and urgency by mentioning that they can get your free report *only* if they take action within the next (say) 3 days. Don't keep it open indefinitely. You can always bring that free bonus back again a while later, but don't leave anything out there indefinitely.

It's fine if they're a day or two late in emailing you asking for the bonus. But if they're more than a few days late, then just thank them for emailing you, apologize that the offer has expired, and let them know that if they keep listening, you will be offering that and more soon. You have to make them honor your offer to some extent. Otherwise, they won't respect your deadlines in the future.

Of course, the key to it is that you create *remarkable reports*, even if they're only a few pages long. They don't even have to be published on Kindle. They just have to offer some form of instant gratification - a powerful benefit or take-away - something they can implement quickly and get some results fast.

How to Lose Friends and Influence Nobody

Add value to others. I was a big fan of a certain podcast. And then I saw that he was speaking at a conference that I was attending. So I walked up to him before his talk and thanked him for making a great show by mentioning very specific things from his show.

I was later having dinner at a local restaurant, and he walked in with a friend. After dinner, I made sure to stop by his table and gave him a few small tips and some feedback about how he can improve his show. One thing I mentioned was how at the end of the show, he was asking his audience to leave ratings and reviews for his show on iTunes (before it was changed to Apple Podcasts). I told him that a better call to action would be to give out his email and ask his audience to email him if they had any questions, comments, or suggestions, and to give away something and build a list.

A few weeks later, at the end of his next episode, he did exactly what I had suggested, and even mentioned me by name and thanked me for it. After that, we exchanged a few emails, found out he lives just a few miles away from me in San Diego, and ended up having breakfast one time. And we almost did a big project together, which would've made us both a good chunk of change, but it fell through due to other external reasons.

My point is that relationships are everything. And you can't fake interest in people. People can sense it pretty quickly if you're being nice to them because you want something out of them.

And if you don't have the time to engage with everyone, at least do it for those who you're already following and getting value from.

And here are a few quick tips on how to lose friends (and customers) and influence nobody (aka, how to annoy strangers and make them unfriend/unfollow/ block you on social media), and then do the opposite ;-)

* Don't complain about your customers on social media. There is a Facebook group for podcast editors that I'm a part of (got an invite from a friend and joined thinking I might learn a thing or two). The amount of whining from the editors in the group about how their customers suck, how much they say "umm" and "aahs" and constantly criticizing the very podcasters who are paying them money, is such a huge turn off for me. And with my half-baked Indian-Canadian-American accent, I shudder to think what these people will be talking about me behind my back if I were to hire one of them to edit my podcast.

So I won't be hiring a single person from that group – like, ever.

* Before you respond to harsh criticism and trolling about you or your company, take a deep breath, give it a few hours, and then try to have someone else from your company respond, or at least write the response for you. If you're the owner of a company and a person trashes you unfairly for no reason on social media, even if they cross the line in their criticism, you can never cross the line, or even approach the line, in your response. Because doesn't matter if you're a solopreneur and a one-person business – when your "business" goes against an individual on social medial, the narrative always becomes "evil business vs. poor customer", and the individual will always win – no matter how unfair it is, or if every one of their accusations is false and their language and tone completely crosses the line.

Always type your response – whether it's to a post on social media or an email – in a text file. Save it. Sleep on it. The next day, trash it and write a completely new, calm, and collected response that does not try to get back at the troll or nasty customers.

* Don't message strangers and simply just say "Hi" and stop there, or "How can I help". You are a total stranger to them – how can they possibly know how you can help them when they probably don't even know your name or what you do? And even if they did, why would they want the help of a stranger? And no one is going to be volunteering a list of all of their business needs so you can pick and choose which ones you can do.

* As soon as you connect with someone, don't DM/PM them your bio, or a link to your website, your lead magnet or make them an offer. Give before you ask.

* Don't complain about your life constantly. It is a big downer especially when people already have enough stress in their lives with the pandemic, their mental health, with bills and possibly declining revenues, and with the health and well-being of their loved ones.

* Don't give out affiliate links every single time you make a simple recommendation to someone about a product or service you use. Makes you look greedy, even if it's a perfectly fine thing to do.

* The fastest way to lose friends, acquaintances, customers, and future customers is to post divisive or harsh content about politics or religion. And sometimes even sports. The world is not black and white – it's a lot of grays when it comes to any topic. So unless politics and religion are part of your core brand, try to stay away from it and keep those two personal. Because no matter what your political views are, about half of your audience will have a different view from you. And in today's heavily partisan climate, you don't want to lose half of your audience because you can't stay away from making political or religious statements.

* On the flip side, be unapologetic about posting about your true passions. Your family and real friends will not un-friend you just because you post too much about what you're truly passionate about - could be podcasting, YouTubing, blogging, vlogging, NFT's, crypto, etc.

An Entrepreneur's Worst Nightmares

The thought of losing your business overnight due to some crazy sequence of external events – like a pandemic, or an earthquake, or because you (or someone from your company) said or did something on social which got you canceled – is an entrepreneur's biggest nightmares.

But what's even worse: Losing your business to a partner, employee, or freelancer - because of a lazy, careless or ignorant mistake.

In my 25 years of doing business offline and online, I've personally seen people lose their business, or take a big hit financially in regaining control of their business for many reasons: a disgruntled ex-employee hijacking the domain name, YouTube account, iTunes, or Apple account, or web hosting account - thus losing access to their domain, YouTube channel, podcast, or server (which they couldn't get back control of because hosting fees had been paid by the ex-employee or freelancer), and so on.

And even if they could eventually get back control of these assets, it might be after a long-drawn court case and several thousands of dollars in legal fees and anxiety-riddled sleepless nights, and usually a heavy hit in their business due to lost revenue.

For the average solopreneur or small-business owner like you and me, we just have to be a lot more cautious, and an extra dose of paranoia is not necessarily a bad thing these days.

So here are the top things you should *never* let anyone else control when it comes to your business:

- Publishing Mobile Apps, Kindle books, YouTube content, Podcasts, and digital products through someone else's Apple, Amazon, or Google account
- Hosting digital media under someone else's AWS account
- Registering your domain names under someone else's domain registrar account
- Buying mission-critical software, services, and plugins in someone else's name or credit card
- Signing up for online services using someone else's credit card
- Hosting accounts under someone else's credit card or an agency's account
- Unrestricted access to company credit card
- Signing authority to buy assets on your behalf
- Allowing one or two employees to hoard all of the intellectual property, business processes, or contacts. Knowledge sharing is critical. And every employee/freelancer/partner must be made to document their work and processes and partnerships.

There's probably more, but you get the idea.

Every time you ask a freelancer or employee to sign up for something on behalf of your company, just pause for a minute and ask yourself: If that person disappeared tomorrow with the account and all of the information and assets created and stored under that account, will it affect your business?

And usually, the answer is a yes for almost everything.

And even if they need to work with a service daily, you sign up for it with your or your business card, so that you're the one paying for it. And create a company domain-based email for all of your employees and contractors to use in all business transactions, so that it is not tied to their personal Gmail or Yahoo id. And that means you can back up and archive email communications.

Write Clickbaity Titles

> **Roberto Blake...** ✔ · 10h ···
> That video that was dying until I changed the title?
>
> It's almost to 40,000 views now after getting only 4,000 in the first day, and is now getting 1000-2000 new views a day and has already earned $600 in ad revenue so far...
>
> Because I changed the title...

Twitter.com/robertoblake/status/1434910069267865602

The idea of Clickbait itself isn't necessarily bad. Sure, it becomes suspect when you use the word "bait" – as if you're trying to falsely get someone to do something. And when someone takes the bait, what follows is usually something unpleasant.

But the overall idea of clickbait is just wanting someone to click on your content – like wanting to get someone to open your email, read your Twitter thread, Facebook post, or blog post – and that's not a bad thing.

However, the darker side of clickbait is when there's a bait-and-switch, where the title promises one thing, and you end up reading/listening/watching the whole content piece, only to find out that there was nothing (or close to nothing) in the content related to the title - and that the whole thing was just a way to get you to visit a page or watch a video just so the publisher can make a few cents off of showing you an ad.

Unfortunately, there are a lot of social media content creators who use clickbait for the wrong reasons, and we tend to only notice those because those are the ones that get popular.

But we don't talk enough about the great work done by marketers and writers in writing terrific curiosity-inducing email subject lines, article headlines, YouTube & Podcast titles.

In the chapter "I Came Home and the Dog Was Bald", I wrote about the story of how Roy H. Williams (Wizard of Ads) came up with that sentence at one of his seminars.

Many years ago, I used that same title as the subject line of an email I sent to my email subscribers, which set the record for the email with the highest ever open-rate and click-through rate that I've ever sent to my lists over the years. The record was broken recently by another email – which was a copy of the original email I sent my list years earlier (your list can change a lot over several years and it's ok to bring out a re-run on occasion).

Curiosity, shock, excitement, bewilderment, emotion – they all work when used in the right doses. But sensationalism for the sake of sensationalism alone, won't work. Make sure that the pay-off in the content consumed is so good that it ties it all back to your title.

Otherwise, you'll leave people with a really bad taste in their mouths about your content, your brand, and even about you. And while you might make a quick buck off of that in the short run, in the long term, it is going to seriously hurt your reputation and your ability to build relationships, grow your audience and make more sales.

So use clickbait the right way – great title, leading to great content, with a great payoff.

Everyone Should Learn Marketing (Even If You're Not A "Marketer")

Imagine you're in a book store and you pick up a book whose cover or title intrigued you. You flip it open to the table of contents to get an idea about what's in the book, so you can decide whether or not to buy it. And you see this...

TABLE OF CONTENTS

* Chapter 1 My Awesome Book: Welcome to Chapter 1. In this chapter, Ravi writes...

* Chapter 2 My Awesome Book: Welcome to Chapter 2. In this chapter, Ravi writes...

* Chapter 3 My Awesome Book: Welcome to Chapter 3. In this chapter, Ravi writes...

If people won't do this to their book, why would they do it to their podcast? (see image below)

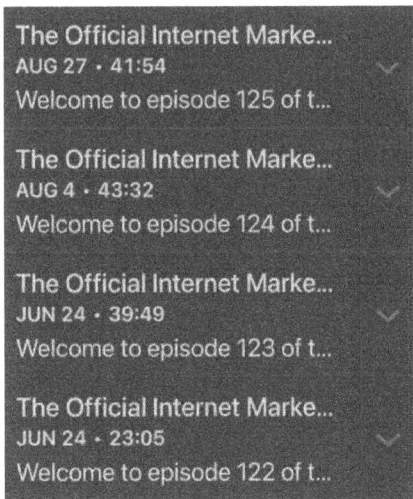

P.S. The above image is a screenshot of the details page of a real podcast.

Probably because they're not aware of how it looks to a potential subscriber, or they didn't know to even look, to begin with, leave alone where to look. And that's usually due to a lack of awareness - and marketing skills.

Whether it is a podcast, YouTube channel, or a blog, one additional skill we need to develop as content creators (in addition to our primary skill) is Marketing.

A big part of marketing is Copywriting, and a critical part of copywriting is coming up with great blog post titles, Podcast episode titles, Email subject lines, YouTube video titles, Book titles, etc. - which is key to getting people to click and check out our content. Without that first click that draws them to your content, nothing else will happen.

Another part of marketing is going one step further and investigating the full user experience ahead of time and making sure it's fully optimized for your audience so that you're not losing your audience or making it hard for them to check out or consume your content.

For a podcast, that would be something like subscribing to your feed in different apps, seeing what a potential subscriber would see in the apps or various podcast directories, what the artwork looks like - not just on a large screen monitor but as a 75x75 size thumbnail on a phone, what happens when they visit your website, can they see your podcast feed player above the fold, can they get to any episode in one click without having to jump around to different posts on your website, etc.

So the next time you click on something – podcast episode, YouTube video, news article, social media post, etc - try to make a note of what made you click.

And learn marketing regardless of your expertise, niche, or skills.

Outbox Marketing

This is the lowest hanging fruit when it comes to getting started with promoting your products: Anyone and everyone you've ever communicated via email –acquaintances, friends, family, business contacts – basically anyone you've ever exchanged an email with.

There will be some exceptions based on your judgment - like someone you've had an unpleasant exchange with, or someone who never replied to you even after multiple emails, or your grandparents, etc. Ignore those.

To everyone else, reply to the last email *you* sent *them*. That means going to your "Sent" folder, and replying to your response.

Keep the same subject line as the original email (your email client will probably add a "Re: …" to the original subject). Do not change it. Replying to the original email and keeping the subject intact will preserve your email thread with them, and they'll know that this is a personal email that you sent manually and not an automated email broadcast that you're sending to a list. Write something like this:

****

"Hey <firstname>,

Long time, no hear! :-)

The last time I sent you an email, I was living in New York and you were working on your website. I hope it's going well.

I wanted to quickly let you know that I've recently launched a free podcast called "SubscribeMe".

I'm planning to have a Q&A segment where I'll be answering questions from my listeners.

The podcast is about Digital Marketing, creating Membership Sites and Online Courses, how to Create, Sell and Deliver Digital Content, Content Marketing, Creating Audio, Video and PDF's and Reports and Kindle books, at https://SubscribeMe.fm.

Or you can also search for "SubscribeMe.fm" as one word, in your favorite podcast app – like Apple Podcasts, Overcast, and even Spotify.

If you have any questions regarding any of the topics above, I would love to answer them on my show. I'm happy to mention your name and website when answering your question.

I also frequently give away my paid content via my podcast. Like in the latest episode, I gave away a free copy of my Kindle book Krush it With Kindle: The Abso-Frickin-Lutely Fastest way To Plan, Write & Publish a Kindle Book to anyone who emailed me a special code within 3 days of it going live.

I'm planning to do more such awesome giveaways, so please subscribe when you get a chance (all subscription links available at SubscribeMe.fm)

I hope you're doing well. Let me know if there's anything else I can help you with.

Cheers!

- Ravi Jayagopal
Freshly Minted Podcaster at https://SubscribeMe.fm

****

So the main takeaways:

- Keep the body and subject intact and actually "Reply" to the last email you sent them

- Personalize it by mentioning something related to your last exchange ("The last time I sent you an email, I was living in New York")
- Ask yourself What's In It For Them (WIIFT) (Yeah, I changed WIIFM to WIIFT). In my example above, that is me saying "Ask me any questions you have and I'll answer them for you and give you a shout-out".
- Also give them a link to your website so that they can listen to it on your website (if you're using a feed player on the home page like I am, at SubscribeMe.fm) and you also have links to subscribe through a whole bunch of platforms on that page.

Be Your Own Sponsor

If you promote an affiliate link or promote a sponsored ad via an ad read, you are sending traffic to somebody else's website. The vendor gets to cookie them for retargeting. They get to convert them into a customer. They get to ask for the visitor's email id by offering a lead magnet, they get to keep most of the profits. Sure, you get paid a little too.

You could probably make more money on a PER-listener basis if you promote an affiliate that results in a sale. But with a sponsorship, you get guaranteed money upfront, regardless of whether it leads to a sale or not. But either way, you don't own the customer. You don't own the relationship for the long term. It is the vendor, to whom you sent your listener, the one who gets to enjoy the relationship and the profits.

Why not do that yourself?
Why not be your own sponsor?
Why not promote your own products and services?

If you promote an ad on a podcast, you get paid just once. DOGPOO. You did that episode once, you got paid once. That's it. You are never getting paid a dime more for that podcast. Sure, the advertiser might sponsor another show. But still, you cannot get paid for what was already done. That's DOGPOO. Do once, get paid only once.

But if you promote your own products and services, you get a customer now, and could keep selling that customer one-time products and recurring subscription-based products, over and over again, for life! Now, that is the perfect example of DOSAA. Do once, sell again and again.

Every product or service you create is an asset for life. And every customer you convert is also an asset for life.

The Best Social Platform

It's the one where most of your target audience is.

It's the one where you get the most engagement.

It's also the one that helps you convert the most (whatever is the end-goal of the conversion, doesn't always mean just a purchase).

If your target audience is kids, they're probably not on Facebook or Twitter.

If they are Baby Boomers or Gen Xers, they're probably not on Snapchat.

"Probably not on" is a tricky phrase. You could make a reasonable guess about that based on general psychographics.

But there's only one way to know for sure: Post content there - high quality with decent quantity – with good consistency, and see what works.

When it comes to building an audience, you have to throw things on the wall and see what sticks. And you have to throw stuff on *all* the walls, not just one.

Email, Twitter, TikTok, Facebook, LinkedIn, Podcasting, YouTube, Blog, etc.

That's where repurposing is extremely powerful, so you can "Do Once, Publish Everywhere".

3 Must-Have Superpowers

3 easy-to-learn-and-master skills that can become your superpowers:

1. Typing
2. Googling
3. Automating Typing

1. Typing

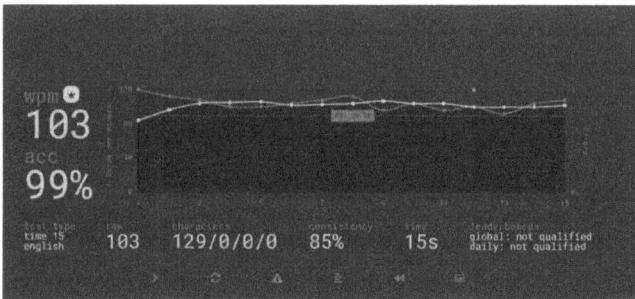

This is a screenshot of one of my typing test results from MonkeyType.com. 103 words per minute (wpm) with 99% accuracy. It's decent, considering my 17-year-old types at 180 wpm.

That's because I taught him how to type when he was 6.

Typing skills matter. When you can type without looking at the keyboard, it's almost like you can now start brain-dumping your thoughts onto the screen at the speed of thought. Ok, not literally, but close enough – you get the idea.

Learning to type will make it so easy to create content fast. Some of the best content starts with written words. It is so easy to repurpose written words – a "script" if you will – into other forms of media. I have written more about this in another chapter titled "Put Your Pen Down, Script It and Rehearse It".

With the amount of content you have to create these days – sending emails, blog posts, podcasts, videos, Kindle books, lead magnets, social posts, Tweets – there's so much relying on your ability to type.

The slower you type, the slower everything becomes. Simply by speeding up the one thing you're doing all day, every day – typing on a keyboard – you can save an unfathomable amount of time and frustration over the long run, think faster, and be in a better flow as you're creating content because your typing skills are not impeding your thought process, and you're not constantly hunched over the keyboard because you have to constantly keep looking at your keyboard to see where the letters are.

So learn typing – like, today. There are amazing free and practically free resources to do this, like TypingClub.com and Typing.com.

And to know where you stand, start with a free typing test at MonkeyType.com.

2. Googling & Searching

Knowing how to Google is like putting your research capabilities on steroids.

With the insane amount of content you have to generate today (like I mentioned in the last section – from blog posts to emails to social posts to scripts for your podcasts, and videos – you have to make sure that what you're talking about is valid, true and accurate. You don't want to be misquoting people, or misrepresenting numbers, or spreading rumors, or propagating untruths. Bad or poor information can not only hurt others because they're now learning the wrong thing and relying on bad information to make their decisions, but it can also make you look unprofessional and unreliable because you couldn't be bothered to do basic research before advising or teaching others, even more so if you are positioning yourself as an expert in your niche.

So to be able to quickly research your ideas, whether it is to get more data, or find out the source of a quote or a news article, is critical.

There is an ocean of tutorials out there on how to Google, but here are some of the ones that I use regularly that have helped tremendously speed up my research.

Dogpoo site:SubscribeMe.fm

To search a specific website. Will bring you results for that keyword only from that website. Very useful to search your website at times, might even be faster than using your own website's search form. Very useful to search a specific site, like Reddit, for specific topics so you can add to the conversation if possible.

You can also use the "-" (minus) sign before the word "site" to exclude a domain from Search.

"cart racing videos"

Putting quotes around the keywords will show you pages that have those words in that exact order. Without quotes, you'll get way too many results that may just have one or more of those words somewhere on the page and not necessarily together.

"marketing course" +free

You want "marketing course" to be together, and must also include the word "free".

"marketing course" -free

Same query, but it should not have the word "free".

"seth godin" filetype:pdf

You want to look for PDF files that have the words "Seth Godin" together. Warning: You might get shady websites that are probably illegally storing a premium PDF. But for the most part, this is a great query to search for PDFs by specific people, especially if you are researching specialized reports on specific topics or from specific authors.

dogpoo @twitter.com

Brings back results from Twitter showing accounts with "Dogpoo" in the username, as well as tweets using it in a hashtag.

LeBron James twitter

Search for a person's or brand's twitter handle – better results faster than doing the same on Twitter.

#throwbackthursday garyvee

To search for all of Gary Vaynerchuk's posts with that hashtag across all social platforms.

camera $50..$100

Search for a keyword within a range of numbers with two dots.

How to search Google for articles written during a certain year range.

Go to google.com, enter your search term, and search first. Then click on the 'News' tab. Click on 'Tools'. Click on the "Recent" drop-down and you can change that and select a specific date range.

related:asana.com

Search for related sites. The above query will show you websites of similar tools, like Trello, Basecamp, etc.

The website Alternativeto.net is also a great resource for finding similar products or services.

Other Searching Tips

Facebook and Twitter have great search features as well, which will make finding people and discussion threads so much more powerful.

And that will help you follow people who are putting out the best content that you can learn from, get ideas for creating content, follow trends, as well as get involved in any interesting discussions to build authority as well as relationships.

3. Automating Typing using Text Shortcuts

For Windows users like me, I use and recommend AutoHotKey.com. My personal AHK shortcut file contains thousands of shortcuts, everything from my email (which is why I never make a typo when entering my email in any form) to my address to support response texts and email bodies, and email signatures.

macOS has a text shortcut tool built-in at System Preferences > Keyboard > Text. You can also use something like TextExpander for Mac.

Here are some of my favorite shortcuts I use all the time.

If I type in "rd" and hit space, it will expand into Ravi@DigitalAccessPass.com.

- "ra" becomes Ravi
- "ja" becomes Jayagopal

- "addy" expands into my full name on one line, home address on next, city, state zip on the third line.
- "smh": https://SubscribeMe.fm (sm for subscribeme, h to indicate it's a link – so all of my link shortcuts end with an "h"
- daph: https://DigitalAccessPass.com
- oneh: https://OneDayOneTime.com
- "luk" becomes "Please let us know if you have any further questions."

- All of my email signatures end with an "s". So for emails I send regarding my plugin S3MediaVault, my shortcut is "s3s" (as in s3 signature), and it expands into this:

  - Ravi Jayagopal
  https://S3MediaVault.com

  My Podcast about Digital Marketing, Membership Sites & Online Courses
  https://SubscribeMe.fm/

  Who is Ravi?
  https://SubscribeMe.fm/ravi-jayagopal

- My main email signature for all generic emails is "rrs"
  - Ravi Jayagopal
  My Podcast about Membership Sites & Online Courses
  https://SubscribeMe.fm/

  Author of 7 Books
  https://SubscribeMe.fm/ravisbooks

  Co-Founder, Membership Plugin & Platform for WordPress
  http://Digital-Access-Pass.com (DAP)

About Me:
https://SubscribeMe.fm/ravi-jayagopal

```
::ra::Ravi
::ja::Jayagopal
::rd::Ravi@DigitalAccessPass.com
::rs::Ravi@S3MediaVault.com
::dptit::Dogpoo & Dosaa: 67 Proven &
Implementable Truths, Tactics & Hacks To
Create Better Content, Promote Your
Products, Grow Your Audience and Make More
Sales
::dph::https://DogpooBook.com
::dps::
(
- Ravi Jayagopal
Check out my new book (8th)
Dogpoo & Dosaa at
https://DogpooBook.com

67 Proven & Implementable
Truths, Tactics & Hacks
To Create Better Content,
Promote Your Products,
Grow Your Audience and
Make More Sales
)
```

Here's a partial screenshot of my AutoHotkey file with all the shortcuts. I currently have 13,128 lines in it. Some of them are multi-line shortcuts, like the "dps" above, which is a shortcut for "Dog Poo Signature" which I'll be using for a little while to promote this book in my emails.

I have entire support/customer service emails that will appear in my email by typing just a few letters. I have possibly saved hundreds, if not thousands, of hours of typing, that too given that I type at 100+ words per minute. So someone who types at a typical 30-40 wpm, will easily save about 3 times as me. And that's a lot of time saved.

And it all adds up over the years as you add email templates and canned responses. And it also cuts down on typos (I see my emails bouncing all the time because there was a typo in the email when someone filled out a contact-us form, and even in checkout forms, which is the worst, because they open a ticket saying and allows you to be a lot more creative, like attaching different signatures to your emails or support ticket responses based on the context.

E.g., when I've just launched a new website, or released a new Kindle book, or doing a launch, or have a new YouTube video, I will use a different signature when promoting the latest thing.

Or if it's related to a specific product or service, I will have links in my signature that promote a specific and related free lead magnet or podcast episode, etc.

Curate Your Feeds (Both Ways)

Aggressively unfriend, unfollow and unsubscribe from all content that is not serving you in any impactful way. Mute or Block as many people as you need to.

There will be times when someone goes through a personal crisis, like the death of a loved one, a pet, etc. And sometimes, during their process of mourning, every post of theirs will be such a sad post and might make you very emotional every time you read those. Don't feel like you are obligated to be a part of everyone else's sadness and anxiety and depression and mourning. We all have our own stuff to deal with, with our pets, loved ones, jobs, and such. No need to burden yourself with everyone else's problems. If you can help, do it, and then mute (on Twitter) and "Unfollow" on Facebook (without unfriending) to still be connected to them without seeing their content for a little bit.

You also shouldn't create an echo chamber filled with only those who think, speak, and act like you. You also need to be aware of other opinions and news from the other side. But when it comes to divisive topics like politics, unless your brand or content is political, you probably already know what the other side thinks. No need to let it aggravate you daily and affect your mental health. Mute/Unfollow anyone whose posts upset you because their views are extremely opposite from yours.

And before it gets to the point of having to think about quitting social media just to maintain your mental health, you may want to first try curating your feed aggressively and fill it with informative, positive, educational, and entertaining content.

If you feel like you need to take a break from a social platform, it's a sign that your feed needs a lot of work. Of course, if you still feel the need to get away from all of it for a bit, just go ahead and do it – it will all still be there when you get back.

Unsubscribe from any newsletters that are not providing immediate value for what you're trying to achieve right now – information overload can cause unnecessary anxiety and stress, because everything you're reading from others will make you feel like you're not doing enough, and that you need to do this, that and the other, and it will take you off-track.

Impostor Syndrome (and how to avoid it)

Per Wikipedia, "Impostor syndrome ... is a psychological pattern in which an individual doubts their skills, talents or accomplishments and has a persistent internalized fear of being exposed as a 'fraud'."

Here are some tips to help avoid being inflicted by that syndrome:

1. Know that you're a *huge* part of everything you've accomplished. Don't hesitate to take some well-deserved credit for every bit of hard-earned success.
2. Be thankful for your journey as well as for everyone else who has helped you along the way, whether it was positively or negatively.
3. Do not exaggerate your life, success, finances, situation, assets, or results.
4. Share and teach only what you've practiced, implemented, and executed yourself. Share only your own results - and what you know to be 100% true.
5. Always be your authentic self, and never show yourself as more than you are or different than you are.
6. If people aren't converting, then don't take it personally. Instead, revisit the other parts of your funnel – like your landing page, core offer, sales copy, pricing, branding, etc. Failure to Sell is not an indictment of your character, personality, or skills.

Fierce, Feverish & Focused

It's amazing when I look at my Facebook feed. So many people posting non-stop, like...

"Tell me how you feel with a GIF"
"What kind of ice cream do you like?"
"Guess which of these concerts that I did not attend?"
"Only a genius can solve this puzzle"
"Post the 8th most recent photo in your phone."
"Ruin a first-date in 4 words"

Ok, so you say it's "social media", so there's nothing wrong with being social, right?

But the line between "purely social" and "purely business" is as thin as it's ever been.

And like with every single decision you make in life, it comes down to your priorities.

You could spend a lot of time (and create a lot of likes and comments and "noise") by posting and participating in cute-and-clever-and-funny stuff about all kinds of the regular stuff. With TikTok, Reddit and Twitter, there is an infinite amount of that kind of content out there.

However, there's only one person who can create content that has your thoughts, ideas, personality, character, back-story, and unique twist on what you know.

So you can still be social, and also add value to your core audience at the same time. You could come up with some kind of a ratio – like say, 30/70 – where 30% of your posts could be cute-and-cuddly, family/dog/cat/beach/vacay pictures, but more importantly, 70% of your posts are something super-targeted and relevant to your target audience, your niche, your expertise, your podcast, your passions, your business, your blog and so on.

Of course, don't just keep pitching stuff all the time either. Fiercely and Focusedly (just made up the word) create content that creates a lot of value to your target audience. Always be thinking What's In It For Them (WIIFT).

Create unapologetically with your 1,000 true fans in mind.

If I asked every single one of your "friends" on Facebook what you do for a living and to name your podcast, product, or website, will they be able to?

Other than my friends and family and Facebook, I do not know what a majority of my Facebook friends do for a living, because I never really see them posting information valuable to their target audience. They're only posting cute-and-cuddly time-pass stuff All. The. Time. And that's fine if you're only using Facebook for "social" purposes. But something tells me that if you ask a lot of them why they're on social media, they will probably tell you it's for "networking" and "connecting" and "relationship building". Umm... OK! I don't think Ice cream questioners and GIF-askers and Joke-sayers have exactly been building a relationship with me, because other than that they're cute/cuddly/clever, I don't know who these people are, what they do for a living, what their core expertise is, what they're passionate about, and what are they good at – except for creating posts that just like-bait posts.

But if you asked those who follow me, most of them can tell you what my core niche is, what my expertise is, what I'm passionate about, and what I'm preaching and practicing - because I'm constantly creating value for my 1000 true fans.

Of course, I also post family pictures and cute-and-cuddly like-bait content, but I keep those to a minimum. Most of my content is just trying to educate or entertain my target audience – made up of those who wish to **make, market, and monetize online digital content with membership sites and online courses**. I always keep it relevant to the subjects that I'm trying to grow my audience in.

You might say that kind of stuff is not supposed to be on a FB personal profile and should be reserved for a Facebook "Page". But I would respectfully disagree because go look at your own "friends" on Facebook. How many "Pages" do you follow and interact with compared to "People"? Probably just a fraction.

Eventually, it comes down to your priorities. If building your 1000 true fans is the highest priority for you, and not just posting like-bait, then just embrace the fact that your "friends" on Facebook – other than your real friends and family – should eventually consist of those who are drawn to you because of what you stand for, what you post, your niche, your topic, your expertise, and your passion.

Digital Sharecropping

Sharecropping is a system of farming where a landowner allows a farmer or family to use the landowner's land, in return for a share of the crops produced.

Building your business on a third-party platform, where *they* own the platform, *they* control the sales, and then *they* pay *you* a portion of the profits, is generally referred to as Digital Sharecropping.

It can work in many industries and for many businesses. For eg., all of my books, including this one, are being sold on Amazon Kindle and will probably make the most sales on that platform (except this one, because I'm launching this one directly on my website with massive bonuses).

However, nothing is stopping me from selling this book on my own website or through other eBook platforms. And that is why my book sales will not get destroyed even if Amazon rejects or bans my book from being sold on their platform.

However, if you are building your membership business on a third-party platform, and something goes wrong with your account, or the platform itself shuts down or gets bought out by another company (that, say, absorbs the talent and IP and shuts the actual platform down), or there is a controversy about your products or services, then your account or website could get shut down and all of your content, your members, and their billing profiles – could all disappear overnight.

They may allow you to export your existing content (or you probably have a backup copy of it anyway), and probably also the contact information of your members. But it is practically impossible to transfer the recurring billing profiles of your paying members out of their system, and into your own system. Such a transfer would make the billing information – like credit card numbers, credit card security codes (CVV), customer names and addresses, etc - very insecure and highly susceptible to fraud or identity theft. So, most companies will not allow you to transfer the secure and private billing information out of their systems and into yours.

That means if you ever wish to leave the hosted platform and move to a different one, you will have to contact all of your monthly paying members and ask them to re-sign up again for a subscription. And when you do that, you could (and probably will) lose a majority of your current, paying members. Some of that could be just them evaluating whether they still need your membership, some of it due to the laziness of not wanting to move over and sign up again, and some of it due to sheer apathy. Either way, you risk losing a substantial portion of your recurring income overnight, simply by moving membership platforms, especially from third-party hosted platforms that store your members' billing information in their systems (like, say Udemy and Patreon).

That ought to make most course creators nervous about betting their future on a third-party platform. And that's why building your own self-hosted membership platform using WordPress and a membership plugin like DigitalAccessPass.com (DAP) (or equivalent), is a great idea for most people.

Here's why you should not use a 3rd party platform and marketplace like Udemy as your main course delivery platform (based on their policies at the time of writing this – please check their website for the latest):

1) They make the rules, and they decide how much you get to keep from every sale.

2) If they help you bring a new customer, you only get 50% of the sale. And on top of that, if there's a Udemy affiliate involved –

i.e., a Udemy affiliate referred your buyer to your course via their affiliate link - you could end up getting as little as 25% of the sale.

Imagine that: If you have a $100 course, you're getting a pathetic 25% of that, which is just $25.

3) Now you might think, "Ok, let me just use Udemy to bring in new customers and I'll slowly bring them over to my site and sell them other products in the future". Not a bad idea. They do get a ton of traffic. They sell millions of dollars worth of courses. You could get organic traffic to your course, which means more exposure to your brand and your course. And then you can bring them over to your site for future courses, right?

Not exactly.

You do get exposure to a new audience - people that you may never have been able to reach before. So it's a great additional tool for acquiring new leads and customers.

But here's the problem: You cannot promote your website as easily as you might imagine, because they have a lot of rules about that: You cannot start your videos introducing your web site; You cannot have your domain name flashing over the lower part of your videos; You cannot have a call to action in your main course videos that bring people back to your web site, etc.

From the research I've done, they frown upon this. You can only promote your website and your other online courses at the end of your course, from what they call a "Bonus" lesson. So if you have 10 videos in your course, the bonus lesson would be video #11. Now guess how many people get to the end of a course? Very few. I once heard Seth Godin talk about how he had launched a course on one such online course platform. And I think he said that less than 10% of the people completed his paid course - something they had paid actual money to buy!

He was puzzled by that, but that's something that we - as online marketers - have known for a while. People don't always consume the digital products that they purchase - not most of the time, and sometimes not for a while. I've done it too - I cannot even begin to tell you about the number of unopened DVDs and CDs I have in my storage room from years ago when big courses were sold on DVDs and CDs - stuff that I sometimes paid hundreds of dollars for.

My point is that if they don't get to the end of the course, then all you've accomplished is worked very hard to send Udemy a new customer, and you will probably just get as little as 25% of the sale.

You might be thinking, "Ok, I'll create a coupon code, generate traffic, and send my audience directly to my Udemy link, so that way I can keep 97% of the sale".

But if you're planning on doing the marketing, why send them to Udemy? Why not send them to your website? That's like me going to the mall to buy a pair of shoes that I see in the window, and they refuse to sell to me and instead ask me to go buy it on Amazon.

If you're going to spend money on ads, and spend time posting on Facebook and Twitter, then why not build that audience on your platform, to your domain? And get incoming links to your own website that will greatly help in long-term search engine optimization (SEO)?

So Udemy essentially doesn't want you to use them for the main reason why you would want to use them: to generate new leads and buyers and bring them over to your website in the long term.

4) Udemy has restrictions on what kind of emails you can send to your buyers. From what I've read, most of these marketplace platforms will not allow you to send your buyers emails with links

that lead back to your site. You cannot send out other offers of your own, or promote third-party products using affiliate links. Your access to your buyer's list is very restricted, and the email list that you build on such a platform cannot be downloaded, imported into another system, and it cannot be sold as part of your company if you end up selling your company. So this rented list is not a true asset for your business.

5) Instead of building your own business, you are essentially building *their* business. They are the ones getting a paying customer. They're just paying you a small commission for all practical purposes. They are the ones who can continue to market other courses from other sellers to your buyers – and they can keep doing this for life. They are building an asset off of your back. It's *their* lifetime customer value that keeps going up, not yours.

6) A lot of courses on Udemy are coupon-driven. Udemy frequently offers courses worth several hundred dollars, for $10. It seems like the "buy any course for just $10" promo happens once every few weeks. Of course, as a seller, you would need to opt-in for this promotion. You have to give Udemy permission to promote your $300 course for $10. And then they seem to practically spam the heck out of all their buyers – and those include your buyers too.

To be honest, I too have purchased a couple of courses on Udemy after they dropped from a few hundred dollars to just $10. And as a seller, it's tempting to opt into this promo, because you know Udemy is going to promote the heck out of these $10 courses, and you certainly don't want to be left out.

But if the course sells for $10, then you're probably going to get paid 1/2 of that because it's not your promotional effort - the $10 promo is their promotion. And you can't maximize the transaction by upselling your buyers, or adding them to your list and selling them other add-ons later.

Guess who gets to do all of that? Udemy, of course.

7) They don't allow you to sell recurring subscription products. Just one-time products.

My point is not about bashing Udemy, the company. Because I think they have a great platform and marketplace, and if we're to ever use a third-party marketplace, I would probably choose Udemy over other options.

I'm talking strictly about *not choosing* to build your membership site or online course on a third-party platform and marketplace. I'm telling you to stop renting and instead own your home.

You could take everything I said about Udemy and replace it with any of the tens of other course-creation platforms - like Ruzuku, Teachable, Skillshare, Digital Chalk, Mindbites, Mindflash, and WizIQ - and most of this would probably be true. I just used Udemy to make a point, because they're quite popular.

Let's flip the coin and see what's on the other side.

You can use Udemy and other such online course creation platforms as a marketing tool –repurpose some old content, old videos, and see if you can leverage that massive organic traffic that you can get from them. And you can try to fly under the radar and use bonus lessons and other legit tactics and try to get them over to your website.

If you have to tiptoe around too much, then I don't know if it's worth it. Because for all that time and effort, you would be better off creating maybe a podcast, or creating any number of courses within your own content library, where even if you sell it for as little as $5, at least you get to keep the entire $5. Plus most importantly, you own the buyer, and their payment profile is in your payment system (like Stripe or PayPal). And if you use a membership plugin like DigitalAccessPass.com (DAP), then you can automatically give each new member an affiliate link right in the welcome email, that they can use to promote your membership, products, and services. Every new member automatically becomes your affiliate, they promote you, which brings in more traffic, some of who will sign up, then each one of those new buyers now becomes an affiliate and they bring in more members, and so on.

That is a great marketing opportunity to use an affiliate program. And you can use all of that to build *your* business and not someone else's business.

So, to summarize…

* Marketplaces like Udemy are great if you're just getting started, don't have an established name or brand. And you're trying to build a name for yourself. And you want maximum exposure for your brand. In that case, create a free course. Also, create a more expensive course that costs like $100 - $300. And then participate in all of their promotions, because at this point, when you're just getting started, making money alone should not be your goal. Your goal should be to get your name and your brand out there in front of as many people as you can.

* Getting that kind of exposure will help you get noticed and build authority. If your course gets thousands of students to sign up, you can leverage those numbers into becoming a mini-celebrity in your niche. Having 1,000+ students on Udemy with high ratings is a great testimonial by itself of your high-quality content. You can use that to build your brand further: Be a guest on podcasts, write a book about how you created it, create an online course about how you did all of this, use that to help others with their marketing, and so on.

So if you don't have your website, then marketplaces like Udemy can be a great starting point to go where there's already traffic, and create your presence. Just like renting a store at the mall, where there are already so many buyers. Like selling on Amazon. Like submitting your podcast to Apple Podcasts, Spotify, and other podcast directories. Like writing a blog post on Medium.com, rather than on your blog.

To leverage a large, built-in audience, Udemy and other marketplaces can be highly valuable. But you have to know where to draw the line when it comes to renting vs. owning. And unless you can bring them all back to your website and onto your own platform, it's very hard to have a successful, long-term business. And you'll be stuck selling one-time products because many of these platforms don't allow recurring subscriptions.

So remember, out of the 3 ways to host your membership site...

1) A Self-Hosted WordPress Site

2) A fully-hosted third-party membership platform

3) A third-party marketplace like Skillshare and Udemy

The absolute best option is to have a WordPress-based site running on your hosting account, running a membership plugin like DAP (there are others like Members, Paid Memberships Pro, Access Ally, etc), where you own and have full control over your content, your members, your affiliates, your emails, and the payments - basically all of it.

And *that* is how you build a successful, long-term profitable online business.

A Tale of Two Timers: A Simple Productivity Hack

Here's a simple hack to keep you focused on your writing (or whatever it is that you're creating, like videos or blogging).

1. Set up a cool-looking visual "Count Up" timer that tracks your overall progress. Every time you start writing, start the timer and turn it off as soon as you're done. I use the "MultiTimer" iOS app.

It's an actual screenshot from when I was writing this very book.

2. Now whenever you're ready to work on your book, start a regular timer on your phone - like a 10- or 20-minute "Count Down" timer. You can do this by saying "<voice assistant>, set a timer for 10 minutes". I prefer at least 20 minutes because when you start a new task, it always takes a few minutes just to settle in and then a few more to gain some momentum. So if that takes 4 minutes, I wouldn't want to lose that momentum after just another 6 minutes. I want to keep it going for at least another 15.

This second timer is to get you to stay focused and keep writing for that specified period.

Here's how these two timers help:

Timer #1 (Count Up) will help you keep track of how much time you've spent working on your book, and will give you tangible visual feedback and a sense of satisfaction, and maybe even a sense of urgency, every time you look at the timer and see how many hours you've already spent.

Now, MS Word has a way to track the editing time of your document. In my old version, on the actual file on your computer, do a Right-click > Properties > Details, and see "Total Editing Time". In newer versions of Word, click the Office button, hover over "Prepare", click properties > document properties > advanced properties > statistics, and look for "total editing time."

In Google Docs, click on the "all changes saved in drive" to see a full revision history with times.

This number accurately tracks the actual document editing time. However, it can't track the non-editing time that goes into your book – like, research time, Google searches, watching videos or reading documents & blog posts, creating images, finding data, searching through your own content trove of podcasts/blog posts/emails/social posts to find the content you can use that you've already created before, etc.

A timer like this tracks all of that, and it's more visually monitorable in real-time and really cool for posting screenshots on social media to both show your progress as well as for self-accountability.

Timer #2 (Count Down) is just to keep you focused on one thing and one thing only, for a short period. It's amazing how we can trick our minds to really lock in when there's a clock ticking. A deadline plus some pressure works wonders for getting things done.

And since it's a short timer, you don't have to worry about whether you can sustain it, and you get to look forward to it being over rather quickly, plus the sense of accomplishment and satisfaction of having crushed it for that short period, and you got stuff done!

This Two-Timer Technique is way simpler and easy to imagine, implement and execute on, compared to the more complex ones like the Pomodoro technique.

And I always like to keep it simple ☺

SAL and JOMO

One of the reasons some of us tend to spend too much time on social media checking out every link to every piece of content that seems interesting is because there is an inherent Fear of Missing Out (FOMO) on great content if we don't read it right it or watch it right away.

We also get distracted and start working on a side-project else while in the middle of working on the main project, because of FOMO – as if we'll lose the idea or the thought if we don't immediately work on it.

Instead, **SA**ve for **L**ater (SAL) and keep it moving.

This way, there's no more FOMO – there's only JOMO (Joy of Missing Out).

Facebook

You can bookmark posts on Facebook. And you can even add them to a list. I've created several lists like "To Answer" (for posts that I want to come back to and respond), "Ideas" (product ideas, content ideas, etc), "For Podcast" (things that I would want to do a deep-dive on my podcast), "For Blog" (ideas for my blog), "Ravi Saved" (whenever I write a long post in a Facebook group so that I can quickly refer back to it later), etc.

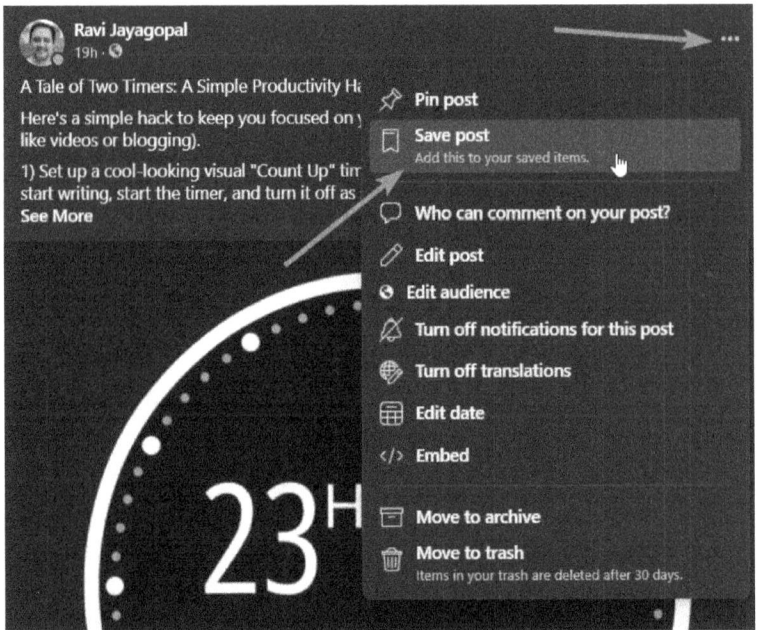

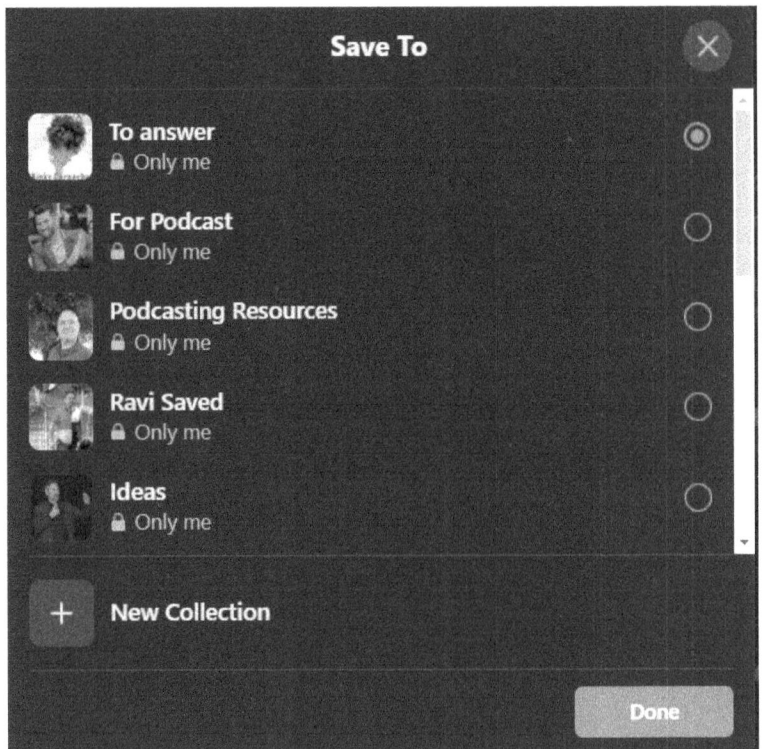

Twitter: "Add to Bookmarks" (I wish they would add lists)

Online article: Add to Instapaper, Pocket, etc (they have browser extensions that make it super-easy). [I loved using love Del.icio.us ("delicious") until they became obsolete.]

Ideas: Never lose an idea or a thought that comes into your head. You can do this by quickly adding it to a list app like Microsoft To-Do (formerly WunderList). You can vet the idea later, just don't lose it.

YouTube: Click on the "Save" icon, then you can add it to your custom list.

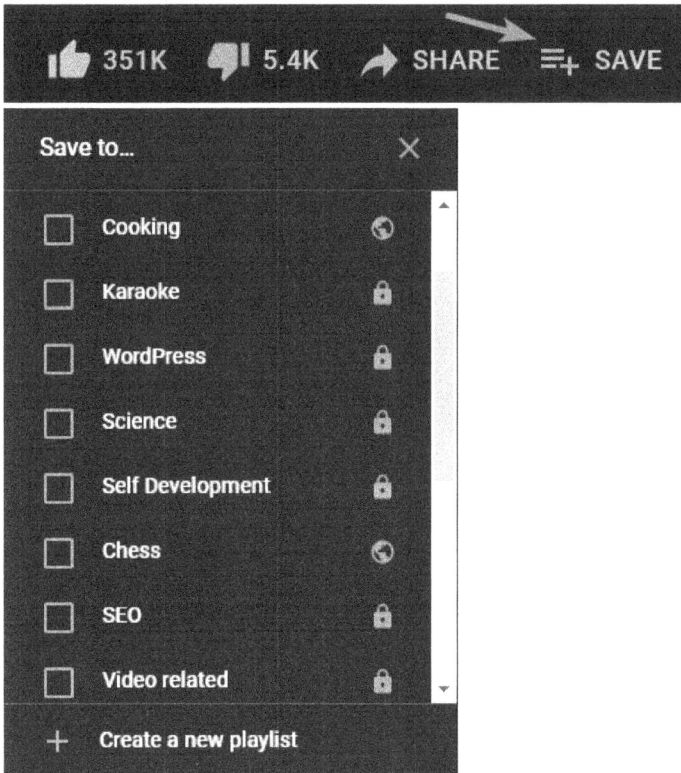

Create Product Images Even for Digital Products

Whether it's an eBook, report, or software, it's not a bad idea to create a product image, because an image turns an intangible digital product into a tangible, visual representation.

Here are some of the product images I've created over the years, for inspiration.

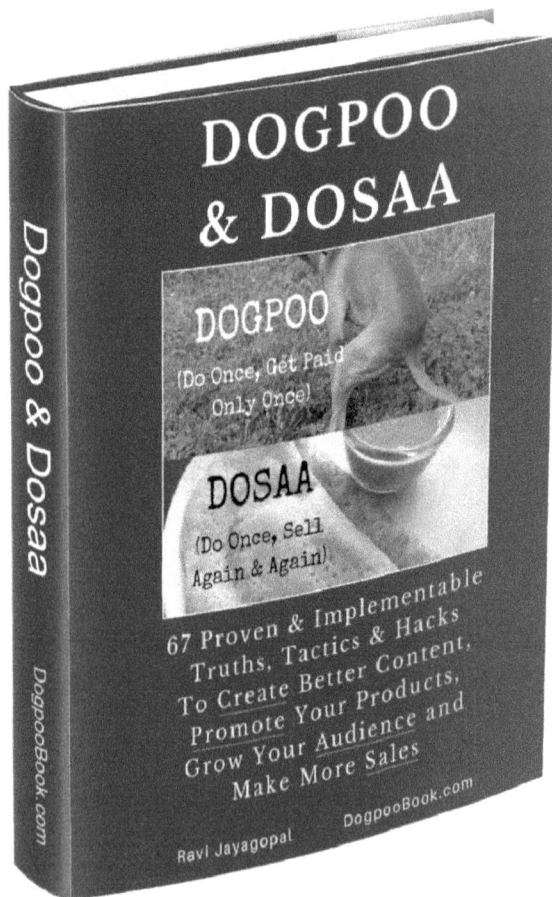

Original book cover created by me, using Canva, for social media and this book's website. It was subsequently changed.

Videos   Ebook   Audio

Image for my course DOPE: Do Once, Publish Everywhere – How to Build Trust, Respect & Influence and Reach New Audiences Using Live Streaming, Video, Audio and Repurposing Content on Multiple Social Media Platforms to visually represent that it had Videos, Ebooks and Audio as part of the course. Created by me using Canva.

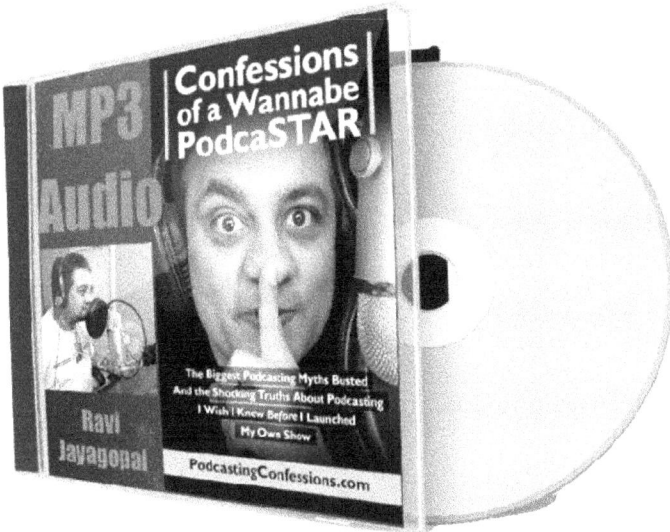

To depict the audiobook for my book Confessions of a Wannabe PodcaSTAR: The Biggest Podcasting Myths Busted – and the Shocking Truths about Podcasting I Wish I Knew Before I Launched My Own Show. Created by me using Canva.

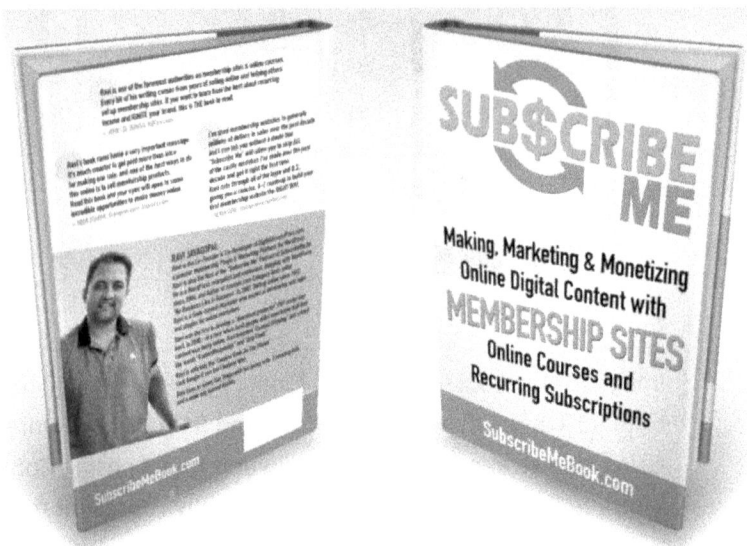

Image for my Kindle book Subscribe Me: Making, Marketing & Monetizing Online Digital Content with Membership Sites, Online Courses and Recurring Subscriptions.

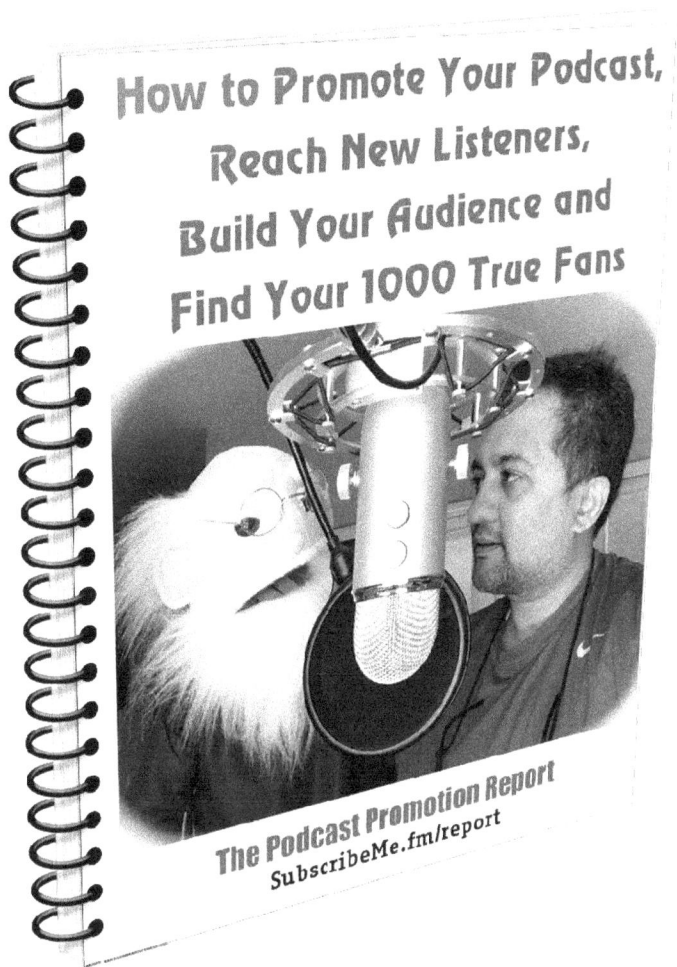

Image to represent by Kindle book and PDF report, Podcast Promotion Report: How to Promote Your Podcast, Reach New Listeners, Build Your Audience and Find Your 1000 True Fans

Image for my book How to Reach a New Audience of 30 Million Listeners with an Alexa Flash Briefing Skill Created in 1 Hour If You Already Have a Podcast (1 Week If You Don't)

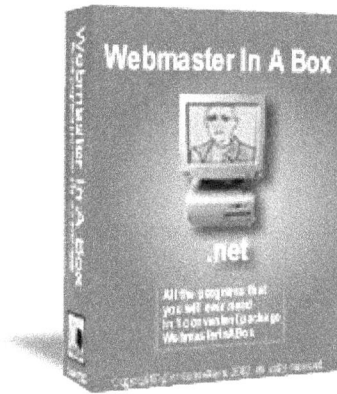

The very first product image I ever created back in 2000 – a software box for my PHP scripts website, WebmasterInABox.net (defunct).

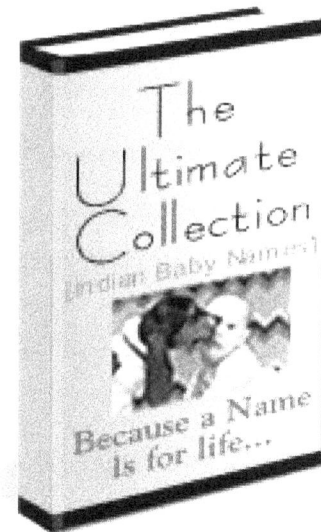

The 2nd product image I ever created back in 2003, to depict the baby names eBook for BabyNamesIndia.com (defunct).

Quick Tips for Your Membership Site

A membership site can be defined as a protected members-only area, which stores your members-only premium content.

This premium content can be a video course, audio course, audiobook, files like PDFs, mindmaps, spreadsheets, zip files, or even images.

And it can be content that you charge a fee for, or give free access – either someone who has signed up for it via a free signup form can access the content) or someone who you have manually given access to using their email.

It could be one-time products, or recurring subscriptions, and everything in-between - like a one-time upfront followed by another one payment, or 3 payments (to facilitate a payment plan), etc.

Here are some quick tips to keep in mind when creating your own membership site. Some of these deserve their own book, but I'll keep it short.

- #1 priority is to build an email list. It can take you weeks (hopefully not months) to create and launch your first product. In the meantime, don't waste the real estate on your home page and the opportunity to start building an email list.
- Start by creating a killer lead magnet, create a sign-up form on your home page, and start driving traffic to it from all of your social and content platforms. I've talked about this in several chapters.

- Selling online is not just about the product or even the price. It's about the entire "Offer". So work on your offer – a lot. Have written about this as well in other chapters.
- Start with a low-ticket, one-time product. While seeing recurring payments come in month after month can be super-exciting, in the beginning, you will not have enough content to charge a monthly membership. So start by selling a one-time product – like an eBook, or a mini video course – and start building a customer list to whom you can promote your next product.
- Give people multiple options in your pricing table. "Ebook + Audiobook" is better than just having "Ebook" as the only option. The Audiobook doesn't have to be ready at the time of launch. Just be sure to mention how soon it will be available after the purchase of the Ebook. And keep your word.
- Read Dan Ariely's Predictably Irrational: The Hidden Forces That Shape Our Decisions, an incredible book about human psychology and how we think about money and make decisions (hint: we're all irrational creatures in one way or the other). This book also has some fascinating pricing experiments that will give you ideas.
- Have an affiliate program. There is no one more qualified to authentically and genuinely promote your products than the folks who have paid for them. Make sure you give everyone who signs up an affiliate link that they can use immediately after signing up to start promoting your product to their audience.
- Having an affiliate program also allows you to approach other list- and audience- owners to promote your product in exchange for a commission. Be sure to give them a "no obligations" free copy first, and let them know that if they like your product, then you would appreciate it if they would share it with their audience using their

affiliate link so you can make sure you compensate them for any sales they send your way.

- If your offer includes a recurring subscription, consider offering a 2-week free trial, where they enter their credit card or PayPal information at the time of signing up, but they will not be charged anything until after the trial is over.
- If your product is priced over $100, consider offering a payment plan which will help them make partial payments over multiple months.
- Once you have a low-ticket offer and a high-ticket offer, one of the things you can try is to sell the low-ticket product on the front-end, and offer the high-ticket item as the upsell immediately after the main purchase. And be sure to discount the upsell and help them understand the value of the offer itself, as well as the discount that they will only get if they buy on the upsell page. And that if they leave the upsell page without buying it, they cannot get that special offer again.
- Don't create too many upsells. Depending on the niche and the strength of your reputation with your audience, more than 1 post-purchase upsell (that happens immediately after one purchase) may not be appreciated.
- See the chapter about "Create First, Sell Later".
- If you happen to follow that strategy and sell a video course, you don't need to have even created the product.
- With video courses, you could even deliver just the first lesson at the time of purchase, and then create and drip the remaining lessons one by one over the next several days. Be sure that your offer reflects the special deal they're getting primarily because of how your course hasn't been fully created yet.
- See the chapter about Video Tips which has everything you need to know about creating and delivering video.

- See the chapter about Bonuses – your offer must have great bonuses.
- When you're getting started, if you don't have any other courses or content other than the one that you're selling, you can offer other bonuses like a free 1-on-1 or group coaching call with you.
- When first launching digital products, you will frequently have a lot of questions on almost a daily basis. It's great to have someone to run your thoughts and decisions by real quick. Sure, you can crowd-source some of it in online communities like Facebook groups, but most of the time, you'll get heavily biased answers because people will usually recommend what they're using right now. And sometimes, 20 people will give you 20 different options and it will only end up confusing you even more. So check out my business coaching program if you want to work with someone who's been there, done that. You'll be able to ask me questions via chat, email, and have regular online calls. If you sign up through this book, just email me at Ravi@SubscribeMe.fm and I'll be happy to give you a good discount.

Minimalism vs. Perfectionism

One of my best friends from work about 12 years ago - let's call him "ST" - was the kind of person who wanted everything to be perfect before he would do anything.

For eg., one day his doctor told him that his bad cholesterol and blood sugar levels were trending high, so he needed to start working out.

Here's what ST did:

- Spent 2 weeks researching whether to join a gym or buy home fitness equipment
- 1 week: Free weights or BowFlex?
- 3 days: Best running shoes? Best-looking workout gear (Adidas or Nike or...)?
- A couple of visits to the local gym to check out their setup, talk to potential trainers that he could hire
- Researching online whether to hire a trainer on Thumbtack kind of websites to come train with him
- 2 months went by and he had still not started working out or even going for a run or a walk

I, on the other hand, am the type to put on the most comfortable, worn, washed-a-million-times shorts and t-shirt, a good ol' pair of sneakers, and start running that same evening (however slowly lol).

I'm not saying I'm this perfect person, or that I'm a fantastic overachiever, or that I don't care about having good gear. I would still do some research later to get a good pair of shoes only because it would impact my feet and knees. But I'm taking action from day one - the research can happen later.

I'm still overweight, but that's not because I procrastinated worrying about the "Setup". I work out every day and I am still overweight because I gotta work out even more and eat even less, etc.

I've seen people waste months or even years looking for things to be perfect, or wait for things to become affordable - like sports and fitness equipment, to video/audio gear, to waiting for a reputable publisher, the perfect eCommerce platform, or best WordPress membership plugin, etc. They go into full-blown "Analysis Paralysis".

I am all about "Get to work now with that you've got" minimalism, whether it is about starting a podcast, or a YouTube channel, publishing a book or launching a WordPress plugin. And that has helped me exponentially more times than it has failed me.

It's understandable to look at the popular video creators, podcasters, and authors and get overwhelmed thinking that you need the same kind of expensive gear and setup and expensive specialists to put out great content.

But if you ask those same people who are celebrities today in their niches, they'll be the first to tell you that they all got started with a bare minimum setup, working with "good enough" equipment, software, and gear.

That's why the "Google was started in a Garage" clichés are... clichés. Because they're true.

A majority of everyday creators - who may not be celebrities, but are quietly crushing it every day with their content - are the ones doing it consistently and fearlessly and using minimalistic software, gear, and outsourcing. And down the road, when they start making money, they upgrade. They don't wait for a year to save up enough to afford those things - they start today, start getting results quickly, making money as a result, and then use that to reinvest.

* No need for professional video camera setup with boom mics and exquisite lighting and sound-proof studio that costs > $5,000.

> => They're doing it with their iPhones and webcams and Android phones and window- or outside lighting with inexpensive <$100 LED lights

* No need for expensive audio gear with mics and mixers costing > $3,000 with mic, mixers to start a podcast

> => They're doing with a <$500 dynamic mic (<$100 mic in my case), recording audio on their laptops, and interviewing guests on Zoom. Some of my favorite indie podcasts I listen to are hosted on Anchor, a free podcast host.

* No need for a "Professional Sound Studio" costing $$$ to rent per hour

> => They're doing it at home in closets and bedrooms, surrounded by blankets and cardboard

* No need to wait for a reputed publisher to pick you

> => They're choosing themselves, writing with whatever tools they've got, some free, some practically free

The stigma that "Self-publishing = Vanity Publishing" is dead - long gone - at least when it comes to the majority of the creator economy.

Choose yourself. Give yourself permission to do whatever it is that you want to do without waiting.

There are incredible tools that are free or almost free everywhere you look, whether it's for creating websites, audio, video, or PDFs.

WordPress, Canva, Google Docs/Open Office, Anchor, Auphonic, YouTube, Slack, Skype, To-Do app, Discourse, Trello, Zoom, Calendly, Headliner, and on and on and on.

Today, there's an abundance of tools, technology, and training.

The only thing that is stopping you, is you.

There are some things for which you still need to wait for the right conditions - like when flying an airplane, launching a rocket into space, or getting surgery.

But for everything else, like Nike says, Just Do It.

You no longer need expensive equipment, software, setup, or support staff to get the job done.

I've been podcasting with a < $100 ATR 2100 mic for 6 years. I've been developing WordPress plugins for 15 years with free developer tools. I've written 8 books (including this one). And created innumerable videos with bare minimum tools, many of them free, some of them more than good enough.

You could wait for everything to be perfect... or you could get going now with what you've got, and with the best "more than good enough" tools.

At SubscribeMe.fm/tools, I've shared all of the best tools I use and recommend.

"Perfection is the enemy of progress." - Winston Churchill. Winston was right. Listen to Winston ;-)

And I say, **Imperfect & Published or Perfect & Never Published**. Choose one.

Native Marketing

When your content is natively published, directly on a social platform, I call that "Native Marketing" (not to be confused with Native Advertising).

The advantage is that the audience doesn't have to leave the current platform to check out your content - they can consume it right there.

You'll usually see people publishing links to their blog posts on Facebook. Instead, publish the whole blog post on Facebook directly on your personal profile.

Share it on your business Page, your own Facebook group, and even in other relevant Facebook groups, by publishing the whole text directly. As long as there are no promotional links to your website or YouTube channel or Kindle page, and the content itself is not self-promotional, most groups will not object to you sharing great content.

Then publish the article as a Twitter thread.

Pick highlights from your content and create short videos and share them on Instagram, TikTok, Facebook, and Twitter. Create a full-length video and share it on Periscope, YouTube, and IGTV. Use something like ReStream.io to live stream to multiple platforms simultaneously.

Split it and share it on Instagram, LinkedIn, and Facebook stories. There's more, and I talk about that in another chapter.

Don't force your audience to have to go to yet another platform just to consume your content. At least, don't make that the primary option.

Don't even make them jump from page to page if you can deliver the content on one page.

Don't split up the content into multiple pages for the sake of page-views or SEO or stickiness.

Post content directly and natively on each social platform, so that those who see your content on that platform can consume it right then and there, without having to leave the platform and go to your website or YouTube channel or wherever else.

And this also allows them to share the content with their network on that same platform.

Struggling Artist, Failed Entrepreneur

Another one of the catch-phrases that I created, is MOMMY - More Offers Equals More Money For You. You simply have to start making offers if you want to make money. Simply sitting on a "treasure trove" of content is not good enough if you don't do anything with it.

I've encountered a lot of people who have created tons of great content, but they've never made a penny from it. One of my podcast listeners whose question I answered on my podcast and also ended up coaching for about an hour, had created an insane amount of content - 10,000 hours of YouTube video watch time, a few million YouTube subscribers, millions of video views, etc. But he was making $0 from all of it. And he was about to call it quits, because he had not paused to think for even an hour few minutes, as to how he could monetize his content.

Sometimes, when someone says they haven't been able to figure out how to monetize their content, it's because they simply haven't put much time into trying to figure it out. If you stop everything else, lock yourself in a room with no distractions, and spend 2 hours just brainstorming ideas on how to monetize it, and then come out and start implementing it even a little bit, there's no way for you to make zero dollars. If you put in the time, effort, and execution, I can practically guarantee you that you'll make a few dollars, even if by accident. It's ridiculously hard to make zero dollars if you have a few million subscribers on YouTube.

I gave him some great ideas on how to get going and start making some money, including asking him to stop spending all of his time creating new content, and take time to package his content into something that can be sold, enabling YouTube ads, creating a membership site, building an email list of his audience by offering them terrific free bonus content, etc. Never heard back from him, and when I checked in with him 2 years later, he had not done a single darn thing I had talked to him about - but of course, he had gone on to create several hundred more videos.

So there are a lot of people who are prolific at creating content or a product but don't know how to monetize it. That's why there's a difference in how we label unsuccessful entrepreneurs vs. artists.

"*Struggling* Artist" vs. "*Failed* Entrepreneur".

If you are an artist, and you are unsuccessful, it's generally considered ok, and you're forgiven because it's almost as if people expected that "of course you're not a marketer, so you didn't know how to promote yourself". Because you are *supposed* to be the artist and you're supposed to be focusing primarily on your skill and creativity, and nothing else. So you are labeled a *struggling* artist.

But if you create a physical or digital product or service, and you are unsuccessful and have to shut down your small business, you will probably be labeled a *failed* entrepreneur with a *failed* business venture) because as an entrepreneur, you're simply expected (fairly or unfairly) to know and do a whole bunch of things other than just focusing on your product. And it can all get overwhelming.

As a solo entrepreneur - which is probably what most will be when they're getting started, you have to figure out how to make money, because you have a business to build and sustain, and you have bills to pay. You also have to build an audience, create the website, sales page, and landing pages, create videos, blog posts, podcasts, and social media posts, do a bunch of content marketing, work on traffic and conversion, SEO, copywriting, list building, sending emails, figuring out online ads, work with JV partners and affiliates, and on and on.

That's why if you're struggling, you have been doing this for more than a year and you haven't gotten anywhere close to where you wanted to get to, you owe it to yourself to find a business coach or mentor.

Here's a quick and shameless plug for my coaching program: Whether it is helping you figure out your niche and get started from scratch, or helping you take the next step and get to the next level, I can help you wherever you are right now in your journey.

Even if it's not me, find someone else. Start by checking with your trusted network if they have any recommendations. Just find a coach – you can thank me in a few years.

Thank You!

Thank you for your time spent reading this book.

If you found this useful, or if you have any questions, comments, suggestions, or feedback of any kind, please see my contact information below. Would love to hear from you about what you thought.

And if you are willing to give me a review about this book, I will proudly and happily display it on DogpooBook.com, with your name and a link to your website/blog/podcast, etc. And I will also give you a shout-out on my podcast if you're OK with that. Or you can send me your feedback and I can keep your name anonymous and share just the contents.

But please do let me know what you think. It would mean a lot to me! Thanks in advance!

My Websites

* I'm a Business Coach and Speaker.

* About me: SubscribeMe.fm/ravi-jayagopal

* Free: Watch my Podcast Movement presentation at SubscribeMe.fm/academy/pm18/

* Free Guest: (lol) If you wish to have me on your podcast, or any other show, just email me. Or go ahead and schedule any slot that's convenient to you, at calendly.com/ravijayagopal/call

* Software & Services I use in my business: SubscribeMe.fm/tools

* SubscribeMe.fm: My Podcast about Making, Marketing & Monetizing Online Digital Content with Membership Sites, Online Courses and Subscriptions

* DigitalAccessPass.com (DAP): I'm the Co-Founder & Co-Developer of DAP, a leading WordPress Membership Plugin & Marketing Automation Platform.

* S3MediaVault.com: Audio/Video Player for WordPress that lets you securely embed private Audio and Video that your members can listen/play in their member's area. It also protects regular files like PDF, Zip, Doc, etc.

* CoolCastPlayer.com: Prettiest & Most Powerful Podcast Player on the Planet – for WordPress.

* CutToTheChase.fm: My 2nd Podcast: Business, Marketing & Tech Hacks For Entrepreneurs and Digital Creators

* Digital Creators Academy: Content, Coaching & Community for Entrepreneurs and Digital Creators.

* 1001TrueFans.com: Small Audience, Big Impact: How to Become a Respected, Trusted & Beloved Expert and Build Your Tribe of 1,000 True Fans — Even If You're Starting with an Audience of Zero Followers, Zero Fans, Zero List and Zero Customers.

* Check out my 8 books at https://SubscribeMe.fm/books

* Get your Apple Podcasts reviews from all 155 countries for free, at PodcastReviews.me

Contact Me

Email: Ravi@SubscribeMe.fm or Contact-us form at SubscribeMe.fm

Facebook: facebook.com/RaviJayagopal

Twitter: twitter.com/RaviJayagopal

Instagram: instagram.com/RaviJayagopal

LinkedIn: linkedin.com/in/ravijayagopal

TikTok: https://www.tiktok.com/@ravijayagopal

I hope you loved reading this book as much as I enjoyed writing it.

Cheers!

- **Ravi Jayagopal**

Ravi Jayagopal / SubscribeMe.fm

Disclaimers: The advice in this book is strictly based on my personal opinions, which were formed from years of personal experience of actually doing stuff online, creating content, products, and services, and marketing them and making money with them since 1997. I do not guarantee or in any way insinuate that you'll get similar results. Most people who read this book will probably never take action, or not take *enough* action, for it to make any difference, and may never get any results from what I've recommended in this book. And there will be a few who will not value my advice, or may not agree with what I have to say, or may not be willing to suspend their disagreement and try out new things. For most of those people, nothing I've said in this book will work. Either way, I do not guarantee any results. But you already knew that.

Disclosures: There are links to a bunch of websites, articles, products, and services in this book. Some of them are my websites; others belong to other people/companies. A few of them are affiliate links where I may be compensated if you go on to buy those products or services. Some of them are direct links and I do not get compensated in any way for recommending them. I never recommend anything for the sake of earning a commission. I would recommend those same products even if they didn't offer any commissions. Some of them do, so might as well use those links, right? There's no additional cost to you, but it does help support my business if you go on to use them. But please do your due diligence before acting on any advice in this book, because I'm not responsible for any actions (or lack thereof) that you take (or don't take) based on my recommendations.

So here's to massive, mindful action…

Cheers!

www.ingramcontent.com/pod-product-compliance
Lightning Source LLC
Chambersburg PA
CBHW061204220326
41597CB00015BA/1347